Bid to Win on eBay
The Savvy Bidder's Guide
Patrick C. Cook

Bid to Win on eBay
The Savvy Bidder's Guide

ISBN: 1-58961-140-3 (Paperback)

This book is printed on acid free paper.

Printed in the United States of America

About the Author

Patrick C. Cook is an accomplished software and Internet web site developer. In 1990 he authored and published a successful software program that aided several hundred thousand in understanding the federal laws concerning consumer credit rights. He has since developed scores of software applications. He began developing Internet web sites in 1992 and has since been closely involved with the Internet on many levels.

In 1998 Patrick took an interest in eBay. At first he sought only to make a few purchases but soon found that he wanted to know much more about bidding in eBay auctions. Over several years he developed the bidding tactics and techniques encompassed in this book and with them, rarely lost an auction. Recognizing that how-to-bid information was taking a back seat to how-to-sell on eBay, Patrick undertook this book project to provide a thorough review of the many bidding tactics available to the eBay auction participant.

Acknowledgements

Thanks Julie, for your loving encouragement, your patience and for your greatly appreciated copyediting.

Thanks Brenda, for your insightful suggestions that helped make this book what it should be, both for myself and for my readers.

Thanks Lisa, for struggling through seemingly endless copyediting.

Thanks eBay, for giving us a great playground by which to tune our competitive skills and, of course, to acquire treasures old and new.

Thanks to the great folks at PageFree Publishing for their diligence, attention to detail and for putting up with me.

> And thanks for your interest and enthusiasm in this subject. Without you, I would have had no one with whom to share my thoughts about winning on eBay.

Preface

Imagine having confidence that you can win eBay auctions.

Imagine never again being locked by the fear of overpaying for an auction.

Imagine enjoying eBay auctions more than you thought possible.

Imagine being a Savvy Bidder.

eBay has evolved into a highly competitive online auction community. As membership continues to rapidly grow, more potential opponents are created. Many eBay members have had the time and experience to acquire strong bidding skills if only by simple practice. eBay sellers have generally become much more knowledgeable of what it takes to sell their wares at optimum prices. Gone are the days of predominantly amateur sellers and inexperienced bidders. eBay is becoming an increasingly challenging playground and it is not likely to get easier.

The evolution of the eBay online auction community makes it necessary to move beyond the basic how-to-bid material. It is no longer sufficient to simply know how to place a bid. Now we must know how to leverage our bids for maximum competitive advantage. We want to escape the financial traps that online auctions set for us. We want to become savvy bidders.

Nor can we always snipe eBay auctions. Snipe bidding, as we will discuss, has its disadvantages and risks. We need to know how to strategically bid at all points during an eBay auction. We need to be able to view the auction's landscape from a wider perspective than would normally be needed for snipe bidding. This protects us from rushing into bidding trying to beat the clock. For these reasons this book is not focused on the snipe bidding tactic. Rather, this book encompasses bidding tactics that may be applicable in mid-auction as well as near the end. But, for those who favor snipe bidding, there is plenty of material within these covers on the subject.

As you explore the bidding principles and tactics discussed in this book, you'll begin to realize that the online auction game is designed to extract the maximum number of dollars from those who think like buyers instead of like negotiators. That should come as no surprise since online auction venues are based on the same objective as countless commercial organizations – make as much money as possible. In online auctions the seller has a built-in advantage - the seller can position prospective buyers to compete with one another which serves to maximize the auction's closing price. The objective then is to compete well and not simply fall into being a buyer. While simply making a purchase on eBay is appropriate for many occasions, there will come a time when you will have to compete for the purchase. So that's what we will discuss. In fact, being highly competitive in eBay auctions is the sole focus of this book.

eBay provides a valuable service to millions and is one of the most engaging person-to-person and business-to-consumer purchasing environments we'll likely see for years to come. What I hope to accomplish here is to help you get smart about participating in online auctions. To do that, I speak frankly to help you be more alert and aware so you can advance your bidding skills.

So now it's time to become more skilled in how you play the eBay game. You must think like a negotiator and shed your retail buying mentality understanding that bidding is not buying. The reward is that you'll have more fun as you reel in trophies won at auction at the lowest possible cost to you. Perhaps for the first time you will understand how competition is leveraged to maximize the auction's closing price. You will see right through the competitive tactics of your opponents, and you will launch tactics of your own. You will understand why fear-based bidding loses auction. You will turn minimum bidding into strategic bidding; strategically leverage proxy bidding and even learn how to use the notorious snipe bid tactic. As an alert bidder you will be keen to the signs of a fraudulent auction. You'll realize that luck can play less of a role in winning eBay auctions than you thought. Best of all, you'll have more fun because you are good at the online auction game.

This book is about how you can bid in eBay auctions intelligently or, put another way, as a savvy bidder. A Savvy Bidder is aware, alert and aggressive. A Savvy Bidder leverages information. A Savvy Bidder is a negotiator.

Since no one is writing for bidders, I will

Among a sea of how-to-sell-on-eBay books and web sites, this book is the first devoted exclusively to helping you become a powerful bidder on eBay and, for that matter, other online auction venues. In this book I do not address selling on eBay – this book is exclusively for when you wear the bidder's hat. However, you'll find that this book also helps you become a great eBay seller because you will better understand how auction participants think.

I am delighted you decided to join me for a while. I am honored to have been given an opportunity to share with you my thoughts and opinions on this subject. Use this book to help you win more online auctions, spend less money and have more fun. I hope your journey through this interesting subject is as rewarding as mine.

Table of Contents

Introduction

When I discovered eBay in 1998 I was searching for Java software development resources. I found a training tape set on eBay that was just what I needed. The auction was receiving heavy bidding and I didn't know if I could bid well enough to win the auction. I placed a bid that was very quickly outbid. If I lost the auction, my alternative was to spend $600.00 for the tape set from the manufacturer.

On the final day of the training tape auction, my wife and I were visiting with our neighbors when the discussion moved to eBay. My neighbor was an avid comic book collector and had developed strong bidding skills on eBay to complete his collection. He preferred to bid in the last seconds of an auction. To him, it made perfect sense to wait until the auction was about to close so that he could estimate the auction's closing price and move in with the winning bid. My neighbor explained that placing bids during the auction was "just costing you money" (because bids raise the auction's current price). That evening, I used the bidding techniques we discussed and won the auction for $200.00 under the retail cost.

I soon discovered other items I wanted to purchase on eBay. I was hooked on the prospect that I could participate in deciding what price I would pay for items I wished to own. But, to maximize my savings I knew I was going have to get good at bidding on eBay.

However, I certainly wasn't willing to overspend while I learned to bid well. So I began reading any material I could find that would teach me how to bid well on eBay. I purchased and reviewed as many books on the subject of eBay as I could find. However, these books glossed over bidding and focused on how to sell on eBay. I found a few web sites that offered tips about bidding, but once again they lacked substance. I even researched articles written by math professors that discussed the mathematics of auctions. These were very interesting articles, but that was game theory – I wanted real world experience.

Observations

I turned to the best source of training – actual eBay auctions. I reviewed many auction listings and closely examined the bid histories of those auctions. Through simple observation, it became clear why eBay auctions are won, and lost.

Current Price Focusing

I landed on an important realization as I studied eBay auctions in search of the winner's formula. I recognized an interesting dichotomy; even though bidders are advised to determine what they are willing to spend for an item, most will place small bid amounts that are far below what they are "willing" to spend if necessary. This is interesting because if a person is willing to spend $100.00, for example, why doesn't he simply plug in a bid for $100.00? Why place the smallest possible bids?

It didn't take long for me to realize what was happening. Bidders were using the auction's current price as their reference point. While I had no doubt that virtually every bidder had a private "not to exceed price" in mind, the actual bid amounts were predominately as low as possible. Human nature, such as it is, wants to purchase a thing at the lowest possible price. In fact, the tendency to bid as low as possible is actually factored into the formulas the math professors use to explain the game theory of auctions.

Ok. No surprise there – we all like to save on purchases. But there's another factor at play here; bidders predominantly treat the current price as the purchase price. Bidders intellectually know that the current price is subject to change in a single-unit eBay auction and that they may not

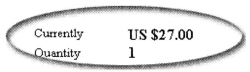

Figure 1 - An eBay screen portion showing an auction's current price.

be able to win the auction at the current price. Yet because the majority of purchases the consumer makes (the consumer comprises the majority of eBay's members), there is an element of the traditional retail purchase that is always present – the price. It is no surprise that an online auction bidder will tend to treat an auction's current price as the *purchase* price, even though he knows better.

Palatable Price Increments

I observed that auctions that predominantly receive small bids often close at a higher price than they might have otherwise. The reason for this is deceptively simple and is, once again, rooted in a human characteristic that commerce has spent hundreds of years developing and exploiting – people tend to accept small price increments easier than large price increments. The upshot is that it is easier to bid again if it just requires a few more dollars. So, bidders often do not form a price target for themselves. Rather they "follow" the current price. As a result, the current price inches its way up in palatable increments, carrying the bidders along.

Fear of Overspending

When people are in a purchase situation where information is not available to help them make a wise purchase, they become protective of their money. In eBay auctions, no one can know the personal value that opponents place on a particular item. Bids amounts are deliberately hidden in single-unit auctions so there is no reference to the valuation of the opponents. During the auction bidders do not know the possible extent of the competition. Add to this the "virtual" aspect of online auctions – there is seldom a brick-and-mortar presence of the seller and it is rare to physically inspect an auction item before bidding on it. Add the concern that the seller is untrustworthy, or even fraudulent, and fear can become a dominant element of online auctions.

The fear of overspending that results from so many unknowns actually interferes with the competitive capabilities of a bidder. A fearful person is competitively handicapped. Our challenge is to overcome such fears. This starts by keen observation and skilled analysis of the information that is available to you.

Bidding is not Buying

The typical retail purchase process is fairly straightforward; select, decide and buy. Well, this doesn't work as well in a competitive purchase situation. Rather, it plays out more like; select, decide, negotiate price and maybe buy. Observation alone demonstrates that eBay bidders try to buy while not fully grasping that they cannot buy until they successfully negotiate the actual purchase price. Bidding is not buying.

The confusion between bidding and buying is perpetuated by eBay itself and its sellers by treating eBay members like retail buyers. eBay has evolved (or devolved) into a retail-like environment with an auction format. This shift to retail-like purchasing works because the typical eBay member is already familiar with it. Our challenge is to understand how purchasing via eBay really works, not how they would have us believe.

The more eBay auctions I examined and participated in, the more I came to realize that those who understood that they were involved in a competitive price negotiation process did much better than those who were simply trying to buy.

Given this, I began to look at how I could think like a competitor, not like a buyer. However, not only does the eBay environment cater to the buyer mentality, but the buyer mentality is well entrenched. This serves to perpetuate bidding as buying. Nevertheless, I resisted my own buyer tendencies and worked to understand the dynamics of online auction competition as a format by which to earn the right to make a purchase, not just to make a purchase.

Bidders are Generally Predictable

For those who appreciate the competitive nature of online auctions, one of the first things he looks for is how can he better understand his opponents. Well, the good news is that eBay bidders are generally predictable. The typical bidder falls into bidding habits that are easily spotted and can be competitively leveraged. Of course, there are many bidders who go about bidding in a seemingly random manner that is often rooted in reacting to the actions of their opponents. My own observation has taught me the competitive value of understanding the habits of my opponents as much as practical. Yet I have also come to appreciate that underestimating the competitive power of irrational bidders leads to losing auctions or possibly over paying.

Virtual Purchasing

An outcrop of eBay's blossoming size is that it has attracted so many sellers that there will often be multiple (or many) auctions for the same or comparable item. For many bidders it doesn't really matter if a particular auction is won because there will almost always be another.

The volume of the same or comparable items up for auction has the general effect of reducing closing prices. When supply is up for a particular item, available competition tends to be spread across multiple auctions. (The number of purchase candidates does not increase in markets just because there is more of a particular product available). In the auction format, competition is essential for optimum closing prices. Since the online auction environment is based on a price negotiation model, persons will tend to migrate to those auctions offering the same or comparable item with a lower current price. As a result, many place bids in one auction only to jump to another in a quest to save money. Many sellers further damage the prospects of their auction's closing prices by simultaneously posting multiple auctions for the exact same merchandise. Add to this the perpetual pursuit of items to sell where eBay auction items are bought and put right back up for sale on eBay.

On eBay any member can bid at any level of seriousness they choose in a single-unit auction, as long it is above the auction's current price. For price-focused people, eBay provides a rich environment where they can engage in purchasing even though their bid or bids may not be competitively strong enough to win an auction. Often, winning the auction isn't even the primary objective. Rather, it is snatching a great price. Thus the *act* of purchasing without assured acquisition, e.g., "virtual purchasing", becomes the dominant activity. These factors combine to make eBay the greatest virtual purchasing environment ever.

At first, you may think this a great thing. After all, it would appear that "auction jumpers" are easily defeated since they do not compete as aggressively as might a highly motivated person who sticks with an auction. Problem is, the noise they produce creates the illusion that competition exists. This influences others to increase their price point. In fact, by the design of the single-unit auction, even the noise increases the current price. This causes "serious" bidders to actually have to pay more due to the bidders who attempted to pay less.

I came to appreciate that this noise is an aspect of the online auction game. It is highly unlikely that eBay or its sellers will ever do anything to suppress such noise. When I wear the seller's hat, I want all of the noise I can get. Doing anything to reduce noise actually damages the auction. From the bidder's perspective, many will regard each bid as an attempt to purchase the item. I know that this may not be the case. This allows me to not be influenced by *apparent* interest and fall into the trap of increasing my own perceived value based on bid activity alone. My challenge, as yours, is to leverage the noise, not be controlled by it.

Fewer Bargains

There was a time when you could find plenty of bargains on eBay. Bargains surfaced for three general reasons:

1. Sellers had not yet learned how to maximize the potential of their auctions, in terms of the closing price.

2. There was less competition overall because there were fewer eBay members.

3. Sellers had the freedom to contact bidders after the auction closed without a winner and strike a deal. Many bargains were picked up this way. eBay eventually closed the door on off-eBay deals.

Having myself been active on eBay since 1998, I remember the bargain days. In virtually every auction I posted as a seller or bid in, there were almost always early bidders who placed low bids. They were playing the odds that they would win auctions that few others found, or that a few desperate sellers would contact them and strike an off-eBay deal.

Now we must compete with a larger population of potential opponents. Prospective bargain auctions often become highly competitive auctions *because* they look like bargains. eBay policy has been changed in an effort to eliminate off-eBay sales. Now, if a seller doesn't want to risk suspension or termination, their auctions must produce winning bidders or be re-listed. But they don't want to lose money.

So more sellers are pushing up their First Bid prices and relying on reserve prices. Given this, and other factors, we need a way to be competitive. We need to have a keen eye for bargains – they're still around. But we need to be prepared to win auctions against greater competitive odds than ever before.

Bidding Tactics Lacking

My observations also revealed that the typical bidder utilizes just a very few bidding tactics. For instance proxy bidding and snipe bidding are commonly used. Even these are generally under utilized. Most bidders are unaware of several other highly competitive bidding tactics. My goal was to identify how these and other bidding tactics could be fine tuned to be highly competitive. I soon realized, however, that bidding tactics are just tools – strategy is much more important.

Getting It Together

Given these observations I formulated bidding tactics that I tested in actual eBay auctions. I learned the value of not becoming focused on the current price and taking a negotiator approach to eBay auctions. I learned to avoid minimum bids and exposing my intentions with proxy bids. I learned how to understand and leverage the habits of my opponents. I learned how to time my bids for maximum tactical advantage.

When I did lose an auction, I carefully analyzed why I lost. What could I have done to foil that sniper? Should I have predicted that a certain tenacious bidder was not going to lose the auction easily? Did a certain bidder place a proxy bid at his full personal valuation? I looked for the bidding patterns of my opponents that I had originally missed and asked how I could have leveraged those patterns. I learned the value of researching my opponents and would even research myself looking for telltale signs of competitive weaknesses. I questioned if a specific bidding tactic would have worked better than the tactic I had actually used. During this self-training period, it didn't matter if I won or lost the auction as long as a specific bidding tactic was proven effective.

I fully recognize that not all of the bidding tactics I present will be valid for all auctions. I also recognize that you could not possibly master all of the bidding tactics available to you simply by reading a book. You must try them when appropriate and only to the extent of your ability at that time – participate in all online auctions within your limits.

As you try the tactics discussed in this book, you will become more skilled with them over time. You will develop your own strategic style, as it should be. Bidding skills take focus, practice, observation of the results and corrective action the next time through.

I would like to extend my sincerest wish that you win every online auction you desire to win. It is also my wish that the savings you realize by becoming a Savvy Bidder pays for this book many hundreds of times over. I encourage you to share your bidding skills with others – there is plenty of room for master bidders.

Be Savvy...

Pat

About this Book

Part 1 of this book, *Foundations*, provides a discussion of strategic bidding. This is where you'll get a sense of the principles on which strategic bidding is based. We also explore the fundamental concepts of auctions as well as the very important target price.

Part 2, *Tactics and Techniques*, discusses bidding tactics in eBay auctions. Here we discuss actual bidding tactics that are the tools of the Savvy Bidder.

Part 3, *The Laws of Strategic Bidding*, apply strategic bidding tactics and techniques in the real world. The laws cut to the chase and offer honest observations of strategic bidding as well as some of the issues found in the online auction game.

A glossary of online auction related terms has been provided at the end of this book to help clarify online auction related terms used in this book.

Throughout the book I have made an effort to provide step-by-step instructions where needed to help you understand a possible strategic approach for a particular online auction situation. I provide realistic examples of auctions to which certain observations are made and tactics applied. Of course, you must adopt the tactics we discuss to your own style. I encourage you to shape the tactics presented to accommodate circumstances relevant to your own auction participation. But the objective always remains the same – win auctions at the lowest cost to you.

I cannot predict every variable and nuance of every auction – you must make strategic decisions based on what you find when you discover an eBay auction of interest to you. What I can do is provide you with the concepts of bidding strategically from which you create your own success.

As I'm sure you realize by now, this book is not written to provide you with the basics of eBay auctions; you can get that information from the eBay web site as well as from the books and web sites that specifically address the mechanics of eBay. To allow us to remain within the scope of this book, I must make the assumption that you are already knowledgeable of the mechanics of eBay or that you will take the time to learn them. Interestingly, you may find that once you have been exposed to the principles of strategic bidding you may actually learn the mechanics more easily because you'll have a context by which to apply them.

This book will not turn you into a habitual snipe bidder, although it will help you become a very good snipe bidder when the tactic is appropriate. You will not be advised to loosen up your wallet or purse and bid with abandon (which is certainly one way to win auctions). However, this book will help you abandon the fear-based bidding common among your opponents.

This book will not teach you how to sell on eBay, although a Savvy Bidder makes a damn good seller because she understands how typical bidders think.

This book will not teach you how to break or skirt around the rules of eBay. A Savvy Bidder does not break the rules – he uses the rules. What you will get here is an education in bidding principles, tactics and techniques. The objective is for you to become a winning bidder by strategically leveraging a position in the auctions in which you participate. This is best accomplished within the rules.

Will you win every auction you participate in with these bidding principles and tactics close at hand? No. There are many highly experienced bidders who have been active in the eBay playground for a while now and they will prove to be formidable opponents should you encounter them. Also, there are many people who bid in eBay auctions who do not have a sense of when to quit bidding and by money power alone they win auctions. In fact, their bidding tactic is their money. But that's ok. If a person is willing and able to pay more than an item is worth to you, or perhaps even worth to them, then they should have the right to purchase that item. You, on the other hand, choose to own an item at a price that is in harmony with your personal valuation, or lower.

Among the readers of this book there will be a tiny percentage that will think that they have found the sure-bet way of winning every online auction. This is not so. In fact, by the very design of online auctions, there is no sure bet. The single-unit online auction is designed to create losers. And, the more losers there are in an auction, the higher the closing price. There are only skills that can be applied to increase your chances of winning online auctions.

Companion Web Site

You are invited to visit **www.savvybidder.com** for additional material for the Savvy Bidder that this book could not accommodate. At the web site you'll find useful resources and information to augment this book. The web site also has links to Internet resources of interest to the Savvy Bidder. Please visit the site when you get a chance.

How to Use this Book

The Auction Venue

This book addresses the eBay auction venue specifically. However, many of the concepts and principles discussed in this book may also apply to other auction venues such as Yahoo and Amazon auctions as well as others.

When applying any strategic bidding principle or bidding tactic to a particular auction venue please take the time to understand that auction venue's processes, rules and policies before forging ahead. In addition, eBay has a tendency to frequently modify its web site, rules and policies, so I strongly encourage you to remain aware of any changes.

This book has not been reviewed by nor endorsed by eBay, Inc. Use your own best judgment when applying any principle or concept discussed in this book.

Auction Formats

This book predominantly applies to the single-unit eBay auction format. This is an auction where one item (a single unit) is auctioned and where there can only be one winning bidder. When a point is made about an auction, assume that the auction format is a single-unit auction unless it is specifically stated that the point applies to the Dutch auction format (where multiple items are auctioned).

Membership IDs

eBay membership ID's are obscured in the graphics of this book. This was done to insure that no specific eBay member is inadvertently associated with a performance or skill attribute (or lack of) that is under discussion.

Gender References

I have made a concerted effort to randomly use gender references. Rather than taking the "him/her", "he/she" approach, or referring to one specific gender throughout the book, I have mixed gender references throughout. When referencing a gender during the discussion of a subject, there is no intention to imply specific capabilities or skill attributes to the gender being referenced at that time.

Book Layout and Conventions

This book is sequenced so that general concepts concerning strategic bidding are discussed first. Specific bidding tactics and techniques are then discussed followed by *The Laws of Strategic Bidding*.

The Laws of Strategic Bidding are presented on the assumption that you have a fairly good understanding of the concepts and principles of strategic bidding as well as the bidding tactics discussed in this book. While most of the laws relate to strategic bidding, some laws discuss issues of interest to the Savvy Bidder.

I have made an effort to not use acronyms, abbreviations or jargon in this book. However, I have coined a few terms. If a term is unfamiliar to you, you may find a definition of the term in the *Glossary of Terms*.

Money values are expressed in U.S. dollars throughout this book. In addition, because cents are important in online auction bidding, I felt it would be appropriate to include the cent designation even if there were no cents involved. For instance, a money value is expressed as $75.00 rather than $75.

Glossary of Terms

In the Glossary you will find most of the terms relating to online auctions as well as the terms coined throughout this book. I encourage you to refer to the glossary frequently for concise descriptions and definitions of terminology related to our discussion of strategic bidding.

Writing In this Book

Do it. Underline. Highlight. Cross out. Write notes in the area provided after each chapter and after each law. Doodle in the margins.

Cross out everything in this book you don't agree with and apply the rest.

Caring for this Book

Dog-ear the pages. Use plenty of bookmarkers. Get coffee stains on it. Such wear and tear means it's getting plenty of use and that you are having fun with the subject.

Part 1: Foundations

Strategic Bidding

We start our exploration by taking a look at what strategic bidding is all about. After some fundamentals, we'll explore the target price. Then we'll consider the bidding budget and how to create a bidding plan. That will take us to a summary of bidding tactics.

The Strategic Way

The objective of the Savvy Bidder is to win auctions at as far below a target price as possible. This requires having a target price in mind. The objective is not just to win auctions at a good price – that goal is much too vague. The idea is to approach auctions in a way that does not get you pulled into a competitive bidding situation without a price objective. Let's start our discussion with explaining what an objective is.

> *An objective is a clearly defined statement of intention to reach a realistic end result within a certain time.*

A valuable attribute of a Savvy Bidder is her dogged pursuit of a clearly defined objective concerning an auction of interest. The Savvy Bidder does not merely hope to win the auction – she expects to win it. The Savvy Bidder does not rely entirely on luck to win the auction – she makes a concerted effort to eliminate luck from the equation. She makes every effort to acquire more and better information than her opponents have and to make better assumptions. In short, the Savvy Bidder is an informed and objective oriented bidder.

The process of strategic bidding is straightforward. First a concerted effort is made to determine a target price for the auction of interest. If that target price is acceptable, a bidding budget is developed. Then the landscape of the auction is explored. This landscape includes the seller, the active participants, the particular situation of the auction and the item itself. Next a bidding plan is established. The plan remains flexible and is used to help select the tactics that will be used to position for the win. Thus a realistic objective is defined and a plan is laid in to accomplish that objective.

The typical bidder will usually know something about an auction item of interest and will have an idea of its value to her personally. Many bidders make some effort to size up their opponents. However, the opponents that receive the most attention are the prominent ones such as the current highest bidder. Certainly, the typical bidder will assess the seller to some degree. But, the Savvy Bidder takes it up several notches. For instance, she makes an effort to determine the probable closing price of the item to better understand what price *may be required* to win the auction. She seeks more in-depth knowledge of her opponents, the seller, the auction item itself and other aspects of the auction. She takes a price negotiator approach rather than a buyer approach. She operates within the scope of her well-formed bidding budget, follows a flexible bidding plan and utilizes tactical bidding to position in the auction. So, although her approach has some elements in common with a typical bidder, hers is a more directed approach.

What's the Big Deal?

So, what's the big deal about bidding strategically? "Why don't I just figure what the item is worth to me, place a bid at what I am willing to pay for it and let it go at that? If I win, I win." Depending on a number of factors, such as the item being auctioned, competition in the auction and your perceived value of the item, you may very well decide that it is appropriate to simply bid your highest price and see what happens. If you win, you win. But, you will not want to take that approach too often because it is not a very effective tactic in many auctions.

The problem with this approach is that your price may be too high or too low with respect to what is <u>needed</u> to win the auction. If you are prepared to pay $500.00, for example, that amount may be more than is needed to win the auction. In addition, since your participation is actually contributing to creating a market for the auction, your personal valuation may actually affect the valuation of other participants in the auction. So, if your personal price is higher than it needs to be, your bidding may actually help pull the closing price up. This is because other participants will have to exceed your personal valuation if they want to win the auction. Alternatively, your price may be too low to compete due to others having formed a higher personal valuation. The idea is to find a personal valuation for the auction item that is low enough to be competitive but not so high as to cause opponents to increase their own valuation.

That you might be willing to spend $500.00 for an auction item is all well and good – this would be your personal price. But the strategic objective is to not compete on the basis of your personal price. Rather to compete with a price that is market based – a target price that has a basis in the current market activity for the auction item of interest.

FOUNDATIONS

The Target Price

A target price is a realistic and probable closing price for an item based on the final price of recently closed auctions within the same auction venue. Alternately, pricing external to the auction venue could be used to establish a target price. However, it is best to consider the recent auction closing prices of the same or comparable item. *The objective is to isolate what the current auction market thinks the auction item is worth because that is the potential closing price range of the auction.* In addition, a target price helps you avoid a personal price opinion as a basis for your competitive participation. This is because your personal price may be too low to be competitive in the auction or may be higher than it needs to be to win the auction.

A target price is a price that has a higher probability of winning a particular auction because it is based on recent price history within the same market or pricing that is external to the auction venue. In this way a target price provides you with a realistic guideline, given the current market. A target price provides reliable information by which to guide your strategic participation in the auction.

It is tactically weak to use another's bid as your own price guide. Doing so makes the assumption that another bidder was actually expressing his true personal valuation through his own bidding – this is not usually the case. One common way of relying on another's valuation is via the current price (displayed on eBay screens as "Currently" or "Current bid"). Assuming bids have actually occurred in an auction, the current price reflects the price bidders have collectively set for the item up to that point in time. When a proxy bid is in place, the current price effectively misleads bidders to form a lower valuation than may be necessary to win the auction. Because of the misleading nature of an auctions current price, you cannot be an effective competitor when you measure your personal price against the current price. We'll delve into this important subject later.

By focusing on closing prices of recently closed auctions as a guide for your own bidding, you avoid relying on specific bidders who may have bid well below the item's probable market value. You also avoid specific bidders who bid well above the item's probable market value during those auctions. And, the closing prices of recently closed auctions were the actual purchase prices, not inaccurate mid-auction pricing reflected by the current price.

A target price effectively eliminates the individual personal valuations of each bidder in the auctions from which you collect the closing prices. Since you have obtained the actual final prices of recently closed auctions, all of the bidding activities of all bidders in those auctions are considered, *but no single bidder becomes your price guide.* By not focusing on any specific bid in those auctions, your target price is not misled by the lower bids and not influenced by the higher bids. The target price, therefore, provides you with empirical pricing information that can be turned into information of competitive value.

The target price, for our purposes, is not what you intend to pay for the item. Rather is used to develop a strategic bidding budget, which will be explained in a moment. Your bidding budget is used to help you leverage a range of dollars. It is important to have a bidding budget so you can defocus on the auction's current price. A bidding budget is not the same as a personal budget. As discussed in a moment, a bidding budget is for strategic purposes while a personal budget tends to be a personal preference budget.

We'll go into depth concerning the target price later in this book. For now just get a sense of how important a target price is to your success in online auctions.

Your Bidding Budget

With a target price established concerning an auction of interest, you are able to determine a bidding budget for that auction. Mathematically, a bidding budget is the difference between the auction's current price and the target price. For instance, if you have determined a target price of $250.00 and the current price is $150.00, you have a bidding budget of $100.00.

It is important to clarify that a bidding budget is not the same as a personal budget. A personal budget is based on factors like what you are comfortable paying or what you can afford for the item. A personal budget tends to be influenced by a simple glance at your pile of household bills. If you go into an auction using a personal budget, the pressures of a personal budget will most surely limit your competitive strength. A bidding budget, on the other hand, is a range of dollars you will leverage to win the auction. The power of a bidding budget should become clear as we go along.

The importance of a bidding budget is that it enables you to determine effective bidding tactics because you know how much money you have allocated to "work" the auction and you are not resistant to using that budgeted money. You manage your bidding budget so that it can be used effectively throughout your participation in the auction. For instance, you might use 25% of your bidding budget early in the auction, and another 50% near the auction's close when competition is likely to be more active. In this example, notice how only 75% of the bidding budget was used. The objective is to manage a bidding budget to win the auction with the least consumption of the budget possible while remaining ready to use that budget fully if necessary.

You may elect to use a portion of your bidding budget to implement stealth bidding tactics such as Adjustment Bids, strategic minimum bids and a few others we will discuss later. This is what is meant by "working" the auction. Because bidders who are trying to purchase the auction item will be less likely to employ stealth bidding tactics, a stealth bid may actually provide competitive positioning. Because the typical bidder is trying to make a purchase, he often loses sight of the fact that the auction is really a competition to earn <u>the right</u> to make the purchase. Thus, the importance of stealth bidding tactics are often not evident to many bidders.

A bidder without a bidding budget tends to become focused on the current price and measures the current price against his <u>personal</u> budget. His personal budget has a "price pain point". Assume you were looking at an auction with a current price of $200.00. You have determined that you will not pay any more than $400.00, which is your price pain point. The $400.00, in this case, is a price you hope the auction *doesn't* reach. Since, in this example, you would prefer to avoid having to pay $400.00, the natural tendency is to bid in *avoidance* of $400.00. One cannot compete effectively when the underlying concern is to avoid his price pain point – a personal budget is more likely to have a price pain point.

The Savvy Bidder uses a bidding budget as a vehicle by which to choose her bidding tactics. Keep in mind that a bidding budget has the foundation of a target price – a probable closing price for the item within that auction venue. Therefore the Savvy Bidder is mentally prepared to utilize all of the money within the range between the current price and the target price. He is able to bid within his bidding budget in an aggressive manner or a stealth manner, as the situation dictates. More important, he is neither current price focused nor operates from a fear of over-spending for the item – both of which free him to participate in a highly completive manner.

Is this making sense so far? Let's consider the next element of strategic bidding.

Exploring the Landscape

Once a bidding budget is determined the Savvy Bidder explores the auction and its players with the objective of uncovering information that will be useful to position in the auction for the win.

During the exploration, the seller is assessed. The purpose is to uncover risks associated with purchasing from that seller. The value in knowing the risks is not just to help you avoid a bad transaction, but also to identify risks that your opponents might perceive which may have the effect of lowering their willingness to bid. If other bidders perceive a risk, such will likely interfere with their competitive strength in that auction. If, on the other hand, you do not feel that certain perceived risks are of consequence to you personally, then you may elect to not let such influence your bidding activity in the auction. In this simple way you may pick up a competitive advantage.

Explore your opponents as well. The objective is to uncover information about the bidding patterns of your opponents that you might be able to leverage against those opponents or, at the very least, to prepare yourself for their bidding. The value here is to avoid reacting to the bidding activity of your opponents. Being reactive simply pulls you into a competitive situation that puts you on the defensive – you want an offensive stance (which is not necessarily being the highest bidder, as we will discuss later).

Of course, you want to uncover information about the item itself. For instance, does the item carry more value than is generally known? Is the item actually of less value than the market generally believes or that the seller is representing it to have? When you have more information than your opponents you potentially have a better competitive advantage, depending on how well you leverage that information. Also, when you have better information than your opponents, you are less likely to overpay for the item. Certainly you always seek to underpay, but not to the extent that you greatly risk losing the auction.

Information is a key element in online auctions. Considering that there is much information that you cannot have, such as the actual personal valuation of each participant in the auction, gathering information can be crucial to winning an auction. Also, you are not allowed to view actual bid amounts during a single-unit eBay auction so you must make an effort to be informed about your opponent's possible motives. Usually, you have only the word of the seller concerning attributes of the item up for auction. With so much missing information, it behooves you to seek out as much information about the auction's landscape as is practical. Information is an important part of the Savvy Bidder's arsenal.

Your Bidding Plan

Strategic bidding is implemented with a plan. A plan is simply a predetermined approach you intend to take given the auction's landscape. An example of a bidding plan might be:

> "Since this auction is offering an item in high demand, I'll wait until the auction nears it close at which time I'll be able to better estimate the auction's closing price. If the auction has not reached the target price, I'll enter a proxy bid with an additional final bid in the last seconds of the auction (a snipe bid)."

Another example of a bidding plan might be:

> "Since this reserve auction is offering an item in high demand and I have a strong desire to own it, I'll ask the seller what his reserve price is. Then I'll place an early proxy bid to bring the current price up to but just under the seller's reserve. This may reduce bidding by less serious bidders. If the reserve is not met near the auction's close, I'll place one or more nominal proxy bids at that time. If the reserve price has been met by another bidder, I'll do a Proxy Discovery Run and then place a new proxy bid if the current price has not exceeded the target price."

For now, don't try to understand the details of the above examples. Just understand that a bidding plan helps you decide what strategic approach you will take in the auction. Next I'll explain why your bidding plan must remain flexible.

If there is anything certain about online auctions it is that nothing is certain. This is why each online auction must be approached with a flexible plan. To illustrate the uncertainty of online auctions:

♦ Most bidders tend to bid reactively in reference to the bidding activities of their opponents and the auctions misleading current price.

♦ Only those bidders who are actually participating in the auction are known. No one knows who will enter the auction and when. There may also be persons lurking who intend to snipe the auction in the last seconds of the auction.

♦ One cannot know the personal valuation of each participating bidder (what they are ultimately willing to pay). Indeed, the personal valuation of many bidders actually increases with the current price so even they may not know what they are ultimately willing to pay. Even if you did know someone's personal valuation, it is always subject to change. And the change in valuation comes as a result of a wide variety of variables that influence the participants at any given time.

♦ Many bidders are caught up in the competition and who, intending to or not, may eventually exceed their original personal price tolerance for the sake of winning the auction (the desire to own is often increased by the effort required to make the purchase).

In online auctions, there are too many unknowns for a rigidly defined bidding plan to be practical. In fact, a bidding plan should change as the situation in the auction dictates. The value of a bidding plan is not in being a rigid map of specific bidding actions, rather is a general course of action based on what you know at the moment. To illustrate a flexible bidding plan:

> "I'll place a proxy bid now at 25% of my bidding budget. If another bidder outbids that proxy bid, I'll remain inactive to see what other bidders enter the auction. Then I'll place a proxy bid at 50% of my bidding budget. If my second proxy bid is outbid, and the current price remains within my bidding budget, I'll prepare to snipe the auction with a bid amount up to the target price if necessary. However, if my second proxy bid is not outbid, I'll increase my proxy bid amount near the auction's close."

This bidding plan example encompassed several "what if" scenarios. In reality, one bidding plan may actually be abandoned and replaced with another plan as the auction's landscape changes. It is important to note however that the target price does not change and neither does your bidding budget. How you utilize your bidding budget should always be flexible and responsive to the situation at hand.

Current Price Fixation

The most obvious state of an auction is the current price which is shown on eBay screens as "Currently" or "Current bid". Those who bid without a bidding budget or a bidding plan are in danger of reacting to the current price of the auction. I dare say that most bidders use the current price as their primary frame of reference for deciding to continue bidding in an auction. This, I believe, has its foundations in retail buying where the buyer usually makes a final determination to buy desired merchandise based on its predetermined price. However, in eBay auctions the current price is not necessarily the price that the article will sell at. Rather, the current price reflects only the current state of the price negotiation for the auction. More important, *the current price does not necessarily reflect what opponent bidders are ultimately willing to pay for an auction article.* It is for this reason that the current price is perhaps the worst reference point one could have concerning participation in an online auction.

With the current price as a bidder's sole frame of reference, he will be tempted to bid just a little bit higher unless the current price is beyond his price pain point. In fact, this is the fundamental premise of auctions – to get as many bidders as possible to be willing to pay a higher price than their opponents. What the participants are willing to pay is *implied* by the current price. This cycle continues until all but one bidder have exceeded their respective price pain points. The end effect is that the auction fetches the highest price it could given the participation of bidders who were interested in purchasing the auction article at that time. The auction format, for all intents and purposes, is a brilliant commercial invention – one that is designed to extract the maximum purchase price from a group of interested buyers by creating and fostering competition.

Many, if not most bidders, regard the current price as the purchase price of the auction item at that time. The problem is that the current price increases with each new bid. This makes the "price" a moving price which forces a continual reevaluation of a new and higher price as the current price escalates. The only obvious option is to bid higher than the current price or leave the auction. The Savvy Bidder expects the auction to close at approximately the market value and can therefore escape continual reevaluations based on the current price. This enables the Savvy Bidder to deploy bidding tactics to help her win the auction strategically.

Strategic Bidding Tactics

As a Savvy Bidder you will utilize bidding tactics. These are bidding methods you use to carry out your bidding plan within the scope of your bidding budget. Here is a brief introduction to the bidding tactics we will discuss in this book:

- The Savvy Bidder realizes the advantages and disadvantages of the proxy bid and thus makes use of proxy bidding for tactical purposes rather than to reduce his competitive workload as it is promoted. The tactical use of the proxy bid leverages a bidding method that is really there to help the auction's current price increase.

- Single-unit eBay auctions can be won by as little as one cent. It therefore makes tactical sense to utilize cent values in bids, but *only when* the use of cents provides a clear tactical advantage.

- Adjustment bids are used tactically to bring the current price back to a whole dollar amount. The tactic is useful for helping all participating bidders think in terms of whole dollars with the objective of increasing your own effectiveness using cents later in the auction.

- While minimum bidding should be avoided, it can be used for tactical purposes. While the typical bidder will tend to place bids at the required minimum bid amount in an effort to minimize his bid's impact on the current price, the Savvy Bidder may use a minimum bid for stealth purposes.

♦ Bidding just below the seller's reserve price is a tactic that leverages the additional burden a hidden reserve price places on the participants in an auction. This is a powerful bidding tactic that will be discussed later.

♦ Placing a last second bid (a snipe bid) is a formidable tactic that every Savvy Bidder should master. This is not to say that snipe bidding should always be used. But, when needed, and done skillfully, snipe bidding is a very effective bidding tactic.

Bidding tactics are discussed in part *Tactics and Techniques* and throughout this book. It is important to clarify that bidding tactics are not the entire answer to winning eBay auctions. They are tools that must be backed up by sound strategic bidding principles.

Summary

There are very basic elements to participating in eBay auctions as a Savvy Bidder:

1. Determine a target price that is based on empirical pricing information of the same or comparable auction item within the same auction venue (or alternatively external to the auction venue). Referring to the closing price of previous auctions effectively disassociates pricing information from the bidding activity of individual bidders in those auctions.

2. Accept the target price or, of course, reject it and avoid the auction (or do not expect to win the auction).

3. Determine a bidding budget so that you have the ability to bid decisively when and as needed.

4. Explore the auction's landscape to acquire information that your opponents may not have. Always seek to increase your competitive strength with information.

5. Develop a bidding plan and change the plan as the auction situation dictates.

6. Keep yourself free from focusing on the current price. The current price is misleading and tends to pull bidders into a price chase that maximizes the auction's closing price.

7. Deploy bidding tactics within the scope of your bidding budget and plan with the objective of leveraging a position in the auction that leads to winning the auction.

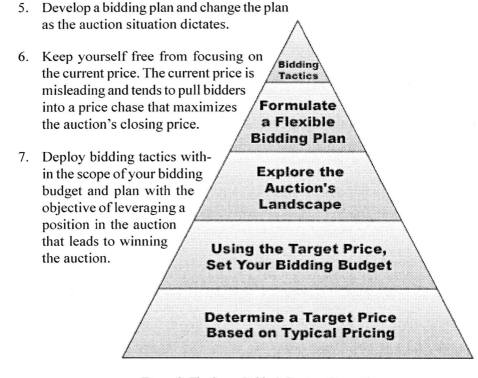

Figure 2: The Savvy Bidder's Strategy Pyramid.

In a nutshell, being a Savvy Bidder means:

> Understanding the auction's landscape, strategically position in the auction by utilizing bidding tactics according to a flexible bidding plan that is within the scope of your bidding budget as defined by a target price.

Conclusion

Strategic bidding proposes to give you a competitive advantage. You make an effort to leverage the information available to help position to win the auction. You attempt to lead your opponent bidders to make bidding choices that are really in *your* best interest. You acquire information about your opponents and try to leverage their bidding habits to work against them. You capitalize on your opponent's lack of information when they do not take the time to explore the auction's landscape. You bid at times and in ways that others do not fully understand to confuse and disarm them competitively. At times you remain silent in the auction and at other times you let your presence be fully known.

This is pretty rough stuff to the average eBay participant. But these tactics are not mean spirited. They are not against the rules, nor are they unfair. Considering that the eBay auction mechanism is specifically designed to create competition to the ultimate benefit of the seller and eBay itself, perhaps fairness is a matter of an individual's perspective. Being a strategic bidder may call for you to be an aggressive bidder at times. This does not mean an overspending bidder, but rather one who seeks every permissible competitive advantage possible. In single-unit auctions, the most common type of eBay auction, there will always be just one winner. The idea is for you to be that winner in your chosen auctions and to be more than the "lucky winner".

Now it's time to explore some fundamentals of auctions that will help you apply the principles of strategic bidding.

Introduction to Online Auctions

This chapter introduces you to several fundamental concepts of online auctions. Understanding these concepts will be important to your future strategic bidding efforts.

Why Online Auctions Work

The auction concept has been around for many centuries and has proven to be a highly successful form of commerce. Online auctions are fairly new on the scene, but are based on the same fundamental concepts that have been in use for a very long time. The basic objective of the auction is to sell tangible goods quickly within an existing, but not well defined, market. In theory, auctions propose to allow the prospective buyers to determine the selling price. To maximize the selling price, prospective buyers are placed in competition with one another. To heighten competition, the single-unit auction creates artificial scarcity by offering one item per auction, and therefore allowing only one participant to win the right to purchase the item. The auction formula is a brilliant form of commerce because it exploits human natures desire for maximum gain at the lowest cost.

Fundamentally, auctions work best when:

- A market exists for the auction merchandise but the market is not well defined.

- Prospective buyers can play a role in setting the selling price (called "Price Participation").

- There is competition among the prospective buyers.

- Artificial scarcity is created which heightens competition.

- All participants in the auction desire to win it.

Of course there are other factors that help auctions work. But the above are the underpinnings of single-unit auctions. In addition there are a number of factors that interfere with how well an auction works. These factors will be introduced throughout this book.

Given an unobstructed ability of prospective buyers to determine the selling price of an auction, the objective of all bidders is usually to purchase the article at the lowest possible price. However the tendency of an auction to close at a lower price is offset by the competition among the bidders. That is to say that competition serves to increase the closing price. Thus, under ideal circumstances, the final closing price is an equilibrium that results from bidders trying to keep their bid amounts down against the competitive effort required to win the auction.

It is important to understand that the closing price of an auction is *not* set by the highest bidder in an auction (with the exception of when the auction receives only one bid). Rather the closing price is established by the collective activity of all of the auction's participants. Assuming the seller does not place a price restriction on the auction (a reserve price) the highest bidder would not likely have bid what he did unless the competition required it. As such, an auction's final closing price can be thought of as the culmination of all bids in that auction with the small bids being equally as important to the closing price of the auction as the larger bids.

In many respects the auction is a sales environment that is based almost entirely on leveraging competition among the prospective buyers. In effect, the auction format capitalizes on that which most buyers prefer to not contend with – competition. Perhaps this is why retail purchasing has been so widely accepted, and is in fact accepted worldwide – there is minimal competition on a purchase-by-purchase basis. In retail someone else predetermines the selling price. In auctions, the prospective buyers determine the selling price (if the seller does not introduce price restrictions). While the eBay venue has made auctions an interesting and challenging method of purchasing, we must not forget that the underlying purpose and intent of single-unit auctions is to maximize the selling price of an item by creating competition among multiple prospective buyers for an artificially scarce supply.

Lack of Information

The auction format is simple in its underlying design, yet often unfolds in a complex manner depending on the quantity, interest and bid activity of the participants. The complexity stems from the fact that key information is deliberately withheld from the participants to achieve an increase in competition. For instance, the theoretical effect of hiding the bid amounts of other bidders during a single-unit auction is so that bidders are forced to call on their own perception of value rather than someone else's. However, as we will discuss, this is not usually what actually happens.

Also no bidder has any way of knowing for certain who is interested in a particular auction that has not yet bid. Thus, the actual participants are allowed to let their own imagination create the fear that they will not win the auction at a price that they would like to pay if they could. The hope, of course, is that this imaginary fear will serve to increase the value perception of those who desire to win the auction, given the threat of competition.

There are other dynamics of auctions as they relate to the lack of information, but the above should suffice to make the point that the effectiveness of auctions is increased because the participants do not have access to information that would otherwise help them compete in the auction. Once could argue that lack of information is a way to assure fairness in auctions, but the fact remains that it's a way to maximize the closing price of the auction. The Savvy Bidder remains aware that, in online auctions, what people are *not* told is as important as what they *are* told. Knowing this, the Savvy Bidder seeks to gain information that is not obvious to his opponents.

Competition

If, upon its close, an auction received only one bid, there was no competition in that auction. It then becomes a straightforward purchase if the lone bidder meets the seller's reserve, should one exist. Of course, the auction format works best when multiple persons compete with one another, each with a desire to own the item.

While an auction is running no one can be quite sure how many participants will become involved. So, the extent of the competition, in terms of the number and strength of participants, cannot be known for certain. This creates a level of uncertainty in terms of how much competition one may have to contend with. It can be said with some certainty that people do not like to compete for their purchases. Add to this the uncertainty of who the competition is or will be and there exists a resistance to the auction format. But this resistance is offset by the possibility of obtaining a much lower price than might otherwise be possible or to acquire merchandise that is not commonly available. It can be said, therefore, that online auctions work despite their format because the purchase and price opportunities offset the purchase effort.

In addition, each bidder is free to express what he will pay for the item above the current price. This permits an individual bidder to gain a competitive advantage by bidding high. By allowing anyone to bid as high as they like, the auction format permits the force of money to secure a competitive advantage that, of course, is to the sellers benefit.

However, in practice bidders avoid high bids. Rather, they tend to bid at the lowest practical amount. This helps a bidder feel he is not overbidding while still being competitive. The fact that high bidding is not a common practice is good, given the manner in which the eBay mechanism ratchets up the current price on each bid.

For example, if two bidders were each to place a very high bid at the same instant, the eBay auction mechanism would increase the current price to the amount of the lower of the two bids. This obligates one bidder to the auction, and perhaps at a price he feels he could have avoided with a smaller bid amount. Thus the auction mechanism actually serves to keep bid amounts down.

To minimize impacting the current price, bidders will naturally bid cautiously which usually results in several bids of lower amounts in lieu of a single high bid. When all bidders take this cautious approach, the auction receives a higher <u>quantity</u> of bids. A higher quantity of bids actually implies a greater interest in the auction which increases the desire to own, which encourages more bids. Meanwhile, the eBay auction mechanism dutifully increments the auction's current price with each bid. Thus, even if bidders take a cautious approach with small bids, the auction format still serves the seller.

Another interesting dynamic of online auctions is that small bids actually increase competition in the auction. This is because small bids are easily to compete against. To illustrate, if an auction has a current price of $100.00 and a minimum bid is placed that increments the current price to $112.50, the $2.50 price increase is relatively easy to cope with by other bidders. A second bidder need only increase his willingness to pay a few more dollars over the $112.50 bid. If all bidders were to place only small bids, each bidder actually makes it easier for his opponents to compete in the auction. Interestingly, even if the second bidder were to place a $1000.00 bid against a $112.50 current price, the current price would still increase only to $115.00 on that $1,000.00 bid, presenting the illusion that the auction is still winnable which, of course, invites more competition. Contrast this with traditional auctions where a $1,000.00 bid would be gladly accepted and would set the auction's current price to $1,000.00. Online auctions mask high bids to perpetuate the illusion that the auction is still within the reach of those not willing to spend $1,000.00, in this example. Online auctions are based on a very clever system to entice competition by making it appear that an auction can be won for less than may actually be necessary to win it. This keeps throngs of persons glued to their eBay browser screens as they eagerly try to buy what they may not be able to have.

By using the current price as the primary factor to determine bidding, the participants enter into a leapfrog situation as each bidder increases what he is willing to pay for the item. This creates a bidding cycle that raises the auction's current price in relatively small amounts. Since it is easier to accept a relatively small price increase compared to a large price increase, bidders are better able to stay in the auction, continuing to feed the cycle with additional bids. This is why small bids actually create competition.

This describes the typical mechanical process of millions of eBay auctions each day. Essentially, persons interested in owning the item keep a constraint on their bid amounts. As bidding occurs, the auction's current price increases, providing evidence that competition exists. Yet the current price often implies that the auction can be won at a lower price than may be necessary. This further enhances the desire by individuals to own the item, up to a price point. Thus, perceived value is heightened by the competitive activity itself while participants are spurred on by the allure of an attractive current price.

On the surface it is obvious that the bidder with the highest valuation for the item (the bidder who is willing to pay more than anyone else for the item) will win the auction. But, the question is to what extent was that bidder's valuation influenced by the bids of other persons active in the auction. If all players were to bid in an auction with no knowledge of any other bid activity, including bid amounts (a closed-bid auction) and bidder identifications or even knowledge that other bids had actually occurred does not exist, then bids are more likely to be closer to the true personal valuation of the bidders. In this scenario, low bidding would be less effective because bidders would not be able to rely on other bids to help make a determination if their bid was sufficient to compete in the auction. However, this is not the case with the typical single-unit eBay auction. In eBay auctions there is just enough information available to help people bid low enough to possibly take a lead in the auction, but not so high as to fear the risk of overpaying.

When one is aware of the dynamics of competition in eBay auctions, he is able to appreciate how auctions achieve the closing prices they do. The Savvy Bidder makes an effort to understand, and leverage, the dynamics of competition in eBay auctions.

Value Perception

Once a person invests herself in the auction by bidding, personal dynamics come into play. Having bid, she confirms in her mind the desire to own the item and is more likely to believe that ownership is possible. She is therefore more likely to accept a new, higher current price each time an opponent places a new bid. Because of her interest in acquiring the item, she is more likely to continuously reassess her willingness to pay an amount approximately equivalent to the auction's current price.

The challenge is that the current price is constantly increasing with each new bid. This forces the bidder to reassess her willingness to pay an amount at least slightly higher than the current price. However, as mentioned, the current price does not necessarily indicate what another bidder is willing to pay nor does it reflect the amount of an existing proxy bid. Since the current price is the most obvious indication of the valuation the participants have placed on the item up to that point, bidders tend to use it as the basis for their own value perception. The current price is then used to decide whether or not to continue to bid. Thus bidders get caught up in a continuous reassessment process using a factor (the current price) that is not necessarily representative of what the auction item can be purchased for. This is an important dynamic for the Savvy Bidder to understand.

Desire to Own

We all know how wanting can cloud judgment. Once we begin to desire something we set in motion a course of events that usually leads to attaining it. Once an online auction participant begins this process, it comes as no surprise that he will continue until he has either won the right to purchase the item, loses interest or the current price has exceeded what he is willing to spend. As you can see there are many ways that the auction format eliminates participants.

It is this process of elimination that also contributes to the success of online auctions. Few like to be told no, you can't have that. Commercialism in our society spends a great deal of energy and money telling us that we *can* have whatever we want. eBay is one of the few commercial environments where people are eliminated as prospective buyers as a matter if course. In fact, if a single-unit eBay auction ad 10 unique bidders participating in it, 9 will be denied the right to purchase that item. What's one way to not be denied the right to purchase a thing of interest? Justify a higher price and bid again.

We would be appalled if another shopper took a piece of merchandise from our shopping cart at a retail store. Sure we could go get another identical product having suffered little more than an affront to our ego. However, the sense of ownership begins once a decision is made to purchase the merchandise and the decision is manifest by placing the merchandise in our shopping cart. We adhere to our *right* to own a thing even before we actually make the purchase (traditional retailers want nothing less). This mind set applies in eBay auctions as well – bidding begins the process of ownership in the mind of the bidder. This is in contradiction to what is actually occurring; bidding actually begins the process of *obtaining the right* to make the purchase – bidding is not buying.

The sense of ownership is a dynamic that, once begun, can sometimes lead to irrational decisions. For instance, a bidder with a strong desire to win the auction could find himself dueling it out in a bidding war with another bidder who also has a strong desire to win the auction. Also, a bidder intent on winning the auction could place a large bid, only to find that his bid actually increased the desirability of the auction item among his opponents. The stronger the desire for ownership among the participants, the stronger the competition in that auction. And the stronger the competition, the higher the closing price of the single-unit auction.

Small Price Changes

We have all experienced the relative ease of spending just a little bit more once we have accepted spending a larger amount. Once we have come to accept the $20,000.00 price tag for an automobile we would like to own, it is relatively easy to justify another $200.00 for an option we can't live without – it's just 1% more. This applies in eBay auctions as well, except that if we don't accept the additional price increase caused by a higher bid, we forfeit the right to purchase the auction item entirely. Imagine forfeiting the car purchase because you can't bring yourself to pay 1% more for an option – just forfeit the option. But, while the auction is running, bidders still have a chance to hold on to the possibility of making the purchase – it often takes just a few more dollars to stay in the game.

Everyone has a price limit. This limit is set by the amount of money available for certain auction purchases or is set by the personal valuation assigned to the item. Certainly you are not willing to pay more than an item is worth to you and certainly you would prefer to pay the lowest possible price. However, when you learn that other people are competing for the same item and that they are perhaps ready and willing to spend more than you, there may be a willingness on your part to pay a higher price. Since there can only be one winner (in the single-unit eBay auction), your alternative is to be the highest bidder or lose the auction to another. *Auctions capitalize on the fact that people are generally willing to "rethink" the price they are willing to pay once they learn of the competition for an item they desire to own.*

Throughout this book we'll call on these auction-related basics as we apply them to strategic bidding. Next let's discuss a very important aspect of strategic bidding, the target price.

The Target Price

A target price is a probable closing price of a particular auction within the market. A target price helps you establish a bidding budget. With a well-formed bidding budget, you are better able to select optimum bidding tactics for the auction. Therefore, the goal of a target price is to provide you with a stable price guideline as the basis for a strategic bidding budget.

The concept of the target price is not the same as the common "maximum price". You will often hear advice that, before bidding, you should decide the most you would be willing to pay for the item. This is certainly good advice, but such advice is crippling to winning auctions at the lowest possible price. So we take it to a higher level and operate with a target price. A target price is a realistic and probable closing price based on the present market. A target price is then used for strategic bidding purposes, not necessarily as a purchase price goal.

A target price, as we are defining it, is not what you would be willing to pay or would like to pay, but the price the prevailing market will probably dictate based on recent performance of the market. This is important because you cannot generally succeed in a market if you ignore the market's behavior. But this is just what the typical bidder does – he overlooks the fact that a particular electronic device, for instance, has a prevailing price of $500.00 and enters the auction thinking he'll win it for $250.00, which is his personal price preference. He may indeed win the auction, but only if he is lucky. Since the Savvy Bidder makes a concerted effort to eliminate as much luck from the equation as possible, the Savvy Bidder needs a better way.

Let's lay some groundwork by first outlining three typical approaches concerning pricing:

1. "I won't know what I will spend until I see how the bidding goes in the auction".

2. "I am not willing to spend any more than $250.00".

3. "I understand that the typical closing price of auctions for this item is $500.00 and will therefore plan my bidding strategy accordingly".

Just by our discussion so far in this book, you can understand why the approach illustrated by statement #1 is not for the Savvy Bidder. Since it has no specific price goal, it cripples a strategic approach and allows the competition in the auction to lead you along. The Savvy Bidder makes an effort be in control, not be controlled.

The approach illustrated by statement #2 is based on the common "determine the maximum you are willing to spend" approach. The risk here is that your personal price may be too high or too low with respect to the price that your opponents are "willing" to spend. If too low, you put yourself on track to under bid, which usually results in losing the auction. If too high, you are on course to overpay for the auction. This approach is based on what you would <u>like</u> the closing price to be rather than what may be realistic given the current market. This approach is also based on such things as how much you can afford or possibly the spending limit your spouse has set for you. It also factors in your personal price pain point – your not-to-exceed-under-any-circumstances price. While these are valid personal issues, they set up a weak foundation for strategic approach to eBay auctions.

The third approach is a strategic approach. Here you understand to what price the current market may take the auction. Once you understand what the market generally thinks the item is worth, you can decide then and there if you have a reasonable chance of actually winning the right to purchase the item, considering your personal financial capability of doing so. Assuming you accept the probable market price, you are positioned to take a strategic approach to the auction.

But, just because you accept a probable closing price does not mean you will seek to pay that price. I do not advocate readily paying the market price for any eBay auction. In fact, I advocate paying the absolute lowest price possible – that's the game. But, when you understand the probable closing price of an auction, you have taken the first step in deciding the best possible tactics to win an auction at the lowest possible price. When you understand the typical closing price for an auction:

♦ You are less likely to be caught up in the snare of price escalation. As discussed in Law *#12: Understand Current Price Escalation*, the eBay auction format snares participants into chasing the current price. By posing the current price as an attractive purchase price, persons are tempted to think, "You mean I could buy that for only…", thereby enticing them to bid.

♦ You are able to establish a bidding budget that you can strategically leverage. Without a bidding budget you will tend to bid with apprehension, which usually results in tactically weak bids.

♦ You are not pulled along with the auction. This frees you of having to constantly reassess if you willing to stay in the auction. This, in turn, helps you remain a strong competitor as well as a sensible bidder.

♦ You have a fairly good idea where the participants will take the auction's closing price. This frees you to consider stealth bidding tactics. The typical bidder does not normally use stealth tactics because such appears to consume one's money with little apparent progress toward making a purchase. Naturally, if a person has little idea what they may have to spend, and are throttled by the fear of overspending, they will not be inclined to spend money (bid) on the premise of saving money.

♦ You are positioned to bid aggressively because you are not fear-bound. When you are confident that the auction will close at its typical market price, you are not locked in perpetual avoidance of overpaying. Auctions work on the basis of allowing the participants to collectively establish a closing price (within the constraints of the seller). Except in special circumstances, the prevailing "price comfort" of the market tends to cap the typical closing price of online auctions. Yet due to the general approach of "pay the lowest possible price", auction closing prices tend to be held down. The end result is that auctions will generally close in the range of the typical closing price for the same or comparable item. The Savvy Bidder understands this and fully exploits its competitive value.

All of the above points have a common theme – pay the lowest possible for the auction. To do that, you need to understand where the auction may go, in terms of price, so that you can work the auction and not be worked by it. In addition, you must avoid a personal price preference as your strategic guide. Only then are you able to free yourself from the snare of price escalation, to think strategically, deploy sound bidding tactics, plan your participation, manage your bidding budget and bid aggressively and with confidence.

Typical Price Objectives

Before we discuss establishing a target price let's take a closer look at the various objectives as it concerns price. There are three general price objectives typically used in eBay auctions:

1. Win the auction at a bargain price.

2. Win the auction at a price you are most comfortable paying.

3. Win the auction at a price that is less than the maximum price you are willing to pay.

The Bargain Price Approach

Expecting to get a bargain price in eBay auctions is frustrating because it is becoming increasingly hard to realize that goal. There are several reasons for this:

- Sellers routinely limit the lower price level with the First Bid and often with hidden reserve prices. Because a large number of sellers have experience selling on eBay, they are now better able to set the First Bid and/or the reserve to a price that is consistent with past performance of the eBay market for the item. Very often this pricing is gleaned from other auctions for the same or comparable item or from the seller's own past experience. eBay makes it easy to research the typical closing prices of the same or comparable item. Any regular seller who expects to make a profit is going to take a few minutes and research the potential closing price based from recently closed auctions. Naturally, the seller is likely to set the First Bid price, and possibly a reserve price (collectively referred to as the "floor price"), accordingly. In this regard, regular sellers often set a floor price that take their auctions out of the reach of bidders seeking to win the auction at bargain price.

- In the single-unit auction, the more actual bidders there are, the higher the closing price (because the current price increases with each bid). eBay membership has soared since the days when eBay was an upstart online auction venue. The greater the number of participants, the greater the potential competition. eBay has reached a membership level that virtually assures sellers a larger audience for their auctions. Winning auctions at an unrealistically low price is getting much harder to do.

The bargain price objective damages a bidder's competitive strength because it tends to confine her to minimum bidding. Minimum bids are not normally competitive because they are easily to outbid. Also the minimum bidder must continuously reassess her personal valuation for the item. This leads to being current price focused which in turn leads to becoming caught up in an ascending price cycle. The cycle is broken only when the price pain point is reached or when the auction closes. Such a bidder takes stabs at auctions, but never seems to consistently win them.

There are still bargains to be had on eBay, if one is intent on locating them. However, regular eBay sellers are now experienced enough to capitalize on typical market pricing. More important, there are now enough prospective bidders on eBay to virtually insure that a bargain auction will fetch a closing price consistent with past market performance. The simple fact is that when there is stiff competition for a "bargain", the price is almost always driven beyond the bargain point. On eBay, if it looks like a bargain, it probably won't be for long or there is something very wrong with the auction.

The bottom line is that going into an eBay auction with a bargain price approach does not usually result in consistently winning auctions.

The Most Comfortable Price Objective

Another price objective is what you are most comfortable paying for the auction item. This objective is subject to a variety of issues. One issue is that you are prone to change your price acceptance as it comes to light that the price you are comfortable with may not be attainable given the competition in an auction. In this case, there are only two possibilities; increase what you are comfortable paying or abandon the auction. Interestingly, once the desire to own sets in, there is a tendency to justify a higher price than what was originally decided. Small current price increments help bidders adjust their comfort level upward in palatable steps.

The mind has the incredible capacity to rationalize purchases once the interest to own has developed. Have you ever found yourself saying: "I'll buy this now and cut back on lunches for a few weeks". Purchase rationalization is one reason why credit cards are big business – buy it now, deal with payment later. In online auctions many bidders get caught up in the process of continuously increasing what they are "willing" to pay for an auction item due, in large part, because the interest to make the purchase becomes stronger the more the person is involved with an auction.

When you are engaged in an auction you see the bidding actions of other bidders. Some will bid very low, others moderately and others occasionally bid high. Each bid is based on the bidder's own level of interest due to factors unique to the individual bidder. It is virtually impossible to place any significance on individual bids because you cannot know the bidder's motivation or price preference. Does a minimum bid represent that bidder's full personal valuation or is he fishing for a bargain? Does a high proxy bid represent the maximum the bidder is willing (or able) to pay or is it an irresponsible bid? When we assign a meaning to individual bids we risk being influenced by the actions of bidders who may not know what they are ultimately willing to pay.

Going into an auction with a "comfortable" price causes one to focus on the current price. This comes as no surprise because the current price is the most visible means of determining if the auction's current price is in alignment with your price comfort. The problem with being current price focused is two fold. First the current price is not necessarily the actual price one will pay. And second, your price comfort level may actually track the current price, up to a point.

In my opinion, taking a comfortable price objective is competitively weak. Such a price objective is subject to change and encourages becoming current price focused. As individual bidders watch the current price increase, some or all of the bidders will increase what they are comfortable paying which creates the very competition auctions need to fetch the highest possible closing price.

The Maximum Price Objective

The maximum amount you are willing to pay creates a dichotomy. On the one hand your maximum price is what you would pay if you had to. On the other hand, you want to avoid your maximum price. The resulting internal resistance may lead to your being overly cautious in the auction. You may then place minimum bids trying to avoid impacting the current price any more than possible so you won't be faced with having to pay up to your maximum price. When all bidders are caught in this "price avoidance" syndrome, the auction may actually close at a higher price than it may have otherwise. This occurs because participants place minimum bids trying to avoid impacting the current price and yet find themselves acclimating to a gradually increasing current price.

I have run across several sources that encourage placing bids at the maximum one is willing to pay in an auction. The logic is that the bidder will actually only pay one bid increment over the <u>second</u> highest bidder. While this is logical, this practice leaves a bidder vulnerable to a number of possibilities:

- A bid at your maximum price will create a proxy bid if your bid is higher than the required minimum bid increment or another's proxy bid, should one exist. As discussed in the section *Proxy Bidding* in part *Tactics and Techniques*, if a proxy bid takes the highest bidder position it creates a target for other bidders. It is not improbable that a bidder who bids at his maximum may actually find himself paying close to his maximum due to other bidders attempting to outbid the proxy (assuming they don't manage to do so).

- When a bidder places a maximum bid in a reserve auction, and that bid is greater than the seller's reserve (assuming no other proxy bid exists), the auction's current price immediately escalates up to the seller's reserve. In this situation, the bidder plunges headlong into becoming committed to purchasing the auction at a price that is at least the seller's reserve price. Yet, the bidder may have been thinking that a healthy bid on a low current price would have given him great protection against subsequent bidders.

But when the current price is escalated rapidly in this way, the competitive benefits of the proxy bid are diminished. In this scenario, the maximum bid actually hurt the bidder competitively because it caused the removal of the hidden reserve which is usually a deterrent to bidding.

♦ When a person bids his maximum, he leaves no bidding budget to use for subsequent bidding – his personal budget for the auction is tapped out. Of course, one could argue that it makes no difference if the entire budget is expended in several bids or in a single bid. This logic assumes, however, that the bidder actually needed to pay up to his maximum to win the auction, which is not known until the auction has ended. It is quite possible that an auction might close at a lower price if a maximum bid were not placed in a single bid. Since a maximum bid represents a competitor taking a strong position in the auction, competing bidders may also introduce strong competition in response, leading to a very rapid escalation of the auction's closing price.

♦ The potential for fraud in online auctions should never be dismissed with the "it can't happen to me" attitude. Assume a bidder places a bid at his maximum in an auction that is being shilled (see *Glossary of Terms*). A large bid, which may become a proxy bid, provides fodder for the shill bidder to take the auction's current price up a large notch. This is done by the shill bidder placing a series of bids at the minimum bid increment until the large proxy is outbid. The shill bidder may actually retract his last bid, which was at a minimum bid increment (the retraction of a small bid does not raise as much suspicion as the retraction of a large bid). The retraction puts the bidder who placed the large proxy back into the highest bidder position leaving the current price up at proxy bidder's maximum bid.

One advantage of a maximum price is that it is not normally flexible in the bidder's mind. Often a maximum price is based on the limits of a personal budget, an appraised value, a retail value or it is the person's price pain point. With some type of price guideline available such as a retail price, a person tends to reason that she will not pay more for an auction item than she would from a retail source. Of course, a personal budget is a very limiting factor and, when ignored, carries all sorts of consequences. It is likely that a bidder will abandon an auction before bidding over the maximum she is willing (or able) to pay. However, it is also possible that she may find herself actually paying up to her maximum for the reasons discussed above.

As you may have guessed, I am not a proponent of bidding to one's maximum in a single bid. However, it is possible to bid effectively through a series of bids that may collectively reach the maximum you are willing to spend. The objective is to leverage the money you have personally allocated to the auction by using it tactically, avoiding consuming that money in a single bid.

In summary, with a target price you escape the often-futile bargain price approach because you are realistic about the probable closing price of the auction. A target price helps you avoid trying to compete with a personal preference price that may not be sufficient to win the auction or, indeed, may be higher than necessary. A target price gives you a guideline to mange money for the auction in lieu of a placing a single bid to your maximum price. The target price concept supplants the less efficient approaches to eBay auctions, in terms of price.

Determining the Target Price

To determine a target price you first obtain a *typical* closing price by investigating recently completed auctions for the same or comparable auction item.

The closing price of single-unit auctions is representative of the collective interest among the bidders that participated. By taking the final price of closed auctions you automatically eliminate the individual personal valuations of each bidder in those auctions. This is important since you do not want to be lead to believe that any single bid represents the market value for the item. You need only know at what price those auctions closed at.

Once you have the closing prices for several or many auctions of the same or comparable item, you have the low and the high closing prices. This gives you the price range in which these auctions closed. Then, take the price that falls in the middle of the low and the high prices. This middle price is the typical closing price. The more auctions you gather closing prices from, the more representative the typical closing price will be.

Assume for instance that you find five eBay auctions for the same or comparable eBay auction item that have recently closed. The closing prices are: $110.00, $125.00, $156.20, $92.00 and $102.50, listed in the order in which you found the auctions. You can see that $92.00 was the low price while $156.20 was the high price. When you add these two values together and divide by two you get a result of $129.00, rounded to the nearest dollar.

$$(\$92.00 + \$156.20 = \$248.20) / 2 = \$124.10$$

Note: Do not include auctions that closed without a winning bidder. Also do not include auctions that were closed with the *Buy It Now* feature (indicated by the closed auction having only one bid and a winning bidder). If these auctions were included, your calculation would be skewed. You only want auctions in which there was competitive bidding and an actual winning bidder.

We take the middle of the low and high values because we want to eliminate the unique factors that resulted in the low closing price and the high closing price. When an auction closes at the low end of the typical market price, the auction may have ended in the middle of the night, or a serious buyer forgot to bid, or perhaps the seller's presentation was of lower quality. Of course, the item could have been blemished in some way. On the high end, the seller could have posted a very enticing auction or the auction attracted a bidder with plenty of money with a strong desire to own the item. Perhaps the auction closed during a peak purchasing period (such as Saturday evening). By taking the middle value you help eliminate the factors that caused the low and high closing prices.

As we discussed in the chapter *Why Online Auctions Work*, eBay auctions work best when they receive competition. This is because competition tends to pull the closing price up which is offset by the participants effort to pay the lowest possible price. Price equilibrium is eventually found in the auction, which becomes the closing price when the auction's period expires. When you take the closing prices of many auctions, the typical closing price more closely represents the market's equilibrium for that auction item. This market equilibrium tends to remain rather stable for a period of time.

Once you have a typical closing price you have one more step – you must accept or reject the typical price. If you do not accept it, your research has saved you from spending your time participating in the auction. If the typical price is too high for you, you will likely not be an aggressive bidder in the auction for fear of exceeding your personal budget. Of course you may find that the typical closing price is very attractive. In fact, you may even find that the typical closing price is lower than you originally thought it would be.

As you can see by our discussion, it is important that you take the time to understand the typical closing price and use that as a guide in lieu of what you would like the price to be, or not be. If you do not look to the market's price level, you will invariably focus on the price opinions of bidders within the current auction (those price opinions being expressed by their bids) – *there is simply not enough information within a running auction to determine a competitively appropriate price guideline*. When such a guideline is lacking, you will tend to follow the lead of your opponents, allowing yourself to be pulled into being current price focused. Put more succinctly, the current auction is the last place you want to obtain a price guideline from.

When you have accepted the typical closing price, it becomes the price that you will base your bidding strategy on – it becomes a target price. As mentioned, a target price is not necessarily the price you will accept paying. Rather, it is a price guideline to help you determine your strategic approach to the auction.

The process of obtaining a typical closing price is the first and most important step toward competitive bidding in eBay auctions. This is because not only have you obtained a realistic typical price, but you have also determined if you can stand behind this price once you start bidding. Once you have accepted the typical price you can enter the auction of interest and bid with a measure of confidence.

Alternate Methods to Determine the Target Price

The optimum method to establish the target price is to research recently closed auctions for the same or comparable item within the same auction venue. Staying in the same venue is important because each market has different players and expectations. A particular brand and model DVD player, for instance, has a different price performance in retail than in online auctions. Retail selling is different than online auctions due to different distribution methods, different customer expectations, different methods of promotion, etc. Retail offers buyers a different level of security, convenience and access to merchandise as well as purchase timeframes.

But it is certainly possible to use retail pricing to determine a target price in an auction for the same or comparable product. However, the resulting target price is likely to be higher than the typical market price in the auction venue. This is because auction buyers try to purchase at a price lower than retail. While a higher than necessary target price won't hurt your ability to win the auction, it may mean that you are destined to overpay in the auction environment.

There will be times when there is simply no historical auction information available for a particular auction item. In that case, you must locate pricing information outside of the auction venue. Below are some ways of establishing the target price when there is no historical pricing information within the same auction venue:

♦ As mentioned, you could establish the target price based on the current retail or street price for the same or comparable product. Use one or more of the many comparative shopping web sites on the Internet to determine high and low pricing. Make an effort to get pricing for the same make and model of product as the auction is presenting.

◆ You could establish the target price based on recently closed auctions for the same or comparable auction item in another auction venue. For instance, you could research historical pricing on the Yahoo auction web site or perhaps the Amazon.com auction site. Use care with this approach because these venues do not have the same quantity of potential buyers as does eBay. The greater the potential number of bidders, the more reliable and consistent historical pricing will be. Also, avoid obtaining pricing information from new person-to-person auction sites and those that do not have a large membership.

◆ For collectibles there are many books, databases and web sites that provide a "book" value for particular items. These are often excellent sources for pricing information. Keep in mind that the pricing information these sources provide is usually based on what collectors are likely to pay to purchase a specific collectible item. The pricing information is not necessarily what an auction bidder will pay. This is because there are other factors an auction bidder considers such as the seller's reputation, lack of experience with the seller, the condition of the item, the often unknown source of the item, risk of fraud, and so on.

◆ You may wish to use an appraisal estimate from product researchers as the basis for a target price. This has disadvantages because it often requires time to perform the appraisal, there is usually a fee involved and it requires the cooperation of the seller. However, for high price auction items, an appraisal may be the best possible option for pricing as well as other reasons. The advantage is that an appraisal provides you with information that your opponents may not have. People generally deal with high-risk purchase situations by reducing the amount of money they will spend, i.e., by lowering their financial risk. It is quite possible that bidders who lack appraisal information will bid too low to be competitive because they perceive a higher risk.

◆ Lacking an alternative, you could establish a target price based on the value you believe the auction item would lend to your existing collection. In this case, the target price is based on your own unique circumstance and not on historical pricing information.

◆ If you intend to resell an auction item, you could set your target price based on what future monetary return you expect or hope the item may fetch. It is wise to perform comparative pricing research, ideally within the same auction venue. One additional step is to reduce the target price by a percentage that allows the profit margin you seek.

◆ Lacking any form of pricing information, either within the same auction venue or outside it, you could set the target price based simply what you are willing to pay for the auction item. The key is that once you establish the target price, avoid changing it while participating in the auction. By remaining steadfast with a predetermined target price, you use it to help you bid strategically in the auction.

Let's take a moment and address how *not* to establish a target price. Never establish a target price according to the bidding actions of another bidder. By doing so you are subject to erroneous pricing information. You cannot know what is motivating a person to bid as she does and you cannot know if a bid represents the bidder's entire personal valuation or something less. It is impossible to know if a bidder has sound knowledge of the auction item, or no knowledge of it at all for that matter. A reliable target price cannot be derived from the actions of individual bidders. By contrast, historical pricing information is derived from the cumulative bids within similar auctions. In a single-unit auction, the only pricing information of any value is the price at which the auction closed because it is at that point that price negotiations ceased and an actual purchase was made.

Discounting the Target Price

As we have discussed you determined the typical closing price by researching recently closed auctions, in the same venue if at all possible. You then obtained a middle value between the lowest closing price and the highest closing price. This is a typical closing price for the auctions you researched. However, certain aspects of the auction you are currently pursuing may make it wise to reduce the target price which I call discounting.

For instance, if the condition is slightly lower than the auctions used for the historical pricing information, you may want to discount the target price to bring it more in line with the specific auction of interest. Below are some additional examples of situations to consider in determining whether to discount a target price:

◆ The seller's terms of sale are restrictive or conflict with eBay's policies. Once again, you compensate for the inconsistency, if such is an issue for you.

◆ The seller has an additional profit center – shipping and handling fees. When shipping and handling is excessive, I offset this additional cost by reducing my target price for that auction (that is, if I elect to bid in the auction at all – my personal policy is to not support a seller's excessive shipping and handling profit center by bidding in such auctions).

♦ The seller's profile points are very low or the seller's feedback has an uncomfortable number of negative ratings. This is a risk factor that you may feel necessitates a discounted target price.

♦ The seller has placed a reserve price on the auction and has not disclosed that reserve price in her auction listing. Further, the seller refuses to tell you the reserve when you request it. Personally, I usually do not bid in such auctions because I choose to not bid blind with respect to a reserve price. If you choose to bid in such an auction anyway, you may elect to discount the target price to give yourself a more confined bidding budget. This will place a constraint on your bidding until the reserve price is met by another bidder. Please see Law #37: *Beware the Hidden Reserve Price*.

♦ From reviewing recently closed auctions in the same auction venue you determine that closing prices usually exceed what you know is the typical value of the auction item <u>outside</u> of the auction venue. Whatever the reason for this, you elect to keep your target price consistent with outside pricing knowing that you can purchase from those sources if needed. By discounting the target price, you build in a limit that helps protect you from overpaying in relation to alternate sources.

The above summarized situations that may call for discounting. Following are some examples of perceived risks that may justify discounting the target price:

♦ The seller's description is sketchy or incomplete.

♦ The item's condition is not clear or is not favorable to you, but would be acceptable at a lower price.

♦ The item is remanufactured, refurbished, "factory renewed", recertified, repaired, out of warranty, etc.

♦ The seller's description lacks key information that is important for making an informed decision to participate in the auction.

♦ For a product that is not factory new, the seller is using a manufactures photo rather than a photo of the actual auction item.

♦ There is no photo of the auction item.

By discounting the target price you are effectively adjusting your bidding budget to account for undesirable situations or perceived risks. Your objective is to determine a target price that is appropriate for the specific auction. You want to avoid discounting too much as doing this may hurt your competitive strength in the auction. For instance, if you felt you had to discount the target price by 50%, then maybe there are too many undesirables or risks concerning the auction. If you proceed with a 50% discounted target price, you are likely to limit your competitive strength. On the other hand, a 10%, 20% or even 25% reduction serves a more useful purpose while helping you remain competitive.

Never discount the target price simply because you don't like the typical closing price. If your price research indicates a typical market price of $500.00, for instance, and you don't like or can't afford that price, you may be better deciding to not participate in the auction. If you were to participate with a discounted target price of say, $300.00, you are likely to lose the auction anyway. Let the target price serve you *before* getting involved in auctions you are likely to lose. Remember that the target price is for strategic reasons, not to dictate what you will be willing to spend for the auction item. There is no sense determining a target price simply to force it into alignment with your price preference – such would defeat the purpose of the target price.

Determining a Maximum Target Price

There will be times when an auction develops into a situation where it is practical to exceed the target price. For instance, new information comes to light during the auction that indicates that the original target price was set too low. For strategic purposes you set a maximum target price.

It is important to clarify that while the target price aids your strategic bidding, a *maximum* target price is the absolute shut off, the safety value. You set your bidding budget based on the typical closing price, not the maximum target price. A maximum target price is *not* used to determine your bidding budget. Rather is used as a last resort should you elect to exceed your bidding budget to win the auction should new information to come to light during the auction.

A maximum target price can be determined in a variety of ways. What I suggest is that the maximum target price be set by adding a certain percentage to the target price. 10% for example may provide you with a suitable contingency price. You may choose to set your maximum target price higher or lower depending on the situation at hand and, of course, your personal budget. You might also consider setting your maximum target price at the street price or at the manufacturers suggested retail price (MSRP) if you are pursuing a product also available from retail sources. For collectible items, you might consider the price found in collectible price guides as your maximum target price with the original target price remaining at the typical closing price.

If you use pricing factors that are visible to your opponent bidders such as an MSRP (Manufacturers Suggested Retail Price), your maximum target price will be more competitive should it be needed. Many bidders will take the time to at least conduct some comparative shopping on an auction item of interest to them. MSRP information is readily available across the Internet. It is natural to expect a bidder to avoid paying more than MSRP in an auction, so the MSRP may very well become the maximum your opponent bidders would bid. Knowledgeable collectors understand the current value of collectibles and bid accordingly. When I run across a vintage camera on eBay, the first thing I do is look the camera up in an online camera price guide that I subscribe to. I rarely bid over the guide's price, considering the condition of the camera up for auction. The price provided by the guide is usually my maximum target price, while I'll set a target price at a typical closing price within the venue.

Benefits of the Target Price

Now that we have discussed what a target price is as well as discounting and a maximum target price, let's review the potential benefits of the target price. Consider:

♦ While other bidders may be working in isolation, in terms of pricing, you are working with a target price that makes use of information separate from the current auction. This helps isolate you from the competitive influences of the current auction.

♦ You are freed from the shackles of current price focused bidding. You can quickly determine where the current price is *in relation to the typical market* price but you do not allow the current price to determine your bidding. This enables you to select bidding tactics that are consistent with where the market may take the auction and not be swayed by the actions of individual bidders.

♦ A target price helps you remain realistic in terms of the possible (or probable) closing price of the auction. In other words, you do not fall prey to believing that the current price is the purchase price.

♦ You have a stable price goal that is not subject to change as competition enters the auction. Remember that competition is a key element to the success of a single-unit auction. It is competition that increases the current price, and ultimately sets the closing price. Your objective is to remain free of being pulled into the competition with a buyer-minded approach. A target price helps you remain focused on the closing price of the auction, which is all that matters in a single-unit auction.

♦ You know when to abandon the auction. Not only have you accepted a target price (which is based on actual market performance) but you know at what point you would overpay in relation to the typical market price.

Perhaps the most important benefit of the target price is that you are able to bid aggressively. Aggressive bidding does not necessarily mean placing high bid amounts, although it may depending on the strategic approach you choose to take. Rather aggressive bidding is done without the fear of over bidding, or the fear of under bidding for that matter. With a target price, you have the ability to bid decisively without the burden of having to reassess your price tolerance with each bid. This potentially makes you a powerful bidder.

Aggressive bidding allows you to utilize the bidding tactics you deem necessary based on the current auction scenario. Here's an example: You place a proxy bid at 50% of the target price with the objective of discouraging several minimum bidders who are accomplishing nothing more than adding to the auction's bid count (which tends to attract more bidders). With this bid you don't have to fret over whether or not you will overpay in the auction – you had determined reasonable bounds when you established the target price. In addition, you aren't concerned about your bid being outbid. In fact you expect it to be outbid eventually (that's why you only bid 50% of the target price). You didn't ponder if you were willing to pay the current price – you do not expect the current price to be the final purchase price. This is just one example of being able and ready to bid aggressively. When you have a stable, realistic, fact-based target price, you are in a position to bid decisively. This is a competitive strength that many bidders simply do not have.

It is vitally important that you understand a key point about the target price – you do not expect to necessarily pay the full target price. Rather, a target price is a price guideline you use to determine a bidding budget by which to deploy tactical bidding. Always seek to pay the lowest price possible in any auction. However, by having a realistic price guideline, you are better able to place bids that accomplish your tactical objective at the time of each bid.

The target price helps you maintain sensible participation in the auction so that you avoid underbidding and overbidding. Underbidding tends to create more bidding activity that in turn helps increase the final closing price. Overbidding creates a challenge for other bidders because it gives them a price guideline. Depending on the auction situation the target price helps you select and deploy the most appropriate bidding tactic, given the specific auction circumstances.

Another benefit of the target price is that is allows you to determine a bidding budget. If the target price is $300.00 and the auction's current price is $200.00, then you have a bidding budget of $100.00 that can be used to position in the auction to win it. I do not propose that you always use your entire bidding budget. But, having a predetermined, accepted and realistic bidding budget is important to strategic bidding.

A bidding budget helps you determine which bidding tactics you will use in the auction. For example consider an auction that is receiving heavy competition. Since you have a $100.00 bidding budget remaining, you might select a bid tactic that utilizes 50% of the budget now with the remainder held for use later in the auction when it likely that competitive activity will increase. Or you might find an auction late in its period and decide to use 100% of your bidding budget to snipe the auction.

The target price frees you from regarding the current price of a single-unit auction as a purchase price. Rather, the current price now becomes an indication of the competitive activity in the auction up to that point, not the purchase price. You are therefore able to determine your bidding budget, which you strategically manage to help you obtain a winning position in the auction.

Tactical Advantages of the Target Price

With a target price and a maximum target price in mind you are ready to participate in the auction. You can use the various bidding tactics discussed in this book to work the auction so that it ideally closes at a great price with you as the winning bidder. There are several tactics that contribute to conditioning the auction to close at or below the target price. Let's review some bidding tactics in relation to the target price.

♦ The first rule of thumb is to never bid up to the target price unless and until it is necessary to do so. Doing so leaves you with no remaining bidding budget for later use. By bidding high, you effectively take one shot and hope it's enough. In addition, a high bid invites competitive bidding since it creates a proxy bid that presents a target for your opponents.

♦ As you are aware, every successful bid increases the auction's current price. To help an auction's current price to *not* increase further, refrain from bidding until conditions change. This will become even more important when an auction's current price is approaching the target price. Of course, you have no direct control over the bids that opponents might place. You can, however, refrain from using up your own bidding budget until the time is right to do so. Also, remember that bidding invites bidding. Bids suggest that the item is desirable to own (at the current price) which encourages additional bids. By bidding only when it will serve you tactically, you help keep the implied interest in the item to a minimum.

♦ A tactic that may prove successful is to place a significant bid very early in the auction (but not so significant as to consume your full bidding budget). By doing so, value opportunists (bargain hunters) may move on to another auction when they realize they are not going to be able to purchase a $200.00 item for $30.00. In addition, those bidders who attempt Proxy Discovery Runs (see *The Proxy Discovery Run* in part *Tactics and Techniques*) may find that they cannot reach your proxy bid and may move on. This tactic attempts to make the auction less attractive to timid bidders and bargain hunters. Keep in mind that the single-unit auction is mechanically designed to invite bidding and then to eliminate all but one bidder – the longer it takes to eliminate bidders, the higher the closing price will be. Certain bidding tactics help eliminate bidders sooner, reducing the impact they have on the auction's current price. Keep in mind that he seller benefits from all bids in her auction.

♦ In auctions where the seller has placed a reserve on the auction and the reserve is undisclosed (see *Bidding Tactics in Reserve Auctions* in part *Tactics and Techniques*), you could employ the tactic where you bid up to, but just under the seller's reserve. Assuming the target price is higher than the seller's reserve, which you made an effort to find out from the seller, you could utilize this tactic to help the auction be less attractive to opponent bidders. With this tactic you remain uncommitted to the auction while setting things up for another bidder to trip the reserve. Since you have a price guideline, you are able to gauge the seller's reserve in relation to the target price.

With a proxy bid at just below the seller's reserve, the "Reserve Not Yet Met" sign remains illuminated which tends to deter bidding. At the same time your proxy bid remains unexposed until another bidder outbids you (who also trips the reserve). The strategic benefit of this tactic is that you utilize a portion of your bidding budget to position in the auction making it more difficult for bargain hunters to secure the auction for themselves. In addition, you still maintain some of your bidding budget to be used, if necessary, to retake the auction should you be outbid.

Should the auction's current price remain under the seller's reserve toward the end of the auction, technically you need only bid a small amount to become the winning bidder. However, your final bid must also account for the possibility of an opponent bidding in the final moments. Consider bidding an amount at that time that you feel will win the auction, but certainly within your bidding budget.

♦ The snipe bid is a powerful tactical bid as we will discuss in the next part of this book. Given that you have established a target price based on recent closing prices of the same or comparable item, you are positioned to better predict the closing price of the auction. Please see Law #30: *The Closing Price is Best Surmised Near the End*. There are exceptions however, so this is only a general rule of thumb. If needed, you also have a maximum target price to use as a snipe bid if you elect to bid at the maximum.

Your success in eBay auctions has much to do with the skillful use of your money as you bid for a winning position in the auction. While taking a price targeting approach will not guarantee that you will win auctions, it may provide you with a competitive advantage that some or all of your opponents may not have.

Part 2: Tactics and Techniques

Bidding Tactics

We will cover much ground in this important part. You will note that this material is positioned after we have discussed fundamental concepts concerning bidding in eBay auctions and before we delve into the laws of strategic bidding presented in Part 3. *The Laws of Strategic Bidding* will help you apply the tactics discussed in this chapter while this chapter will help you understand the various bidding tactics available to you.

The primary role of bidding tactics is to carry out your strategy. As discussed in the chapter *Strategic Bidding*, a strategy is the approach you take to position in an auction for the win. Bidding tactics are tools that you use in your strategy and should never be used without a clearly formed strategy concerning a particular auction.

If you come across a bidding tactic that you are uncomfortable with or don't understand – then don't use that bidding tactic! I say this because if you use a bidding tactic timidly, you will likely not pull it off successfully. Or at least, you may not fully realize its benefit.

If you feel that you would be hurting the feelings of your fellow bidders with a particular bidding tactic, and that concerns you, then don't use that tactic. You cannot bid effectively in any online auction in which you are concerned about the feelings of your opponents. eBay auctions are every person for themselves. You stand alone among your opponents. You expend your own time and your own money. You must be as ruthless as you deem necessary without breaking the rules. But, you must also not use any bidding tactic in a reckless manner. Always bid wisely and with purpose.

The Savvy Bidder understands that strategic bidding augments the power of his money in online auctions. In other words, the skilled use of bidding tactics and techniques improves your competitive edge. The objective is to take each bid beyond simply being an attempt to purchase the item. Work to have each and every bid provide you with a tactical advantage.

Let's start our discussion of bidding tactics with some thoughts about positioning tactics.

Positioning Tactics

An important fundamental of strategic bidding is to position to win rather than simply bidding to make a purchase. Of course, to purchase at the lowest possible price is the ultimate objective of your participation in online auctions. To achieve this objective, it is important to not compete simply as a buyer. Buyer-minded bidders also want to win auctions and certainly want to win auctions at the lowest possible price. However to the buyer-minded bidder the most obvious method of dealing with competition in an auction is to outbid the opponents to attain or retain the highest bidder position.

Positioning is a matter of placing bids at times, and of amounts, that give you a particular tactical advantage. Your tactical advantage may come immediately after your bid or may come later in the auction. You may choose to take a position early in the auction or late in the auction depending on your strategy.

Most bidders think that the best position to have is to be the highest bidder. However being the highest bidder in a single-unit auction is important only at the instant the auction closes. Being the highest bidder during the auction is not necessarily the best position to have. This is because the highest bidder is the target bidder whom opponents focus on. Certainly, you will need to become the highest bidder for the auction's close. However, you can use bidding tactics to imply a particular level of interest (or disinterest), a particular level of competitiveness or to encourage your opponents to make decisions that are not entirely in their best interest.

Positioning also involves helping your opponents underestimate your intentions, your budget or your bidding abilities. If successful, this results in some of your opponents disregarding you as a competitor. However, we need to be realistic that not all participants in auctions are observant. There are many who enter an auction and simply bid with the intention of making a purchase. To such an opponent the actions of other participants are relevant only if he is out bid. Therefore never assume your opponents are paying attention. Don't be surprised if a tactical bid does not produce the outcome you anticipated. At the same time never assume your opponents are ignorant of what you are up to. Some opponents are very astute. Your objective is to try positioning tactics when they are appropriate, but never put complete trust in their outcome.

Following are some examples of how you might utilize bidding tactics in different situations to position in an auction:

♦ A position tactic can be to pose as an easily outbid participant in the auction. To illustrate, early in the auction you place a minimum bid that is quickly outbid and then perhaps place second or third minimum bid, which are also outbid. Here you display a pattern of being an easy to defeat bidder. Later in the auction, you demonstrate a different bidding pattern that opponents may not be expecting. For instance, you place a strong proxy bid near the auction's close. It's not unlikely for opponents to start picking away at your proxy bid with minimum bids under the assumption that you are an easily outbid minimum bidder as you earlier demonstrated. But, by doing so, they become current price focused which is not the most effective competitive position to be in.

♦ Snipe bidders do not need to be active during an auction – they intend to take the auction in the final seconds of the auction (snipe bidding tactics are discussed later in this chapter). One positioning tactic might be to place a bid in mid auction to indicate to the other participants that you intend to compete for the auction as a "normal" bidder. However, you actually intend to snipe the auction. This is particularly valuable if you are known as a snipe bidder in your auction community.

♦ Another positioning tactic is one where you place a bid very early in the auction that was outbid and you have not bid again since. Here you are making an effort to fool opponents into believing you do not have the budget or the interest to sustain continued bidding. The objective is to let your opponents believe you have left the auction so as to imply less competition.

♦ A position tactic can be one where you have bid up to, but just under, the seller's reserve. The tactical objective is to try to keep the auction in the period of reserve-not-yet-met *and* let bidders who bid below your proxy be confronted with an immediate outbid notice. This situation tends to dissuade bidders from continuing to participate in the auction because it presents a frustrating situation to those who simply want to make a purchase. This tactic will be discussed later in this chapter.

♦ Of course, you can position in an auction with a strong proxy bid. The advantage is that you fend off bidders who have a current personal valuation that is below your proxy bid. The disadvantages are that the current price increases with each of your opponent's failed bids. Also you become the one to outbid, the target. In addition, a proxy bid, once it is outbid, implies a personal valuation. Some bidders may assume that your personal valuation (according to your proxy bid) is all that you were willing to pay for the auction. Such opponents may believe you have bid your maximum and can be defeated once your proxy is outbid. They may therefore disregard you as competition once you lose the highest bidder position, assuming you do not respond too quickly.

♦ A bidder in an auction may place a bid with cents. This causes the current price to adjust to the cents used in the bid. For example a bidder places a bid for $35.51 in an auction with a current price of $34.00. The current price is then set to $35.51. The next minimum bid requirement is $36.51. This helps subsequent bidders think in terms of cents. By placing an Adjustment Bid, you set the current price back to a whole dollar. This is a form of positioning because your objective is to try and preserve the use of cents for your own bidding later in the auction.

♦ Positioning may come late in the auction. You may choose to monitor the auction, assess the participants and place a winning bid only at the most appropriate time. The most appropriate time might be in the final day, hour or minute of the auction. In effect you place a bid in the auction at the time when you feel you can make an educated guess, based on your observation and research that the final closing price auction might close at.

♦ In situations where a seller has posted two auctions for the same item and that are running simultaneously, you have the option of pursuing the auction that is taking less bidding – the underdog auction if you will. In this situation, a seller has effectively divided his available market (the bidders interested in purchasing the item) between two auctions. This tends to cause bidders who are seeking to purchase the item to migrate to the auction with the lower current price (bidders are generally current price focused). This situation results in one auction effectively stealing bids from the other with the effect of both auctions having a higher probability of each closing at a lower price. What's most important is that one of the two auctions will be favored more than the other as the interested bidders oscillate between the two auctions. Observing which auction is less favored allows you to deploy the appropriate bidding tactics.

No one can predict the actions of the participants in any online auction. You cannot know the personal valuations of those who are bidding and you cannot predict what bid amounts and bid methods will be used. Therefore you cannot rely on the effectiveness of any single bidding tactic. However, if you attempt to position in auctions, you are more likely to realize tactical advantages than if you simply try to purchase the item.

Notes:

Patrick C. Cook

Proxy Bidding Tactics

The proxy bid is, without doubt, seldom used as effectively as it could be. We'll begin our discussion of the proxy bid with an overview of how it is mechanically processed and then we'll move into some ways to use the proxy bid for tactical purposes. By the end of this section you should be able to appreciate how the proxy bid could be used competitively.

The Mechanics of the Proxy Bid

A proxy is a bid of an amount greater than the required minimum bid increment. When a bid exceeds another bid (and is equal to at least one minimum bid increment), the amount of the bid over another's bid (or over the minimum required bid) is used by the eBay mechanism to automatically place future bids on your behalf in response to new bids. The "excess" amount becomes your proxy bid. I refer to this excess amount as a "proxy fund". eBay will automatically bid from your proxy fund for as long as it holds out. Of course, as opponents place their bids, each bid that is placed on your behalf decreases your proxy fund by the amount of *the opponents* bid plus one minimum bid increment. When your proxy fund is exhausted or the auction closes, proxy bidding stops.

Let's consider a simple example of the proxy bid. An auction is currently at $50.00 and there is no current proxy bid. You place a $90.00 bid. eBay accepts your bid and raises the auction's current price to $51.00 (the $50.00 current price plus one minimum bid increment of $1.00). Since your $90.00 bid was more than the required minimum bid, this leaves $39.00 to be used as your proxy fund. To continue our example, another bidder then places a $60.00 bid. eBay immediately places a $61.00 bid on your behalf (the other bidder's $60.00 bid amount plus one minimum bid increment of $1.00) thereby outbidding this new bidder. Yet another bidder places a bid of $75.00 and eBay immediately places a bid on your behalf of $76.00 which leaves you with a proxy fund of $14.00 ($90.00 minus $76.00). Finally, a bidder places a $95.00 bid, which is a higher amount than your $90.00 proxy bid. At this point in our example, your proxy fund is exhausted and eBay allows the $95.00 bidder to take the highest bidder position.

The proxy bid is touted as a convenience that allows persons to bid in an auction without actually attending to the auction for as long as the proxy bid holds out. Essentially, a proxy bid is permission for eBay to bid on your behalf. You never specifically ask that a particular bid be used as your proxy bid because it is assumed that you want eBay to bid on your behalf when you place a bid that is higher than the minimum required bid and higher than another bidder's bid amount.

Proxy bidding is purely a mechanical process. Once you bid to create a proxy fund, eBay uses your proxy fund to outbid subsequent bids that are placed by other bidders where those bids are lower than your proxy bid. You can't choose under what conditions eBay will place a counter bid using your proxy fund. You can't decrease your proxy bid (unless you retract your proxy bid), but you can, not surprisingly, increase your proxy bid amount.

A scenario concerning proxy bidding that is often misunderstood is when a bidder places a single bid that outbids an existing proxy bid, the auction's current price is immediately increased by the full amount of the proxy bid that was outbid. Take for example an auction that has a current price $100.00 and an existing proxy bid of $150.00. If a bidder places a $200.00 proxy bid, which is greater than the existing proxy bid, eBay immediately raises the auction's current price to $150.00, the full amount of the existing proxy bid. It is easy to see why an auction's current price can increase quickly in auctions taking proxy bids.

Whether or not an existing proxy bid is exceeded by new bids, a proxy bid can have a significant impact on the auction's closing price because the proxy is automatically and immediately used to outbid new bids which, of course, increases the current price. For example, if a new bid is lower than an existing proxy bid, the auction's current price is raised to the amount of the new bid. For example, the auction's current price is increased from $110.00 to $112.50 when a bidder enters a $112.50 bid in an auction with a proxy bid greater than $112.50.

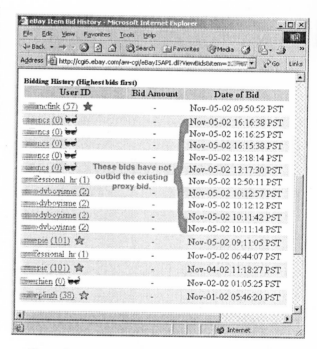

Figure 3 - An eBay screen portion showing several bidders attempting to outbid a proxy.

The most significant disadvantage to a proxy bid is that it sets up a target for opponent bidders to find and outbid. An existing proxy bid must be outbid if another bidder is to have any chance of winning the auction. So, it comes as no surprise that another bidder who intends to win an auction may attempt to take the highest bidder position if the bidder can justify the escalating current price. As illustrated in Figure 3, it is quite possible that an existing proxy bid will be picked away at by bidders until one of three things happen: 1) a bidder outbids the existing proxy bid, 2) bidders give up trying to outbid the proxy bid or 3) the auction closes. In all cases, while the auction is still running, all bids against a proxy bid increase the auction's current price. The current price is indicated on the eBay auction listing screen as "Currently" or "Current Bid".

- The proxy bid system is a great money maker for eBay. The mechanics of a single-unit auction are designed to "pull up" the final closing price of the auction to as high as it can go given the participants in the auction. Proxy bidding is a key factor in this price escalation process because the proxy bid is used to increase the current price as new bids are submitted (as long as the new bids are lower than the existing proxy bid). With the absence of a proxy bid in an auction, the auction mechanism does not have a bidder's money to work with and price escalation can only occur at an amount that new bids allow. If the new bids are minimum bids, i.e., not proxy bids, the auction's current price is pulled up more slowly.

- When a bidder takes a buyer approach to eBay auctions, the proxy bid seems to serve a useful purpose to allow eBay to fend off new bidders on his behalf. It is easier for a bidder to simply enter a proxy bid at the amount he is willing to pay for the auction and let eBay do its thing. This is fine for auction participants who simply want to make a purchase with minimum involvement with the auction. However, the Savvy Bidder understands that a proxy bid can also be used for tactical purposes, which is explored next.

Tactical Proxy Bidding

Generally, there are several occasions when a proxy bid might provide a tactical advantage:

1. The proxy bid may prove handy in reserve auctions (where the seller did not disclose the reserve amount in her auction listing, but that is learned by asking the seller). In this situation a proxy bid could be placed just below the seller's reserve price. The objective is to fend off low bidders while conditioning the auction for another bidder to trip the seller's reserve. This tactic is discussed in detail in *Bidding Tactics in Reserve Auctions* later in this chapter).

2. A proxy bid, *when outbid*, implies a personal valuation. Knowing this you may want to occasionally place a proxy bid during the main portion of an auction to give the impression that you are unwilling to pay a price higher than your proxy bid implies. This impression is given only if your proxy

bid is outbid *and* you do not quickly respond with more bidding. Bidders reviewing the bid history of the auction are able to see your bid (but not the bid amount). They know that you have been outbid because a bidder with a later bid is now the highest bidder. Many bidders will assume from this that you were knocked out of the auction (if you do not respond quickly). Certainly, if the auction has exceeded your target price, the assumption would be accurate. Otherwise, the tactic is to place a proxy bid and let it be outbid with the objective of getting opponent to not regard you as a competitive threat.

3. A snipe bid is usually a bid that is greater than the required minimum bid, i.e., a proxy bid. The objective, of course, is to submit a snipe bid with an amount high enough to come out the winning bidder once all bids have been reconciled once the auction closes. With a snipe bid that is high enough to qualify as a proxy bid, the auction venue will, in a matter of milliseconds, bid on the bidder's behalf during the final reconciliation of all outstanding bids. The final second (snipe) bid will need to withstand the possible bids of other bidders, including the possible bids of a few other snipe bidders. The proxy bid can prove its worth for snipe bidding.

The Risks of Proxy Bidding

I personally do not like to entrust my money to the auction machine unless doing so provides me with a tactical advantage. The auction machine knows only one thing; if another bidder places a bid, use my money-in-trust to outbid that bidder and keep doing this until my proxy fund is exhausted or the auction closes. Since I cannot alter these mechanical functions, I am left with no option but to allow it to carry out its duty. For this reason consider a few situations where you may *not* want to have a proxy bid in place:

♦ Assume, for example, you had a $250.00 proxy bid in place that represents what you are willing to pay for the auction item. Another bidder then places a bid that outbids your $250.00 proxy bid. Your personal valuation (expressed by your proxy bid) is effectively exposed. You might prefer that no one know your personal valuation since it may indicate what you think the value of the item is. This is especially true if you bid the maximum you are willing to pay for the item. Since the personal valuation of one bidder often influences the personal valuation of other bidders, the auction might generate more interest than it may have otherwise. By placing a proxy bid in an auction, if your proxy bid is outbid, it implies that the item may have a higher market value than other bidders may have otherwise thought.

♦ Suppose you have a $150.00 proxy bid in place in an auction with a current price of $50.00. A bidder mistakenly places a $1000.00 bid intending to place a $100.00 bid. Your $150.00 is exposed by the bidding error. Most bidders will retract a mistaken bid quickly. A few bidders just disappear and let the auction close with the bad bid left standing. Whether or not the mistaken bid is retracted, the amount of your $150.00 proxy bid is exposed, at least temporarily.

♦ What if a particular bidder has the habit of following you from auction to auction because they assume that you are a knowledgeable bidder of certain auction items. This "stalker" places a series of small bids until your proxy bid is outbid, confident that you are an informed person. At that point, the bidder has an idea of what you might be willing to pay for the item. It's a way of obtaining information about your valuation, which may very well be based on sound knowledge of the market. Once your proxy is outbid, that bidder can discern the amount of your proxy bid because he takes the highest bidder position away from you. Of course, such a bidder can also wait for another bidder to outbid your proxy bid.

♦ If shill bidding is occurring in an auction in which you have a standing proxy, the shill bidder could place bids until your proxy is outbid and then stop. The shill bidder's logic is that if at least one bidder is willing to pay a certain amount, there may be others with a similar or higher personal valuation. The shill simply raises the auction's current price to just slightly over your proxy amount and lets other bidders take it from there. As mentioned, the current price implies market value so by the shill bidder increasing the current price he also accomplishes increasing perceived value. It is also possible that you will reassess your personal valuation and bid again. An existing proxy bid is valuable to a shill bidder because he can use the eBay proxy mechanism to raise the auction's current price without himself placing high proxy bids. In effect, a shill bidder would be able to use an existing proxy to help mask the fact that the auction is being unfairly manipulated.

♦ If you would rather your personal valuation for the auction not be exposed, then a proxy bid should be avoided. Or, put more accurately, a proxy that is equal to your personal valuation should be avoided. As mentioned above, once a proxy is outbid, observant bidders can easily discern the approximate amount of your proxy simply by reviewing the auction's bid history if your proxy was outbid by another.

♦ If, on the other hand, a proxy bid you place *is* your full personal valuation and if that proxy is outbid, then it is not an issue because you will not care to continue bidding. But, exhausting your bidding budget too soon is not usually the best competitive approach.

Avoid Exhausting Your Bidding Budget

♦ A proxy bid can possibly serve to indicate a lower market value for the auction than may actually exist. Take for instance a situation where you have a target price of $200.00 for a particular auction that has a current auction price of $100.00. If you were to place a $150.00 proxy bid you may create a period of time where subsequent bidders are outbid and, in doing so, bring the current price closer to the auction's typical market value. The key with this tactic is to not respond quickly if and when your proxy bid is finally outbid. In effect your proxy bid implies that those who continue to bid beyond your proxy bid are risking overpaying for the auction. For this tactic to have the intended effect:

1. Your proxy bid amount must be sufficient enough to imply a potential market value but not exhaust your bidding budget. A $50.00 proxy bid in an auction with an obvious market value of $200.00, for instance, does little to imply a probable market value.

2. Your proxy bid amount must be close enough to the auction's market value to cause bidders to worry that they would over pay if they try to outbid your proxy. For example, a $150.00 proxy bid on an auction with a probable $200.00 market value may cause concern in the minds of opponents who try to outbid your proxy.

3. You do not respond quickly to your proxy bid being outbid. This implies that you knew what the item was really worth. Keep in mind that many bidders tend to rely on the opinions of the auction's participants, those opinions expressed through bids.

♦ It is very easy to quickly exhaust your bidding budget with proxy bidding. The Savvy Bidder makes an effort to utilize his bidding budget for an auction such that enough remains should bidding become competitive, which often occurs near the end of an auction. Many bidders who run through their budget quickly will simply reassess what they are willing to pay. In fact, another way of thinking about the purpose of an auction is to convince the prospective buyers that their original thinking was wrong concerning how much they could have purchased the item. In a way, the proxy bid system encourages bidders to place bids at their full budget with the possible consequence of having to accept a higher price than was originally accepted.

- The Savvy Bidder makes an effort to understand the auction's potential market value before bidding in an auction. This helps him not get caught up in the process of rethinking what he is willing to pay as the auction proceeds. In addition, by conserving his bidding budget throughout the auction, he has some budget remaining should he realize that he underestimated what the market was willing to pay for the item. He is then better able to stay competitive without exceeding a price higher than he had originally accepted.

How Much to Proxy Bid

The process of placing a proxy bid is simple enough – it's like any other bid, just with a higher amount than the minimum required bid and another bidder's proxy bid, if one exists. The key is to know how much of a proxy bid to place for it to give you the maximum tactical advantage. Consider:

- As discussed, a bid placed at the required minimum bid amount is not a proxy bid. Placing a $125.00 bid, for example, on an auction with a $125.00 minimum bid requirement is not a proxy bid.

- If you place a proxy bid of an amount that is just a few minimum bid increments, your bid may not serve a tactical purpose – it is simply a "safe" bid that happens to have a small proxy fund. A safe proxy bid is often not worth the effort because 1) it impacts the current price without serving a useful tactical purpose and 2) it is easily outbid providing very little competitive advantage. There are exceptions as will be discussed. But generally you want a proxy bid to serve a tactical purpose. In this scenario, you may be better off simply placing a minimum bid, depending upon your tactical objective.

- A proxy bid with a high bid amount could cost you more money than may have been necessary should the auction close with you as the winner. This is because other bidders may try to bid against your proxy bid, only to raise the auction's current price *by their full bid amounts* if their bids are lower than your proxy. Try as they will, they may not be able to exceed your high proxy bid, but they will increase the auction's closing price in the effort. If one or more bidders keep bidding, who perhaps really desire the item, they could raise the auction's closing price significantly. A high proxy bid is a target – a target to beat.

♦ Conservation of your bidding budget is important. You'll want to retain enough of your bidding budget for the period during which bidding becomes more competitive. You will need to use your own discretion in this area as some auctions receive more bidding than others, depending on market interest. The important rule to keep in mind is to always retain enough of your bidding budget to be able to place a winning bid when the time is appropriate.

Let's see if we can apply these points with the following examples. Let's assume, for example, that you are considering placing a proxy bid in an auction with a current price of $500.00. There is no reserve on the auction. Your research indicates that the typical closing price is $800.00. The auction is at its halfway point with 3 days remaining. There have been 16 bids placed so far. There have been 3 bidders who have shown a determination to stay in the auction with several bids each.

What tactical advantage do you wish to realize with a proxy bid at this time?

What will your proxy bid be?

The amount of a proxy bid should always be determined based on more than a guess. In addition, <u>when</u> you place a proxy bid and the tactical objective you have for the proxy bid is important. Before placing a proxy bid in mid auction, consider what objective you wish to achieve with your bid.

♦ If you are trying to become the highest bidder in mid auction, then your proxy bid will need to outbid any existing proxy bid, if one exists. Consider the benefits and drawbacks of being the highest bidder in mid auction.

♦ Do you intend for your proxy bid to reduce competition in the auction? If so, a larger proxy bid may provide a better tactical advantage.

♦ Do you want only to announce your presence in the auction? If so, a small, easily outbid proxy bid may be all that is required. In fact, a bid at the required minimum bid will be sufficient to accomplish this objective.

♦ If you want to imply a personal valuation that is lower than the typical market value, then a proxy bid will need only be of an amount that will accomplish the deception. This tactic intends to throw your opponents off by implying you know something they don't. Of course, you return to the auction at the appropriate time and take the win.

Conclusion

The proxy bid is advertised as being able to reduce your effort in an auction. However, you can use the proxy bid for much better reasons, such as helping you leverage a winning position. Positioning is simply a matter of setting things up so that you can place a winning bid at the appropriate time. Positioning often entails influencing your opponents to make assumptions about your competitiveness or to take actions that are not in their best interests.

A proxy bid can be a useful bidding tactic such as in undisclosed reserve auctions, as a shutout tactic, implying a lower personal valuation than you actually have, to influence opponents to misjudge the item's market value or to throw opponents off balance. However, more often than not, a proxy bid presents a target that other bidders may use as their own guideline. With each bid placed against a proxy bid, whether or not that bid takes the highest bidder position, the auction's current price, and ultimately the closing price, increases. Since the objective of the Savvy Bidder is to purchase items at or below the target price, it makes sense to not impact the auction's current price with bids that provide little or no competitive challenge to opponents.

When used for tactical purposes, the proxy bid can be quite valuable. But it is important to think of how the proxy bid can be best applied so as to gain a tactical advantage. A proxy bid should not be used simply as a convenience, letting eBay do your work. Doing so simply hands money over to the eBay machine that is essentially used to help increase the auction's closing price.

Notes:

The Proxy Discovery Run

As illustrated in Figure 4, a Proxy Discover Run is a sequence of bids in close proximity. Such bids are usually minimum bids. The objective is to learn (discover) the proxy bid amount of the current highest bidder. Figure 4 shows that the bidder who performed the Proxy Discovery Run eventually found the existing proxy bid, which had been placed on Nov-27-02 17:41:55 PST (third line item from the top) and then placed one more bid (second line item from the top).

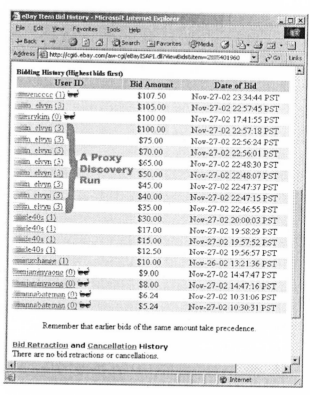

This bidding sequence is often used in an attempt to determine the proxy bid of another bidder and to do so without placing a bid any higher than is absolutely necessary to become the highest bidder.

Figure 4 - An eBay screen portion of a closed auction showing a Proxy Discovery Run.

To illustrate a Proxy Discovery Run;

1. Assume the current price of an auction is $100.00.

2. A bidder places a $105.00 bid only to find his bid is immediately outbid by an existing proxy bid of another (the amount of a proxy bid is kept secret during the auction). Of course, the current price increases to the bidder's $105.00 bid. The bidder wants to know what he must bid to attain the highest bidder's seat, but doesn't want to risk placing a proxy bid any higher than necessary.

3. The bidder places another bid at $110.00, which increases the current price to $110.00 since that bid still is lower than the existing proxy bid. But again he does not outbid the existing proxy bid.

4. The bidder places yet another bid of $115.00 and perhaps another at $120.00. With each bid *that is lower than the existing proxy bid*, the current price of the auction is increased to the amount of his bid.

5. Let's assume that on the next bid the existing proxy bid amount is finally outbid. The bidder attains the highest bidder position.

In the above example, the bidder placed a series of bids for $105.00, $110.00, $115.00 and finally $120.00. The existing proxy bid was found to be an amount over $115.00 but less than $120.00.

In the above example, had the bidder placed a high proxy bid of $150.00, for example, he would have immediately outbid the existing proxy bid, but would also be left with a $150.00 proxy bid in place. This bidder may actually need to pay up to his $150.00 proxy bid amount if other bidders bid up to, but not over his $150.00 proxy. This is the very situation the bidder is attempting to prevent by placing a series of small bids.

Once a bidder who performs a Proxy Discovery Run discovers the amount of the existing proxy bid, the bidder may stop bidding at that point or may place an additional bid to enter his own proxy bid. The end result is that the bidder learned what bid was required to take the highest bidder position. It is fairly obvious what a bidder is trying to accomplish who utilizes the Proxy Discovery Run – he is making an effort to expose an existing proxy bid while not obligating herself to a proxy bid higher than necessary. It also serves to minimize the impact her own bids have on the auction's current price (at least on a bid-by-bid basis). I would not doubt that with each new bid of a Proxy Discovery Run the bidder is reconsidering if she would be willing to pay another minimum bid increment. By placing a series of small bids, she plays it safe.

As illustrated in Figure 5 eBay places no restrictions on the number of bids a person can place in an auction. You'll run across auctions where a bidder places many sequential bids in close proximity in search of the amount of an existing proxy bid amount.

You'll also encounter bidders who run several Proxy Discovery Runs at various points in the auction – each time the bidder was outbid, the bidder launches into yet another Proxy Discovery Run.

It is not difficult to realize that many bidders who perform Proxy Discovery Runs are actually using another bidder's valuation as a reference point. By specifically locating another bidder's proxy bid amount, the bidder effectively adopts the valuation of an opponent. Because no bidder can know for certain if proxy bid actually represents the true valuation of another, a Proxy Discover Run could be a tactical mistake.

The user of a Proxy Discover Run tries to minimize his risk of over bidding in the auction when a proxy bid exists. He also tries to minimize the impact on the current price, at least on a bid-by-bid basis. On the surface these seem like tactical advantages. However, a series of bids in close proximity usually indicates that the bidder was attempting to keep his costs to a minimum.

Bidding History (Highest bid first)		
User ID	Bid Amount	Date of Bid
estindle (1)	-	Nov-04-02 05:22:33 PST
estindle (1)	-	Nov-03-02 08:54:07 PST
andbean (0)	-	Nov-03-02 14:14:37 PST
andbean (0)	-	Nov-03-02 14:14:22 PST
andbean (0)	-	Nov-03-02 14:14:15 PST
andbean (0)	-	Nov-03-02 14:14:08 PST
andbean (0)	-	Nov-03-02 14:14:00 PST
andbean (0)	-	Nov-03-02 14:13:52 PST
andbean (0)	-	Nov-03-02 14:13:43 PST
andbean (0)	-	Nov-03-02 14:13:36 PST
andbean (0)	-	Nov-03-02 14:13:29 PST
andbean (0)	-	Nov-03-02 14:13:22 PST
andbean (0)	-	Nov-03-02 14:13:15 PST
andbean (0)	-	Nov-03-02 14:13:08 PST
andbean (0)	-	Nov-03-02 14:13:00 PST
andbean (0)	-	Nov-03-02 14:12:49 PST
andbean (0)	-	Nov-03-02 14:12:43 PST
andbean (0)	-	Nov-03-02 14:12:35 PST
andbean (0)	-	Nov-03-02 14:12:25 PST
andbean (0)	-	Nov-03-02 14:12:17 PST
andbean (0)	-	Nov-03-02 14:12:08 PST
andbean (0)	-	Nov-03-02 14:11:45 PST
andbean (0)	-	Nov-03-02 14:11:37 PST
andbean (0)	-	Nov-03-02 14:11:30 PST
andbean (0)	-	Nov-03-02 14:11:21 PST
andbean (0)	-	Nov-03-02 14:11:07 PST
ster123 (208)	-	Nov-02-02 17:44:35 PST
estindle (1)	-	Nov-03-02 08:53:32 PST

Figure 5 - An eBay screen portion showing a long series of bids by a single bidder.

This may signal others that this is a timid bidder who can be easily overwhelmed by aggressive bidding. In addition, a bidder who relies on the Proxy Discover Run bidding sequence is at a decisive disadvantage near the end of an auction where there may not enough time remaining to complete a series of minimum bids. A bidder who relies on the Proxy Discovery Run may find herself frantically placing multiple small bids as the auction's clock rushes toward closing the auction.

Tactical Uses of the Proxy Discovery Run

I do not advocate relying on the Proxy Discovery Run. I have found that locating another's proxy bid in <u>mid</u> auction does not generally serve a tactical purpose. However it can be a useful tool near the end of an auction just prior to placing a snipe bid. For example, in an auction with five minutes remaining, you may elect to perform a Proxy Discovery Run to determine the amount of a current proxy bid. Once found, you place a snipe bid. If you use this tactic, you might want to get a little extra mileage out of your Proxy Discovery Run by deliberately consuming the remaining time, leaving yourself enough time to place the final decisive bid. Bear in mind that if other bidders are also bidding in these final moments, you will need to remain alert to the rapidly changing landscape, which your bids are affecting as well.

A Proxy Discovery Run in the final moments of an auction serves to infuse bidding activity into an auction. This has the possible affect of confusing other bidders as they bid against a rapidly changing current price, which is often their primary frame of reference. Many bidders tend to chase the current price, so a rapidly increasing current price can present a difficult challenge for them. By using the Proxy Discovery Run at this time you are making the auction busy with the possible effect of confusing your opponents. If the tactic works, other bidders may meet with so many failed bids that they give up or consistently fail to take the highest bidder position. This is an example of you taking advantage of those bidders who are focused on the current price. However don't get yourself so occupied with the tactic that you miss the opportunity to place your final winning bid.

Conclusion

Use the Proxy Discovery Run for tactical purposes when appropriate. But, avoid using it in mid auction simply to find another bidder's proxy bid amount. Doing so implies you are a fear-based bidder. It also ratchets up the current price for nominal tactical gain. Employ the Proxy Discovery Run near the end of an auction when it will serve to determine an existing proxy bid and with the added benefit of making the auction so busy for current price focused bidders that they can't compete well.

Notes:

Bidding Tactics in Reserve Auctions

When seller places a reserve on his auction, that reserve price is either disclosed or undisclosed in the auction listing. A disclosed reserve simply means that the seller wrote a statement in his auction listing what the amount of the reserve price is. An <u>un</u>disclosed reserve means that the seller has not stated in his auction listing the amount of the reserve price.

When a reserve price is disclosed all bidders and prospective bidders in that auction know the seller's minimum acceptable price and can bid accordingly. Fortunately for the Savvy Bidder, most sellers <u>do not</u> disclose their reserve price. This creates opportunities to use the reserve price to the disadvantage of opponents.

Why I make the distinction of a reserve price being disclosed or <u>un</u>disclosed will be apparent in a few moments. For now let's take a few minutes and review the effect a reserve price has on eBay auctions. This will help you understand how you can use a reserve price for tactical purposes.

Reserve Prices Discourage Bidding

Whether a reserve price is disclosed or <u>un</u>disclosed, a reserve price presents a barrier to those interested in purchasing the auction item. This barrier occurs for several reasons:

1. The seller is placing a "floor price" on the auction with a reserve price. This is because the seller has specified that there can be no winner of the auction unless at least one bidder places a bid at the reserve price or higher. For the bidders who do not know what the seller's price is *and* are not clear what they would be willing to pay for the item, they are not certain if they should even bid in the auction. This often results is actually not bidding in an auction where the reserve price is not yet met. If bidding does occur, such bids are often weak.

2. While every seller has the right to set a minimum selling price, a reserve price is a form of predetermining a selling price, much like retail. A predetermined price is somewhat contradictory to the purest intent of the auction format where the decides the selling price. While there certainly needs to be a provision to help the seller not lose money on an item, a reserve price nonetheless regulates the market's ability to determine the final selling price.

3. A reserve price is often discouraging to a bidder who places a bid below the seller's reserve. Even though bids below the seller's reserve are readily

accepted by the eBay mechanism, the highest bidder cannot win the auction unless he bids at or above the seller's reserve. In effect the bidder is advised that her offer (her bid) is too low to earn her the right to purchase the item – but her offer is still accepted and used to increment the current price. In a very real way, her failed bid is used to her disadvantage.

4. A reserve price adds a level of competition in addition to the participants. In effect, while the reserve price is not yet met, bidders enter into competition with the seller as well as other prospective buyers. A reserve price therefore makes winning the auction a bit harder for as long as the reserve price is not met.

Let's draw an analogy to the reserve price. Assume you are in a retail store and you find a product you want to purchase. But, some stock boy has neglected to place a price sticker on the product and the shelf is missing the UPC label. You know that the product has a price, but you don't know what that price is. You can estimate what the price might be based on your experience. But you cannot make a final purchase decision unless you know the actual price. Perhaps a bit annoyed, you'll likely go up to the courtesy counter and ask for a price check on the product which will be provided in a matter of fact way. The lack of a price interfered with your purchase and you had to expend time and energy doing a task that is expected of the merchant. It's no different in online auctions – if the seller won't tell you his minimum price (his reserve price), you are less able to make a purchase decision and you have to work a bit harder to purchase that item. In this sense, undisclosed reserve prices actually deter bidding.

The dynamics that occur in a hidden reserve price auction are interesting:

1. If the prospective bidders do not know the typical market price of the auction, they must trust that the seller's reserve price is "fair". It's logical to assume that such bidders will have to rely entirely on the seller's representation of the auction item. The better job the seller does in his presentation, the lower the resistance of bidders accepting the seller's reserve price as "fair", which they don't know. With a hidden (undisclosed) reserve price, if the seller fails to convince the prospective buyers, the seller essentially damages the prospects of his auction.

2. And if prospective bidders generally *do* know the typical market price for an auction item, it is logical to assume that they will bid according to the market price, not the seller's reserve. In this case, the seller's hidden reserve actually interferes with the auction because a market price is known as established by past auctions.

A seller setting a hidden reserve price presumes (often mistakenly) that persons interested in his auction will trust that his reserve price is fairly representative of what the item should sell for. If the prospective buyers do not trust the seller's price judgment, for whatever reason, then there is a natural reluctance to bid in that seller's auction.

It is little wonder why reserve auctions receive less bids, at least in the early period of the auction. I have long known that auctions with no reserve price generally receive more bids. In fact, I would routinely post my auctions with no reserve because I wanted my auctions to receive bids, and any bid would do. I have no preconceived notion that "non-serious" bids are of any less value than the "serious" bids in my single-unit auctions – all bids are of value because all bids increase the auction's current price and all bids promote competition. The simple fact is that bids create competition and competition increases the auction's closing price. See law #10: *Bid Begets Bid*. When I had to set a reserve price I always revealed the reserve price in my listing. This is because I want my auctions to present minimum barriers to bidding.

Competition in an auction is important for three reasons:

1. Bids confirm in the mind of the prospective buyer that the auction is desirable to own by the fact that others also wish to own it. A bid is an expression of interest to own (it is not necessarily an expression of one's actual value). A seller who does not realize this is losing money.

2. If there are no bids in an auction with an undisclosed reserve, the implication is that bidders can afford to wait before bidding since there is no competition to contend with at the moment – the lack of bids delays competition. A seller that presents any barrier to bidding is potentially reducing competition in his auctions. Reduced competition often results in a lower closing price.

If there is any interest among the prospective buyers to own the item, a bid will eventually be placed despite the fact that the auction has a hidden reserve price. The important dynamic to keep in mind is that bidding often gets started later in a hidden reserve auction compared to a non-reserve auction, or an auction where the reserve price is stated in the auction's listing (is disclosed). With each auction day that passes with no bids, the lower the auctions closing price is likely to be.

Of course, this dynamic does not always pan out this way. Depending on the demand for the item as well as the reserve price that the seller sets, an auction may very well close at a price that is consistent with the item's market value. It is important to not assign any rigid truths to every situation, in this case a reserve auction, because the dynamics of the online auction environment are often influenced by other factors.

The Secret Reserve

As mentioned earlier, when a reserve price is set for an auction the seller will either disclose his reserve price in the auction's listing or not. Usually, a reserve price is not disclosed. Somewhere someone came up the theory that a secret (<u>un</u>disclosed) reserve price encourages bidders to bid closer to the price they are willing to pay for the auction. This may have been a true statement were it not for the way the current price is formed on eBay.

In traditional auctions, if an auction's current price is $200.00 and a bid is placed for $400.00, for instance, the auctioneer sets the current price to $400.00, not something less. If the next bid were $500.00, then the auction's price is set to $500.00 and so on. It works a bit different in eBay single-unit auctions. Using the same example values as above; if an auction's current price is $200.00 and a bid is place for $400.00, the current price is set to the next minimum bid increment, or $202.50 according to eBay's minimum bid increment scale. The $400.00 bid is then held as a proxy. If another bid is placed for $500.00, the current price is set to $400.00, which is the amount of the existing proxy bid. In this way, *the current price fools bidders to believe that bidding is actually occurring lower than it is*. This serves to help draw in new bids. Regardless of whether or not a reserve price exists, if the current price is not representative of the actual bid amounts, bidders tend to resist bidding to what they are willing to pay. Add to this a hidden reserve and bidders have yet another purchase barrier to deal with – not only are they mislead by the current price, but not knowing the seller's minimum price, they are required to bid blindly with respect to the undisclosed reserve price.

It's little wonder why bidders become current price focused since it is the most visible form of pricing information. Keeping in mind that most think they are making a purchase via an eBay auction, they naturally want to know the price they are expected to pay. When a reserve price is hidden, the current price becomes even more important which, as we discussed, is not necessarily the price that will win the auction. For lack of better information, bidders tend to remain focused on the current price, not the seller's reserve price. In effect, the eBay auction process actually defocuses bidders from a sellers hidden reserve. When the seller hides his reserve, he helps perpetuate focusing on the current price, which tends to keep bid amounts down because the current price tends to fool bidders into believing they can purchase the auction item for less than they may be able to.

When a reserve exists on an auction, the last thing a seller should want is for his participants to be fooled by the current price. If the current price does not escalate to his reserve price, the auction closes with no valid winner. A hidden reserve, given the way the current price is formed in eBay auctions, is self-defeating. This is why I always disclose my reserve price – I want my auction participants to think in terms of what they need to bid to win my auctions, not be fooled by the often erroneous current price.

The Dynamics of Reserve Auctions

The reason for delving into the subject of reserve auctions is to help you gain an insight into the dynamics that often result. The Savvy Bidder is interested in such observations because it will often shed light on how to pick up a competitive advantage. Let's continue our discussion by taking a look at bidding tactics in reserve auctions.

As Savvy Bidders we can only hope that eBay sellers continue to think that hidden reserve prices are actually good for their auctions. It is actually preferable that our opponents continue to be current price focused and operate in the dark in terms of the seller's reserve price. The reason for this is two fold:

1. The competitive strength of most bidders is stifled when they do not know what minimum price (the reserve price) they must meet to win the auction.

2. Most bidders become even more focused on the current price when they do not know the reserve price. The current price, as we have discussed, fools bidders into believing they could purchase the item at a lower price than they may be able to.

Given this, you may be able to use an undisclosed reserve situation to gain a tactical advantage. The tactic involves not "tripping" the undisclosed reserve in an effort to keep the auction in a state where opponents are uncertain what to bid and if they should even bid at all. Consider the dynamics of an auction where the reserve price has *not* been met compared to when the reserve price has been met:

Reserve Not Yet Met	Reserve Price Met
Bidders face a barrier (the seller's reserve price) that must be met or exceeded before any bidder can win the auction. In effect a bidder's personal valuation is secondary to the minimum price demand of the seller. This is contrary to the intent of the auction format.	A critical pricing guideline (the reserve price) become a non-issue. Bidders can now find their personal valuation/price equilibrium. This encourages those bidders to bid to win if they are willing to spend at least the auction's current price.
The current price is effectively meaningless since there can be no winner until the seller's reserve is met.	The current price takes on a new meaning. Once the reserve price is met, bidders actually place more value in the current price as a purchase price guideline – there can now be a winner. This potentially creates additional competition in the auction.
No one is committed to purchasing the auction. So each bidder has less concern about losing the auction. Bidding may get off to a slow start.	At least one bidder is committed to purchase the item when the auction closes. Competition exists.

Table 1 - Comparison of dynamics in a reserve auction.

The bidder that places a bid (or multiple bids) that meets the seller's reserve price, whether or not that reserve price is disclosed, is the bidder who shifts the auction into a new set of dynamics. Once the new dynamic takes hold, the bidder who "tripped" the seller reserve, has likely created more competition for her self. Most bidders know this and avoid being the one to spark competition.

Let's continue our discussion by exploring how the Savvy Bidder leverages the bidding dynamics in reserve auction that we have been discussing.

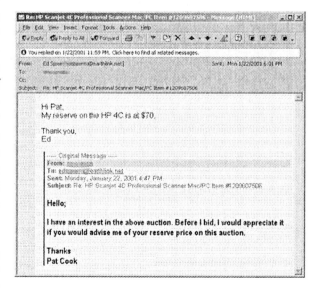

Figure 6 - An e-mail message requesting the seller's reserve price.

Tactics in Undisclosed Reserve Auctions

As you recall, an <u>un</u>disclosed reserve price is where the seller has not stated her reserve price in her auction listing. As such, the reserve price is unknown to the prospective buyers.

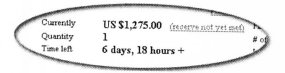

Currently	US $1,275.00	(reserve not yet met)
Quantity	1	# of
Time left	6 days, 18 hours +	

Figure 7 - An eBay screen portion showing an auction where the reserve price is not yet met.

In reserve auctions where the seller has not disclosed her reserve price, ask the seller by e-mail what her reserve price is. It helps to place a bid in the auction before making the request. Bear in mind that a bid below the seller's reserve does not commit you to purchasing the item but demonstrates your interest to purchase the item. You might want to place the lowest bid amount you possibly can to avoid tripping the reserve. Mention in your e-mail to the seller that you are bidding in her auction and would like to know her reserve amount. Usually, sellers will provide this information upon request, especially if you are an active bidder.

If you are provided the reserve amount, you potentially have an enormous advantage over those bidders who do not know the reserve. Use some discretion though. A seller once gave me the wrong reserve price (he had forgotten the exact reserve he had set). I then bid *below* his stated reserve and wound up becoming the highest bidder by exceeding his actual reserve price. I still won the auction but my intended tactic was damaged. Of course, by knowing the reserve you can decide if you will continue to participate in the auction.

One bidding tactic is to place a bid (which might be a proxy bid) *just below* the seller's <u>un</u>disclosed reserve price (which you know). The tactic proposes to add an additional barrier to opponents bidding in the auction. By additional I mean that your proxy bid adds to the competitive situation. Now all bidders in the auction, at least for the moment, have four levels of competition:

1. The uncertainty of a hidden reserve price, which is not yet met.

2. Your proxy bid (which did not trip the seller's reserve price).

3. A misleading current price, and

4. All of the other elements of the eBay auction format which create uncertainty.

By placing a proxy bid up to, but just under the seller's reserve price, you actually created more competitive barriers for your opponents to deal with.

"As we discussed in the section *Proxy Bidding Tactics* earlier in this chapter, a proxy bid creates a target whereby other bidders may attempt to discover your proxy bid amount. Of course the current price increments with every bid, whether or not another bidder succeeds in outbidding your proxy bid. Normally, you would avoid a mid-auction proxy bid for this reason. But, this situation is a bit different. Here you are placing a proxy bid just below the seller's reserve price. In this case, it doesn't matter if other bidders treat your proxy as a target. In fact, you expect them to do so. When a bidder finally does outbid your proxy, that bidder will trip the reserve price, which is the point of this tactic.

When using this tactic you'll want to be sure to place a proxy bid that is one minimum required bid below than the seller's hidden reserve (which you know from your e-mail inquiry). Even when you know the reserve amount, you don't want to trip the reserve. Rather, let the "Reserve Not Yet Met" sign remain illuminated to help opponents remain focused on the current price – and defocused on the reserve price. Yes, the objective is to allow the current price to continue to fool opponents that they could win the auction for something less.

If a bidder has not exceeded the seller's reserve by the end of the auction, you know precisely what bid will be required to met the seller's reserve, possibly giving you a decisive advantage over those opponent bidders who may not know the reserve price.

"Should you decide to snipe the auction, if another bid has not met or exceeded the seller's reserve in the final seconds of the auction, you know precisely what snipe bid will be required to met the seller's reserve, making you a formidable sniper.

When a seller's reserve is not known to you because the seller would not tell you his reserve you may elect to simply wait out the auction until another bidder trips the seller's reserve. As we discussed earlier, the auction enters a new set of bidding dynamics which you can leverage. At that time, you can deploy other bidding tactics as you deem appropriate.

Personally, I do not attempt to bid in a seller's auction where the reserve price is not yet met, is undisclosed and is not provided me upon request. The simple reason for this is that I choose to not bid blindly, in terms of a reserve price. If I have any interest in pursuing such an auction, I'll return to it at a later point to see if the reserve has been met by another bidder.

Another reason for not bidding when I cannot know the seller's reserve is because I fundamentally disagree with hidden (<u>un</u>disclosed) reserve prices – if the seller is not willing to tell his participants his minimum price, then I choose to withhold my bidding until the reserve price is known to me. I do not go to my friendly neighborhood retailer and shop without price information provided by the retailer. Nor will I do so in eBay auctions. More fundamentally, I do not care to get caught up in a current price chase which, as we discussed, is not a reliable price guideline.

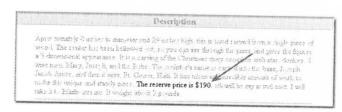

Figure 8 - An eBay auction listing where seller states his reserve price.

Tactics in Disclosed Reserve Auctions

You can also use the tactic of bidding up to but just under the seller's reserve price as described above in auctions where the seller has disclosed his reserve price. But, the tactic has a slightly different tactical objective.

As in an auction with an <u>un</u>disclosed reserve price, you place a proxy bid amount that is one minimum bid *below* the seller's reserve (which is disclosed). As before you don't want to trip the reserve. Rather, your objective is to keep the "Reserve Not Yet Met" sign remain illuminated. Just as in <u>un</u>disclosed reserve auctions, by placing a bid just under the seller's reserve price, you introduce an additional level of competition in the auction – your proxy bid. Now bidders have you to compete with you plus they must bid up to at least the seller's reserve price if they intend to win the auction. This tactic will prevent opponents from taking any form of position in the auction *unless* they bid at or above the seller's reserve price. This forces at least one bidder to have to accept the seller's reserve price, which may be hard for some to do.

Bidding at or over the seller's disclosed reserve price is certainly what those bidders will do if they accept the seller's reserve price and wish to win the auction. But the true objective of your tactic is to force such a bidder to become obligated to the auction by having to bid over your proxy bid (and thus at or over the seller's reserve). With this bid the "Reserve Not Yet Met" indicator goes way and the new bidder is the highest bidder who is now obligated to the auction. Of course, you have been knocked out of the highest bidder position, but that's ok because the Savvy Bidder does not place a high value in being the highest bidder except at the instant the auction closes.

One benefit of not tripping the seller's reserve price, even when the reserve price is known to all bidders, is to remain non-obligated to purchasing the item for as long as possible. This affords you the ability to abandon the auction at any time should you discover an auction that if offering the same item for less or has no reserve price on it. Yet, at the very least, you hold territory in an auction of interest to you. You can simply forget about the previous auction confident that you will not be obligated to it when it closes. This tactic proposes to introduce as much competition in the auction yet leave you free to abandon the auction as you see fit.

Conclusion

While reserve prices are understandable and will be with us for as long as online auctions are posted, sellers who operate under the assumption that an hidden reserve price is good for their auctions have actually provided the Savvy Bidder with an opportunity to leverage the dynamics that occur while the reserve price remains unmet. The tactics discussed in this section are based simply on how you can leverage the seller's reserve price by understanding and exploiting the dynamics that occur in reserve auctions.

A final thought on the subject of reserve auctions; there once was a time on eBay when a bidder who bid below the seller's reserve intended to send a signal to the seller that he had an interest in purchasing the item at something less than the seller's reserve price. The seller could then elect to contact the highest bidder, albeit a non-winning bidder, and negotiate a selling price "off-eBay", as such deals became known. Back then whether or not a reserve was disclosed was of less importance because there was still a chance of purchasing the item in an "off-eBay' transaction.

These days eBay forbids "off-eBay" transactions that stem from an auction listing because it cuts eBay out of its final sales fee. It is an offense that could lead to suspension or termination of either or both parties involved. However, by eliminating off-eBay transactions, eBay effectively reduces the number of bids in a hidden reserve auction. After all, if bidders know that the seller won't be contacting them to make a deal should the auction close with no winning bidder, why bother bidding below the auction's reserve price (which is usually hidden). A reduction of bids reduces competition in the auction. This in turn reduces the auction's closing price, generally speaking. So, this policy effectively repels bidding that might have gotten the competition started that in turn may have lead to the auction closing with a winning bidder. And, no winning bidder means no eBay final sales fee and a free re-listing by eBay. But, I'm sure eBay knows what it is doing with this particular policy.

On the other hand, the effort to forbid "off-eBay" transactions does encourage sellers to set a realistic reserve price. Back before the policy change, I imagine it was not unusual for a seller to set a very high reserve price (keeping it hidden, of course) so that there would probably be no winner. Then, one or more bidders could be contacted after the auction ended and a deal struck. The off-eBay deal would most certainly look very attractive compared to an impossibly high reserve.

Despite this change in policy, seller's generally continued to adhere to the habit of not disclosing their reserve prices which keeps bidders blind to the seller's minimum price. In fact while posting auctions, eBay's form continues to assume that the seller does not wish to reveal her reserve price, further perpetuating the assumption that hidden reserve prices are actually of benefit to the seller. This will continue for as long as sellers fail to understand that the more the bidders know in terms of pricing, the better they will perform as buyers. Retail merchants figured that out hundreds of years ago and pricing information is so embedded in traditional retail that all U.S. retailers are required to comply with the Uniform Pricing Code (UPC) system.

In the meanwhile, the Savvy Bidder can capitalize on her opponent's lack of pricing information, which serves to weaken their competitive capabilities. By thinking of the reserve price as a tactical benefit, the Savvy Bidder is able to use the reserve to position in reserve auctions. And positioning can be accomplished whether the reserve is undisclosed or disclosed. The underlying tactic is to help perpetuate the opponent's focus on the current price, defocus on the reserve price and hope that opponents consequently take a weak position. The hidden reserve is actually a marvelous invention – for the Savvy Bidder.

Notes:

Break Time

Are you getting a sense of strategic bidding? Notice how the Savvy Bidder thinks differently than a buyer? The bidding tactics we have discussed so far are the same bidding methods that other bidders use, but we're looking at them with more of an eye toward leveraging these common bidding methods for competitive positioning.

We see that the proxy bid can be used to leverage a position in the auction, not just to let the eBay auction mechanism do our work for us. You understand now that a proxy bid hands the control of your money to a machine that consumes your money to optimize the auction's closing price. And you see how being the highest bidder with a proxy bid makes you the target, the one to beat.

We looked at how to leverage a seller's reserve price, whether or not that reserve price is made known to the participants of the auction. You see now that a reserve price creates certain dynamics that, if understood, can be strategically leveraged. You see now how an undisclosed reserve price perpetuates focusing on the current price that spoofs bidders into believing that they can still purchase the auction item. This is accomplished by revealing 1) erroneous pricing information (the current price) and 2) hiding real pricing information (the reserve price). And you see how the current price effectively defocuses bidders from a hidden reserve price. Lacking critical pricing information, bidders consequently bid somewhat blindly. But, now you see how you can leverage these dynamics.

While these bidding tactics make sense, you also know that they do not apply to all auction situations and you know that the results will vary depending on a number of circumstances in the auction. What you can rely on, however, is that if you don't at least consider tactical approaches to auctions, you gain competitive advantages either by shear money power (as eBay and seller's would like it to be) or by luck. If you have plenty of money, you have all you need. If you are lucky person, you're in good shape. But, for the rest of us...

As we continue, we'll take a look at minimum bidding and discuss how that too can be leveraged for competitive position. We'll discuss the tactical use of cents in bids as well as the Adjustment Bid. Then we'll delve into the notorious, but awesome, snipe bid tactic.

Ready for more?

Minimum Bidding Tactics

In the single-unit eBay auction format all bidders are required to place a bid that is at least one minimum bid increment higher than the current price of the auction. The minimum bid increment is determined by eBay's bid increment scale that can be viewed at eBay's help section of its web site (or see *Minimum Bid Increment* in the glossary of this book). The current price plus the minimum bid increment is considered a "minimum bid". A bid that is lower than the minimum bid cannot be placed. In addition, a minimum bid does not create a proxy bid.

To illustrate a minimum bid, Figure 9 shows an auction with a current price of $860.00. In this case a bid of at least $870.00 is required (the current price plus at least one minimum bid increment of $10.00). A bid of $870.00, in this auction example, will not create a proxy bid. Of course, a bid higher than the minimum bid could be placed; in which case, a proxy bid would be created.

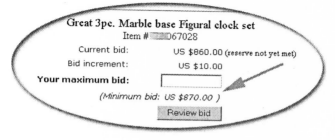

Figure 9 - An eBay screen portion showing the required minimum bid amount.

By reviewing the bid histories of closed eBay auctions (when bid amounts are revealed) you can see the propensity for bidders to place minimum bids. There are several factors that contribute to this:

♦ As illustrated in Figure 9 the eBay auction listing presents a bid amount that is equal to one minimum bid increment higher than the current price (represented on the eBay page by the term "Current Bid" or "Current Bid"). This current price amount is presented even if there is an existing proxy bid in the auction.

♦ A minimum bid has the smallest possible impact on the current price. Bidders who are current price focused prefer to make the smallest impact on the current price with their bidding.

♦ A minimum bid is a "safe" bid because it increases the current price only by the amount of the minimum bid. This is also true even if there is an existing proxy. Since a minimum bid is *not* considered a proxy bid, the current price will only increase the current price by the amount of the minimum bid. In this way the bidder does not venture too far with his bid.

♦ A minimum bid presumably preserves one's money. The logic is that one is spending less by placing a bid that is $1.00 over the current price as compared to placing a bid $20.00 over the current price, for example.

As we continue our discussion of minimum bidding we'll explore how minimum bidding may actually result in a higher closing price of the auction than may have otherwise occurred. This is based on the fact that the mind can adapt to small price increases easier than large price increases. We'll also discuss why minimum bidding is not normally competitive bidding.

Less Is More

When an auction receives all minimum bids there is a good chance that the auction will close at a higher price than had a few bidders placed higher bids during the auction. There are two basic reasons for this:

1. More bidders are rewarded with becoming the highest bidder. For most becoming the highest bidder is part of the fun of eBay auctions. Obtaining the "winning" position encourages continued participation in the auction.

2. Since the current price is rising relatively slowly, participants are not given price shock. Since it is relatively easy to accept small increases, this helps bidders maintain an interest in the auction. The current price implies that it is still possible to win the auction.

Proxy bids in an auction tend to repel bidders who are price conscience because evidence comes to light that competition exists. In fact, when an existing proxy outbids a bidder, it is often the only indication that there is immediate competition. To illustrate, one may place a bid in an auction with a $500.00 current price not knowing that there is a $1000.00 proxy bid in place. He is, of course, immediately outbid by the existing proxy bid. But because the auction required a minimum bid of "only" $510.00 (the current price plus a $10.00 minimum bid increment), the bidder was enticed to bid even though his bid would fail to obtain the highest bid position. His bid sets the current price to $510.00 with the new required bid becoming *only* $520.00 thereby continuing to entice new bids.

This is discouraging for most. On the one hand, the current price made it appear as if only a certain bid was required, only to find out that the bid was not sufficient after all. And, as a reward, the current price is increased by the person's own bid. In other words, he actually caused the auction's eventual closing price to increase, but was given no position in the auction. In this way the current price implies one thing yet delivers something else.

But, we are not discussing this to complain about it. Rather, to understand how the process works. Of importance is to understand that the current price makes the auction seem attractive, enticing new bids. In addition, the current price reduces price shock by incrementing is relatively small amounts as bids occur. It is not hard to understand why this process actually attracts minimum bidding.

Now let's consider the same auction example with a current price of $500.00 and a minimum bid requirement of $510.00 and with no proxy in place. Now a new bidder gets the "Congratulations. You are the Highest Bidder" message when he places a bid for $510.00. He did not have to place significant bid to get a "winning" position in the auction. The bonus is that he did not significantly impact the current price with his minimum bid. With no proxy bid in place, the current price actually delivered on the promise that "You could buy this auction item for only $510.00", in this example.

This is all well and good from one individual's standpoint. But now add several or many others who also bid at the minimum. Each is better able to take a "winning" position and without impacting the current price any more than necessary. This is encouraging and often spurs the participants to keep bidding. It is relatively easy to take (or retake) the highest bidder position in auctions that consist of all minimum bidders. The auction provides all participants with an active and rewarding experience. Everyone is having fun. But at a price.

Current price focused bidders find it relatively easy to justify the minimum required bid increment. For instance, a minimum required bid of $1.00 in an auction with a $90.00 current price is only a 1% increase – another buck is not difficult for most to justify. Please see Law *#12: Understand Current Price Escalation* for a complete discussion of this topic.

In fact the small-price-increase approach is effectively applied in many areas of our lives. For instance, taxes are slowly raised over time to reduce the chances of anarchy. (To reduce rebellion, the IRS took 20 years to integrate employer withholding of income tax into our society, e.g., the W-2). The Post Office raises its first class postage rates by a few cents every couple of years rather than a much larger increase every five or ten years.

The process of slowly raising prices has always worked in our commercial society. Merchants know it works, politicians know it works and the IRS knows that it works. eBay and it's prominent sellers also know it works. eBay auction buyers are more likely to acclimate to a higher price over time if the price is raised in relatively small increments, which is exactly what the current price mechanism is designed to do. Small increases are "absorbed" much easier than large increases.

The method by which the eBay mechanism increments the current price persists this small-price-increase approach. The current price is almost always incremented only by the minimum increment per eBay's minimum bid increment scale (See *Minimum Bid Increment* in the Glossary). There are two occasions when the current price increments by an amount larger than the minimum required bid: 1) when a bid outbids an existing proxy and 2) when a bid is placed that is equal to or greater than a seller's reserve price, should one exist. Other than these two occasions, the current price is incremented in small amounts. This serves to help keep bidders interested in the auction.

When all bidders in an auction are minimum bidders, each contributes to maintaining the opportunity for their opponents to be able to take the highest bidder position. In this way minimum bidding actually helps the auction close at a higher price than it may have otherwise. Since it is easier for bidders to justify small bid increases, each bidder is better able to stay in the auction, continuously adjusting the willingness to pay just a little bit more. This bidding cycle continues and over the life of the auction increasing the chance that the current price will reach a higher amount than it may have otherwise. It can therefore be assumed that minimum bidding is good for eBay and its sellers, in terms of the closing price (which is what matters to eBay and the seller). However, it is not necessarily good for the bidder who ultimately wins the auction.

Minimum bidding also increases bidding activity in the auction. As the *number* of bids increase, the apparent market value of the item increases. This has the effect of increasing the perceived value of the item in the minds of those interested in it. The more activity an auction receives, the more activity it fosters (See law *#10: Bid Begets Bid*).

But let's be realistic. The bidder who ultimately wins the auction will likely be satisfied that she won the auction at the price she did. This is because, in part, the winning bidder acclimated herself to the gradually increasing current price throughout her participation in the auction. To her, it is irrelevant that the auction might have closed at a lower price had the auction not consisted of minimum bidders, herself included. This is perhaps why the effect of minimum bidding is not recognized as an issue. But, as savvy bidders, we are aware of the dynamics of minimum bidding and look for ways to leverage it.

Minimum Bidding is Not Normally Competitive

Minimum bidding is not a trap the Savvy Bidder wants to fall into unless there is a clear tactical advantage. Minimum bidding is not normally competitive. Consider:

♦ A minimum bid is easy to outbid because it allows opponents to capture the highest bidder position with less apparent investment, which encourages continued participation. Remember that most bidders perceive being the highest bidder as "winning" the auction. (Please see Law *#3: Never Think of Yourself as "Winning"*). The tactical objective is to *not* perpetuate making it easy for opponents to gain a foothold in the auction.

♦ A minimum bid implies certain characteristics of the bidder, depending on the interpretation by the opponents in the auction. It may imply a bidder who doesn't have the financial wherewithal to win the auction or is fearful of spending his money. It may imply a bidder who is unsure of what the typical market price is and therefore is testing the auction with minimum bids.

♦ A minimum bid always increases the auction's current price. If the auction's current price is to be impacted by a bid, that bid might as well serve to gain a position in the auction – a minimum bid does not normally achieve any positioning benefit of lasting value.

♦ A minimum bid exposes the bidder's interest in the auction and does so without taking a strong position in the auction.

♦ A minimum bid as a snipe bid risks not being an effective snipe bid. As we'll discuss in *The Snipe Bid Tactic* later, a snipe bid should be several minimum bid increments higher than the current price to be effective against possible existing proxy bids and other last second bids.

A bidder who favors minimum bidding performs a lot of work for questionable competitive gain. He gets caught up in a cycle that often consists of outbid and be outbid. As this cycle plays out, the eBay mechanism dutifully increases the auction's current price. But, the current price is increased such that it does not produce price shock.

It is important for the Savvy Bidder to understand the dynamics of minimum bidding if for no other reason than to not be a minimum bidder unless minimum bids are used for tactical bidding. There are circumstances where minimum bidding could serve tactical objectives, as we'll discuss next.

Tactical Minimum Bidding

At first glance it might be difficult to realize how minimum bidding might be useful as a bidding tactic. As mentioned, a minimum bid is easy for opponents to outbid and possibly get rewarded with becoming the highest bidder. To understand how to tactically use minimum bids we must think in terms of positioning, not simply as buyers. Let's expand our thinking a bit and explore how minimum bids might be useful for strategic purposes.

♦ Consider using a minimum bid to "test" your opponent bidders. Place a minimum bid and check if it was sufficient to take the auction away from the current highest bidder. If one bid does not acquire the highest bidder position, place one or more additional minimum bids until you just outbid the current highest bidder. But don't consume too much of your bidding budget in the process and remember that your minimum bids are increasing the auction's current price. Then stop bidding and watch for any reaction. The sooner he reacts the more determined he is likely to be. With this tactic you may be able to acquire useful information concerning the intentions and even the bidding methods of an opponent bidder. Keep in mind that your tactical objective is ferret out competition, not to become the highest bidder.

♦ If you are a respected bidder in the eBay community (or known as a winning bidder), just your membership ID in the bid history may be enough to intimidate those bidders who know about you (or who take the time to explore your past bidding activities). Obviously, the only way to get your ID into the bid history of the auction is by placing a bid of at least the minimum required bid, even if you do not take the highest bidder seat with that bid. A minimum bid in an auction is sufficient to broadcast an interest in the auction. Perhaps your presence may intimidate weaker opponents.

♦ A minimum bid may be assumed to have come from a bidder who is apprehensive about spending money on the item. By placing a minimum bid you may not be perceived as a competitive threat. However, in reality your bid is part of a positioning strategy. When you win the auction your opponents may find that they underestimated your competitive strength.

♦ Consider placing a minimum bid just prior to a proxy bid. The minimum bid tests if there is currently a proxy bid in place. If a proxy bid does not exist, place your proxy bid. If a proxy bid does exist you may want to perform a Proxy Discovery Run to determine the proxy amount. Once the existing proxy bid is outbid, make one more bid at your proxy amount. However I suggest that the final bid not be another minimum bid. By doing so, you will have expended a portion of your bidding budget only to leave yourself with a weak position.

To the observant bidder a series of minimum bids indicates that you were searching for an existing proxy bid, much as an apprehensive bidder might. However, since no bidder can view the actual bid amounts while the auction is running, no bidder can determine if the last of your Proxy Discovery Run bids was higher than a minimum bid. Thus, with this tactic, you look like an apprehensive bidder, yet leave a proxy bid that is uncharacteristic of an apprehensive bidder. However, re- member the potential disadvantage of owning a proxy bid – you be- come the target for other bidders to try to outbid (see *Proxy Bidding Tactics* in this chapter).

Conclusion

In the preceding discussion we explored some of the dynamics associated with minimum bidding. We discussed how the current price works to reduce price shock which serves to entice new bids. When all bidders in an auction are minimum bidders, the auction may actually close at a higher price than it may have other- wise. As a Savvy Bidder you'll want to avoid this cycle and focus on positioning in the auction by perhaps utilizing minimum bidding to help ferret out information or sway your opponents. Avoid being lured into placing minimum bids because the auction presents itself as easy to bid in and win. Use minimum bidding to gain a useful competitive edge.

Notes:

Bidding Tactics with Cents

Ever wonder why a retail price is $19.95, not $20.00. Or $99.99 instead of $100.00? Or why big-ticket merchandise is priced at $1,995, not $2,000, for instance? What retailers are attempting to do is defocus prospective buyers from a whole dollar amount, which carries more emotional baggage. By lowering the price slightly the merchant keeps his price optimized while helping to keep the mind away from a price that might raise some flags. Thus a slight drop in the price shifts the buyers mind to a more palatable price. This retail pricing method is a way of fooling the mind and has been in use for a very long time.

Despite how retail pricing is presented to consumers, we tend to think in terms of whole dollars. When the electric bill comes in, most of us say to our spouse that the electric bill is $110.00 when it may in fact be $109.36. We tell our friends that the new car we're interested in buying is $25,000 and avoid reciting the lengthy price of $24,783.00. It is easier to think and communicate in whole numbers. This is carried into eBay auctions. For proof of this simply view the bid histories of any number of closed eBay auctions. The vast majority of the bids are in whole dollar values. In other words most bids do not have a cents value.

Why would a person bid $50.00 in an auction rather than $49.99? Why would a person place a bid for $500.00 rather than $499.95? The simple answer is because the bidder is thinking is terms of a purchase at a price acceptable to him at that time, not in terms of a competitive price. This is one of the common results of taking a buyer approach to online auctions. The exception is when a bidder is specifically interested in including cents in a bid as a competitive tactic. And even then you'll commonly find very low cent values such as 3 cents or the common 50 cents.

As a Savvy Bidder you know the value of cents. However, *you want to help your opponents continue to think in whole dollar amounts*. This is because using cents in bidding is a viable competitive bidding tactic that you prefer to keep available for your own use if at all possible. One way to help keep your opponents on the whole dollar is to not yourself throw the current price off the whole dollar value by placing a bid with cents. Fortunately there are a couple factors that work in your favor to help keep bidders thinking in terms of the whole dollar:

1. Bidders who are current price focused tend to use the current price as their price guideline when deciding to bid. A current price of $300.00, for example, is clear and makes it easy to decide if to bid. At this current price, eBay requires a $5.00 minimum bid increment. So, it is easy to simply bid the $305.00 minimum required bid.

2. Retail makes the mind work harder with its cent values, such as $19.95 – auction buyers tend to follow the easier path of thinking in terms of whole dollar values.

3. eBay's minimum bid increment scale is set to use a whole dollar amount as the minimum bid increment except when the current price is less than $25.00 and in the range of $100.00 to $250.00 (see *Minimum Bid Increment* in the Glossary of this book). This tends to keep the current price on the whole dollar.

Since the typical bidder tends to think in whole dollar values and because eBay's minimum bid increment scale facilitates this thinking, a whole dollar bid is predominant.

When the current price is set to include a cents value, bidders are reminded that cents in their bids may have a competitive value. In this case the mind is directed to think in terms of cents rather than thinking in terms of the simpler whole dollar value. When the current price includes cents you may want to consider placing an Adjustment Bid to set the current price back to a whole dollar value (the Adjustment Bid is discussed following this chapter).

As will be discussed in the Adjustment Bid tactic, when the current price includes cents, the current price will tend to retain that cents value assuming that bidders continue to bid to eBay's default minimum bid increment. The exception is when the minimum bid increment is 25 cents. The important principle to remember is that *the current price will tend to retain a whole dollar value or will tend to carry a cents value from one bid to the next.*

Assuming that the current price is on a whole dollar, for instance $95.00, consider *not* using cents in your bidding unless your bidding tactic specifically calls for cents. In this manner you actually bid with less competitive strength to help your opponents remain competitively weaker (by not reminding them of the competitive value of cents). Of course there are other competitive elements to a bid such as the timing of the bid, the amount of the bid and so forth. So, you are not giving up all of your bid's competitive strength by avoiding the use of cents in most of your bids. However, because the current price tends to retain a whole dollar value, you are not aiding your opponents by reminding them of the tactical value of cents in their bids.

Avoid using the cents in your bids in an effort to preserve the strategic use of cents for when it will serve your competitive position in the auction.

Notes:

The Adjustment Bid

There may be times when you want to influence opponents to follow a pattern of bidding that is less competitive for them. For instance, a bidder who uses cents in his bids may gain a competitive advantage over bidders who bid on the whole dollar. Auctions are often won by cents alone. The purpose of an Adjustment Bid tactic is to bring the current price back to a whole dollar value.

When an auction's current price includes a cent value, for instance $110.33, it is because a bidder placed a bid that included a cents value. (Sellers don't normally specify a First Bid with a cents value, except perhaps a value of 50 cents.) When the current price includes cents the current price will usually retain the cents value if subsequent bidders bid to the minimum required bid or place new bids of a whole dollar value. For example, if an auction's current price is $44.22, the minimum bid increment will be $1.00, requiring a bid of at least $45.22. Notice how the 22-cent value was carried over. Another example would be a current price of $260.78. In this case the minimum bid increment would be $5.00 thereby requiring a bid of at least $265.78. Once again the cent value was carried over. You can see how the cents value is retained in the current price as long as the bidders bid to at least the minimum required bid or bid a whole dollar value.

It is better for the current price to not remind participants of the competitive value of cents. The Adjustment Bid tactic returns the current price back to a whole dollar value.

Let's explore a few examples of the Adjustment Bid so that you know what bid amount will be required should you choose to use this tactic from time to time. We'll start with a very simple example based on an actual eBay auction.

The eBay auction shown in Figure 10 has a current price of $26.55. In this current price range, the eBay minimum bid increment is $1.00. So, a new bid will have to be at least $27.55 ($26.55 + $1.00). If you were to place a bid of $27.55, the cents would be carried over to the new current price. However, you want to get the current price back to a whole dollar. That whole dollar value can't be $27.00 because that would require a bid that is lower than the required minimum bid. The next whole dollar value is $28.00, so that will be our bid amount.

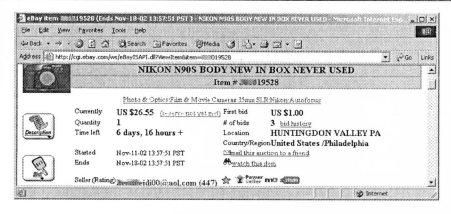

Figure 10 - An eBay screen portion showing a current price with cents.

Determining the bid amount of an Adjustment Bid is a simple four-step process. Using the example auction shown:

1. The current price is $26.55
2. The minimum required bid increment is $1.00
3. The minimum bid is therefore $27.55 ($26.55 + $1.00)
4. Take the next whole dollar value over the minimum bid which is $28.00

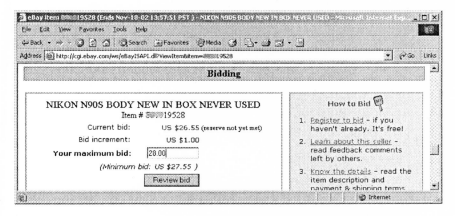

Figure 11 - An eBay screen portion showing a bid amount at the next highest whole dollar amount.

Note in Figure 12 that when we placed the $28.00 bid, the auction's current price was set to a whole dollar amount of $29.00, but our bid was outbid by an existing proxy bid. This doesn't matter since our only objective was to adjust the current price to a whole dollar amount.

Figure 12 - An eBay screen portion showing the resulting current price after a bid at the next highest whole dollar amount.

Before we explore another example, there are two important things to remember about an Adjustment Bid:

1. An Adjustment Bid will accomplish its objective whether or not it makes you the highest bidder. In other words, if a bidder has a proxy bid in place, the current price will still be set to a whole dollar value even if your Adjustment Bid does not outbid the existing proxy. Of course, you will not take the highest bidder position (which is not the objective of an Adjustment Bid anyway).

2. Your Adjustment Bid will not create a proxy bid as long the amount you bid is less than 2 minimum bid increments. In other words, a bid amount that is *less than* 2 minimum bid increments over the required bid is not sufficient to create a proxy bid. Thus an Adjustment Bid accomplishes its objective, but does not leave you with a proxy bid.

Let's look at another example. Assume an auction has a current price of $110.23. Using the Adjustment Bid formula:

1. The current price is $110.23
2. The minimum required bid increment is $2.50
3. The minimum bid is therefore $112.73 ($110.23 + $2.50)
4. Take the next whole dollar over the minimum bid which is $113.00

A bid of $113.00 will set the current price in this example to a whole dollar value and not leave you with a proxy bid.

Ready for another example? Assume an auction's current price is $99.99 (some bidder got clever or the seller has set a retail-like First Bid price).

1. The current price is $99.99
2. The minimum required bid increment is $1.00
3. The minimum bid is therefore $100.99 ($99.99 + $1.00)
4. Take the next whole dollar over the minimum bid which is $101.00

A bid of $101.00 will set the current price to a whole dollar value. Once again, you have not created a proxy bid in this example.

Let's try one more example. This time the auction's current price is very low where eBay's bid increment scale specifies a minimum bid increment of 25 cents. This example has been made the last example because you may find that placing an Adjustment Bid on such a low current price does not yield as a significant competitive advantage as might an Adjustment Bid at a higher current price. Anyway, let's do the example.

Assume an auction's current price is $4.10. eBay's minimum bid increment is 25 cents in this current price range. You want to bring the auction's current price to a whole dollar value.

1. The current price is $4.10
2. The minimum required bid increment is 25 cents
3. The minimum bid is therefore $4.35 ($4.10 + $.25)
4. Take the next whole dollar over the minimum bid which is $5.00

But this is technically not an Adjustment Bid. If you were to bid $5.00, the current price will be set to $4.35 *and* you will have created a proxy bid. This is because the $5.00 is equivalent to more than 2 minimum bid increments according to the eBay minimum bid scale. In fact a $5.00 bid, in this example, is actually equal to over 3 minimum bid increments. So you might as well simply place a $5.00 proxy bid. While the price will be set to $4.35, if and when another bidder outbids your $5.00 proxy bid, the current price will be set to $5.00 accomplishing the same objective as an Adjustment Bid.

You can see that calculating an Adjustment Bid is not hard at all. You simply need to bid at the next whole dollar value *over* the minimum required bid amount. The exception is when the eBay minimum bid increment scale is less than $1.00 as the final example illustrated.

Conclusion

The tactical objective of the Adjustment Bid is to get the current price back to a whole dollar value. You typically want an Adjustment Bid to accomplish just that one objective and not leave you with a proxy bid. The value of an Adjustment Bid is that it will work even when another bidder has a proxy bid in place.

Try the Adjustment Bid when the occasion calls for it. You may find that most of your opponents will then bid in such a way as to keep the current price on a comfortable whole dollar value. Should a bidder place a bid later in the auction using a cents value, place another Adjustment Bid. Normally, an Adjustment Bid should not consume much of your bidding budget. At any rate, the Savvy Bidder expects to spend some of his bidding budget making these small adjustments to the auction's landscape.

Notes:

The Snipe Bidding Tactic

The snipe bid is the most controversial bidding tactic used in eBay auctions. The snipe bid is hated by a great many eBay members and adored by those who have found the tactic effective. While the snipe bid is a highly effective bidding tactic, it is also the riskiest bidding tactic. Let's talk about it.

The objective of a snipe bid is actually very simple – place a bid close enough to an auction's closing such that opponents do not have enough time to respond to the snipe bid. The closer the snipe bid is to the auction's close, the less time opponents have to determine that a bid was placed and place a bid in response. For example, if a snipe bid is placed with 20 seconds remaining in the auction, it is less likely that another bidder will realize that a snipe bid was placed while the auction is still running and have time to place a bid of his own. 5 seconds and there is virtually no chance that an opponent can reciprocate. Figure 13 illustrates a snipe bid. Notice that the auction closed at 06:49:43 and that the final bid was place at 06:49:23, with just 20 seconds left in the auction.

Figure 13 - An eBay screen portion showing a snipe bid 20 seconds before the auction closed.

The snipe bid tactic relies on the auction mechanism resolving all bids at the instant the auction closes. Once the auction has closed the auction mechanism blocks new bids and resolves any outstanding bids to determine the winner. If a previously entered proxy bid exists when the auction closes, any new bids are resolved against that proxy. This reconciliation process occurs in milliseconds and is completely automated by the eBay computers. Thus the tactic of a snipe bid is to submit a bid that is processed by the auction mechanism once the auction has closed and hopefully, resolves to be the winning bid.

Generally, the snipe bid tactic is disliked. Of course it is most disliked by those who lose an auction to a snipe bidder. This comes as no surprise because snipe bidding exploits the precise closing time of an auction and the inability for other participants to respond due to a precise closing time for the auction. Thus, the participants who took the time to bid "normally" while the auction was running are often outbid with a single bid that they did not see coming nor could respond to.

In an effort to make online auctions more "fair" some auction venues automatically extend the auction's closing time if a bid is submitted within a certain time prior to the auction's close. While based on good intentions, extending the auction is unfair manipulation, in my opinion. This is analogous to a seller being permitted to continuously keep extending her auction because she wasn't satisfied with the estimated closing price. If sellers were allowed to keep extending their auctions near the close, bidders would quickly loose confidence that auctions are winnable given the ability of the seller to delay an auction's close. Extending an auction because a bid came in near its close effectively robs bidders of their confidence that they could be the winning bidder. This is important because people do not normally bid for something to do – they want to win the right to make a purchase. If the possibility of making that purchase is continuously moved beyond the buyer's grasp, well, you get the picture.

Fortunately eBay does not extend an auction's closing time due to snipe bidding. It is curious why eBay has not adopted the policy of extending the auction when a bid is placed close to an auctions close. Perhaps eBay recognizes that last minute bidding increases the potential of a higher closing price, generally speaking. In other words, eBay makes more money in final sales fees by allowing bidding right up to the instant the auction closes. Now before you pooh-pooh this thought consider the logic.

The potential for an increased closing price of an auction is rooted in the risks a snipe bidder accepts. Consider:

♦ The snipe bidder must make an educated guess as to what would be an appropriate amount for his snipe bid. If the guess is wrong, there is no chance to try another bid in that auction. What's the most obvious way to avoid guessing wrong? Guess high. But, not too high to avoid bidding excessively. One must remember that the snipe bidder herself cannot reciprocate if it turns out that another bidder also sniped the auction with a higher bid amount or if there was a proxy bid in place that was higher than the snipe bid itself. So, the most obvious course of action is to set a snipe bid at a higher amount. 3 to 5 minimum bid increments above the current price is not uncommon for a snipe bid.

♦ As you are aware, if a bid is placed against an existing proxy bid, and that bid is *lower* than the existing proxy bid amount, the auction's current price is immediately raised to the amount of the new bid. Such a bid could not win the auction but would still raise the auction's current price. Taking an extreme example to illustrate this scenario, assume an auction has a current price of $100.00 with an existing proxy bid of $200.00. A snipe bid is placed for $150.00. This snipe bid is less than the existing proxy bid. The auction's current price is immediately raised to $150.00 even though the bidder does not take the highest bidder position. The bid failed but still impacted the auction's current price. Following this logic, if a bidder places a snipe bid against an existing proxy bid and that bid is less than the existing proxy, the auction will close at the snipe bid amount. As such, eBay makes more money on the final sales fee of auctions that are hit by snipers that <u>fail</u> to outbid an existing proxy. Now that's how to make money!

♦ In reserve auctions, if a bid is placed that is *greater* than the seller's reserve the auctions current price is immediately raised to the reserve price. Because the majority of sellers do not disclose their reserve prices a bidder may place a bid thinking she will obtain a healthy proxy bid in relation to the current price. For example, an auction's current price is $250.00 with an undisclosed reserve price of $500.00. A bidder places a $550.00 bid expecting to receive very good protection with the proxy bid which, in this case, would appear to be $300.00. That $300.00 may fend off many opponents, or so the thinking goes. But, the auction's current price is immediately set to the amount of the reserve, in this example, $500.00 (Please see Law #37: *Beware the Hidden Reserve Price*). Now, assume that this $550.00 bid was a snipe bid. The auction closes at the seller's reserve price of $500.00. This is a problem if the snipe bidder did not expect the trick of setting the current price to the seller's reserve. I wonder how many snipe bidders have been caught off guard with this method of escalating a reserve auction's closing price. Once again, this increases eBay final sales fees.

♦ If two <u>snipe bidders</u> hit the auction, the eBay auction mechanism will play each bid against the other during the bid reconciliation (and in milliseconds). While one snipe bidder may win the auction, she may win at a much higher closing price than she expected. This is because the other snipe bid drove up the closing price. What an ideal way to realize a better final sales fee than to allow situations where two bidders guess high because neither expected another snipe bidder. And, by the time the winning snipe bidder realizes what happened, the closing price is set. (This exact scenario happened to me once. I placed a snipe for $150.34 in an auction with a $120.00 current price (I know, I bid too high). Turns out another bidder also snipped the auction at $140.00. I won the auction at $142.50, higher than I anticipated.)

One must assume that eBay makes more money from final sales fees by allowing snipe bidding. Even if allowing snipe bidding results is a paltry one tenth of one percent average increase in auction closing prices, it adds up over millions of auctions. I have not observed eBay do anything that doesn't have its roots in income generation. The sellers of sniped auctions also benefit financially, but not on such a broad scale as eBay.

That eBay allows sniping to continue without extending auctions is all well and good. But the real purpose of our discussion so far has been to point out how snipe bidding can be a risky bidding tactic. In summary:

♦ A snipe bidder himself cannot reciprocate if it turns out that another bidder also sniped the auction with a higher bid amount or if an existing proxy bid outbids the snipe bid.

♦ The snipe bidder must correctly determine what would be an appropriate amount for the snipe bid. To win the auction, a snipe bid must be greater than an existing proxy and greater than a reserve price. The estimate must be correct since there is no chance to try another bid in that auction. A guess that is too high may result in overpaying for the auction. A guess that is too low may result in losing the auction.

♦ As mentioned if two snipe bidders hit the auction, the auction mechanism will play each bid against the other during the bid reconciliation. While one snipe bidder may win the auction, she may win at a much higher closing price than she expected. Note that if two snipe bidders place a bid of the exact same amount, the *first* bid received takes precedence. In this case, the snipe bidder who placed the second bid to be received loses the auction and has no ability to bid again.

As you can see, snipe bidding is not without its risks. If you thought that snipe bidding is the definitive way to win eBay auctions, you are mistaken. If you are good at snipe bidding, the tactic can highly effective, but should not be your only bidding tactic. When used sensibly, the snipe bid can prove to be a formidable bidding tactic. But what does it take to be good at snipe bidding? Consider:

1. You must be able to estimate the probable closing price of the auction.

2. You must be willing to attend to the auction when it is about to end.

3. You need to be able to make bidding decisions quickly. There can be very little value reassessment (such as when a bidder, being focused on the current price, repeatedly runs through the "am I willing to pay the current price" decision cycle). When intending to snipe an auction, you must have already considered the target price.

4. You must manage your bidding budget during the auction. If the only bid you intend to place in the auction is a snipe bid then managing your bidding budget is not a primary concern. However, if you bid several times in the auction you'll want to conserve an appropriate portion of your bidding budget for the snipe bid.

5. You need to have a sense as to how well your Internet connection is performing at the time of your snipe bid. You must also be ready to accept the fact that the eBay web site may be malfunctioning or that the Internet is bogged down by heavy traffic.

6. You need to know how to work your resources. For instance, running multiple browser windows, working a countdown timer (if you choose to use a countdown timer). When using the snipe bid tactic, you must be ready to think and move quickly.

7. And finally, you will need to be an aggressive bidder. You must not be afraid of bidding. You cannot question your every move as the auctions landscape changes. A snipe bidder must be a confident bidder.

When to Snipe an Auction

The Savvy Bidder considers the landscape of the auction and selects the snipe tactic when certain conditions suggest that it might be effective. Below are a few conditions that might indicate that sniping the auction would be an effective bidding tactic. However, there is no precise rule for deciding to snipe an auction and is a matter of personal judgment. Consider these scenarios:

♦ The auction is receiving very heavy bidding. As such, normal bidding may not provide any significant competitive advantage compared to sniping the auction. Bidding during the auction exposes your bids to your opponents giving them the advantage of responding to your bids. A snipe bid hides your bidding activity until no opponent can reciprocate to your bids.

♦ The auction has at least one bidder who persistently takes the auction back when she is outbid. It is obvious that such a bidder is determined to win the auction. Problem is you do not know the personal valuation of this bidder (what she is willing to pay). In addition you choose to not try to find out this bidder's personal valuation through bidding because the nominal gain of information would not be worth the impact on the auction's closing price.

♦ An auction has a very determined bidder who continuously retakes the highest bidder position. This bidder likes to perform Proxy Discover Runs (see *The Proxy Discovery Run*). If you were to place a proxy bid this bidder may try to find your proxy bid and outbid it if it is lower than what he is willing to pay. You may elect to snipe the auction in an effort to render this bidder's favorite bidding tactic useless or, better yet, to pull such a bidder into the time consuming process of performing a Proxy Discovery Run when time is rapidly running out.

♦ There is a bidding war raging. You choose to let the bidding war run its course and then snipe the auction. If you were to jump into the bidding war, you would introduce yourself as another competitor that may entice the warring bidders to bid even more aggressively than they already are. By sniping the auction, you stay out of the battle.

♦ An auction has an undisclosed reserve price. You have inquired of the seller and have obtained the reserve price, which is lower than the target price. So far the auction has received bids that are less than the seller's reserve. You may elect to snipe this auction rather than indicate your own interest with a bid during mid auction. The strategy in this case is to a) not indicate that there is another bidder (you) who is interested in the auction and b) to not impact the current price with a bid that is less than the seller's reserve and which may provide minimal competitive value. You may elect to snipe this auction with a bid amount that is equal to the seller's reserve or just slightly over the reserve – such a bid would be sufficient to win the auction (assuming no one else also sniped the auction with a higher bid than yours).

♦ Your bidding budget is very tight. For example, you have determined a target price of $375.00 for an auction. Because the item is in demand, the auction's current price quickly reaches $350.00. In this example you have a remaining bidding budget of only $25.00. This may not be enough to leverage during normal, mid auction bidding. A snipe bid may allow you to take a final shot with a limited bidding budget. This is assuming, of course, that the auction's current price has not exceeded the target price. In addition to active bidding, a seller may have also placed a high First Bid price on an auction. This sets a floor price that is near the typical closing price for the same or a comparable item. Thus, the seller constrains your bidding budget. A snipe bid may be a way to get maximum use from a limited bidding budget.

♦ Of course, you may decide to snipe an auction simply because it's a bit more fun. Snipe bidding is a thrill. There's nothing like sniping an auction with zero seconds left in the auction – I did it once.

Estimating an Auction's Closing Price

The key to successful snipe bidding, believe it or not, is not just how near the auction's close you place your snipe bid – that's the fun part. Rather, snipe bidding requires skill estimating the auction's closing price. There are several ways to estimate an auctions closing price.

1. First and foremost, determine a target price for the auction. As discussed in chapter *The Target Price*, the target price is based on the typical market price for the same or comparable item. Alternatively, pricing external to the auction environment is used if there is no market history in the auction venue. While the target price is used primarily to help you determine a bidding budget, it also provides other benefits. In the case of estimating the closing cost of an auction you are going to snipe, the target price provides a guideline as to where the auction participants might take the auction's closing price. This is based on the reasoning that most auction participants will probably avoid paying more than the typical price of the item.

2. If it is apparent that there is an existing proxy bid in the auction, you might want to "discover" that proxy bid before placing your snipe bid. This minimizes guessing with your snipe bid (remember, you'll have no opportunity to bid again). What you might do is perform a Proxy Discovery Run (see *The Proxy Discovery Run*) to determine the proxy bid, assuming that your bidding budget has the room. Make sure to occupy the time up to your planned snipe bid when performing your Proxy Discovery Run – you might as well get an additional benefit. By introducing activity into the auction, you help create a moving target to your opponents. Also, you will not look like a snipe bidder to your opponents, so they may regard you as simply a

normal bidder who is uncertain about what she is willing to pay in the auction as evident by placing a string of minimum bids. Your true objective, however, is to determine the amount of an existing proxy bid so that you can posture for a winning snipe bid.

3. Keep an eye on those minimum bidders, not as competitors, but as bidders who impact the auction's current price. I have observed that minimum bidders rarely win auctions that are sniped. This is simply because their bids do not have enough strength to compete with a snipe bid that may be 2, 3 or 5 minimum bid increments over the current price. However, their bids do increase the current price. In addition, minimum bidders are often occupied with deciding to bid or not, entering their bid and refreshing their browser to see how they are doing in the auction (probably using only one browser window). As such, minimum bidding very close to an auction's close is not normally effective because it is not an efficient use of what little time remains in the auction. However, such bids do change the auction's landscape so you must be watchful.

The real skill of snipe bidding is in predicting an auction's closing price. Obviously this is much easier to do near an auction's close that earlier in the auction. One reason for this is because many of the persons interested in purchasing the item have presented themselves by the time the auction is near its close. Of course, one never knows if one or more snipers lie in wait.

Since the majority of bidders in online auctions take a buyer approach it comes as no surprise that "buyers" will place one or more bids at various points in the auction rather than wait to bid near the auction's close. To the buyer, there is no apparent benefit in waiting to bid near the auction's close. Also, the time pressure of the auction's clock tends to make bidders feel rushed near the auction's close. The bidders who feel most rushed are those who are not sure what they are willing to pay for the item and, consequently, are current price focused. These factors work in the favor of the snipe bidder because it helps make the auction's probable closing price a bit easier to predict.

You don't need to make a perfect guess at the closing price. You just need to get close. If you estimate too low, you'll likely lose to an existing proxy bid or to another sniper. If you estimate too high, you risk another sniper's bid dramatically increasing the auction's final closing price when the auction mechanism reconciles all bids upon the auction's close. Consider your various resources for estimating the auction's closing price:

♦ The target price provides important typical market price information.

♦ The apparent demand for the item as indicated by the activity in the auction thus far and the bid histories of other auctions for the same or similar item.

♦ The type of bidders in the auction. For example, are most bidders in the auction minimum bidders? Are there one or several proxy bidders in the auction? The type of bidders who are participating will help you estimate the probable closing price.

♦ Consider the auction's bidding activity since the auction began. Did the bid activity begin early in the auction, at mid point or late in the auction? High demand for the item may result in an early start to bidding activity and continue right up to the auction's close.

Develop your ability to estimate an auction's closing price. This will help you place snipe bids that are high enough to win the auction while minimizing the risk of overpaying for the auction. The snipe bid is a bidding tactic that attempts to submit a bid that is not just another competitive bid, rather is a bid that is targeted to out perform the participants in the auction, including other snipe bidders. To do this, your snipe bid amount must be in the "sweat spot" – not too high and not too low. Estimating the closing price of an auction you intend to snipe is an important element of effective snipe bidding.

How to Snipe Bid

Let's get to what you came for – how to snipe bid. Here's the general process I follow to snipe bid:

1. A few minutes prior to the auction's close I make sure I am still signed into eBay. This allows me to place a snipe bid in the final seconds of the auction without being hindered by the sign in process. To check that I'm still signed in I click the *My eBay* link at the top of the eBay page. If I am taken directly to the *My eBay* page with no sign in request, I know that I am still signed in. I then click the Back button of my browser to go back to the page I was on before testing the sign on. If the sign in has expired, I complete the sign in page which then takes me to the *My eBay* page and then I click the Back button twice to return to the page I was on before testing the sign on.

2. I set up two browser windows. One to monitor the auction and one to place the snipe bid. I make sure *both* browsers are signed in (see *The Double Browser Bidding Technique* in this chapter).

3. I decide at what time I will place my snipe bid and I get my electronic countdown timer running (Radio Shack catalog # 63-878) so that it will chime a few seconds before the time I have decided to place the snipe bid.

4. With 5 to 10 minutes remaining in the auction I watch the activity in the auction. I use one of the two browser windows for looking around (but not the browser that is signed in). I take this time to estimate the closing price of the auction. Also, I review the participants in the auction to get a sense of which opponents might be aggressive bidders or who might use cent values in their bids. Because I have the countdown timer running, I do not continuously refresh either browser watching the current price. I do refresh periodically to monitor the auction activity.

5. At about 30 seconds prior to the time I intend to place my snipe bid I enter the snipe bid amount in the second browser window (the browser that is signed in). But I don't submit it just yet. I don't use a particular rule of thumb concerning how many bid increments to snipe bid over the current price. I will decide the snipe bid based on the auction's activity or probable activity. At times I will snipe bid 3 minimum bid increments over the current price and other times 5 or 6 minimum bid increments. It depends on how aggressive I feel the snipe bid needs to be given the auction's landscape. However, I always use cents in a snipe bid but never use 50 cents. I also avoid 1 and 3 cent values since they are commonly used. And finally, I avoid cent values with two identical numbers, such as 33, 66, 99 and so forth. In other words, I avoid using "easy" cent values. For example, I choose cent values that do not easily come to mind such as 26, 43, 51, 78, 92 and so on.

6. With my bid amount entered in the signed in browser window (but not yet submitted), I continue to monitor the auction, watching the activity in the auction. I am prepared to increase my snipe bid amount (in the second browser window) if necessary. However, I do not keep asking myself if I "am willing to pay the current price" as the current price increases. In other words, I bid in accordance with the target price and do not consume valuable time fretting over what I am willing to pay for the auction.

7. When my countdown timer chimes, I switch to the signed in browser window and submit my snipe bid. If I'm feeling confident in my Internet connection, I'll delay submitting my snipe bid until the last possible second. Keep in mind that I am prepared, am not sweating over how much to bid and do not feel rushed. I consistently snipe bid with 4 to 10 seconds remaining in the auction, at times with just 1 or 2 seconds remaining.

8. Now that the auction has closed, I review the auction's bid history, which now shows the bid amounts. I assess how well did I predicting the closing price of the auction? On the rare occasion I lose the auction, I determine why. If I lose an auction that I sniped, I do not get upset. I know the risks associated with snipe bidding and, when I choose to snipe an auction, accept the outcome gracefully. But, I have not had to practice such good sportsmanship all that much.

Foiling the Sniper

As Figure 14 illustrates, *always assume that an auction will be sniped*. Be prepared for another's snipe bid by thinking like a snipe bidder. What snipe bid amount might another place in an effort to predict the best snipe bid? Will a snipe bidder bid very high because the item is in high demand? Will a snipe bidder bid too low because the auction's low activity seems to indicate an easy win with a snipe bid? In the end, there is virtually no way to know if an auction you intend to snipe will be sniped by another. Therefore, be prepared by thinking as another snipe bidder would think and then, select the best snipe bid amount and snipe bid timing you can.

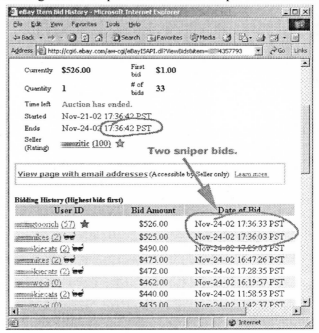

There are a couple of tactics that you might like to consider in an effort to foil

Figure 14 - An eBay screen portion showing two sniper bids.

other snipers. One tactic I like to use is the "pre-snipe double proxy". Having managed my bidding budget I have some money remaining to leverage near the auction's close, I might place a small proxy bid with about 5 minutes remaining in the auction. This gives the weaker opponents something to occupy their time with.

But, its primary purpose is to create doubt in the mind of other prospective snipers – they may question if they are able to accurately predict a winning snipe bid. Then, perhaps with 2 minutes remaining in the auction, I'll place a second small proxy bid, or even a minimum bid, *even if my first proxy bid has not been outbid*. These bids are placed with plenty of time remaining for potential snipe bidders to ponder what's going on.

With two bids to my credit a prospective snipe bidder sees my eBay membership ID listed twice in the auction's bid history. The obvious (and correct) conclusion is that my second bid increased my previous proxy bid. But, how much I increased my proxy is unknown – that's the key. I look like a very determined bidder and it appears as if I had reconsidered what I was willing to pay for the auction. The objective of the "pre-snipe double bid" tactic is to create doubt that a prospective snipe bidder will be able to choose a snipe bid amount that a) that wins the auction and b) doesn't cause him to overpay for the auction. The unknown is a powerful competitive tool. There are several laws that discuss leveraging the unknown. For instance, laws *#25: Keep Your Opponents Off Guard*, *#27: The FUD Factor* as well as a few others.

Let's consider an example auction to illustrate this tactic. Assume an auction with a current price of $100.00. Bidding is active. The target price is $125.00. The auction will close in 5 minutes and you intend to snipe the auction. Since you have $25.00 remaining in your bidding budget (the difference between the target price and the current price) you have only a few dollars to leverage. So, you place a $107.50 proxy bid (3 minimum bid increments over the current price). This bid places you as the highest bidder. After a minute or so you place a second bid. This time, you want a bid to be the smallest amount possible. You place a $110.00 bid (1 minimum bid increment over your previous proxy bid). With 10 seconds remaining in the auction you place a snipe bid for $117.67 (3 minimum bid increments over your last proxy bid plus a few cents for good measure).

The objective of this tactic is to throw your competitors off by introducing extraneous bids that may serve to confuse the bidders and occupy their time. Because bid amounts cannot be viewed during a single-unit eBay auction, and since this tactic introduces a proxy bid *that you increased*, prospective snipe bidders may believe that the auction is out of their reach. As good as this all sounds, there is a risk with this tactic. It may cause a very determined snipe bidder to bid higher than necessary. This may result in a significant escalation of the closing price, especially if you also snipe the auction. The objective of the "pre-snipe double bid" tactic is to confuse and intimidate prospective snipe bidders, but that objective will not always be reached. When using this tactic keep your two "pre-snipe" bids as small as practical. Remember, you are not trying the win the auction with these pre-snipe bid bids – you are only trying to convince prospective snipe bidders to not trust their own judgment as to what snipe bid amount to use.

A second tactic in an effort to foil other snipers is to place a minimum bid very near the auction's close. The objective of the "pre-snipe minimum bid" tactic is to indicate that you are just a typical bidder who isn't going to snipe the auction, helping to relax bidders poised to snipe the auction. The "pre-snipe minimum bid" tactic is especially valuable if you have previously bid in the auction. Your objective is to indicate that you are bidding "normally" and that you are not considering sniping the auction. This tactic hopes to convince another prospective snipe bidder that a lower snipe bid amount will suffice. Of course, observant opponents can check your bidding history and if they see that you favor the snipe tactic they may brace themselves for your snipe bid. This is why the Savvy Bidder shows no pattern (see Law #31: *Leverage Bidding Habits*).

A side benefit of the "pre-snipe minimum bid" is for you to get an indication if the auction has an existing proxy bid. If it does, you have gleaned important information to help you set your snipe bid amount and without consuming any more of your bidding budget than necessary.

I suppose I needn't remind you that these same tactics can be used by other sniper bidders to throw *you* off. Keep in mind that snipe bidders are usually skilled bidders. Such bidders know how to estimate an auction's closing price and they know how to size up the participants in an auction they target. It is quite possible that many snipe bidders will include spoofing tactics to throw off their opponents, which includes you. Don't fall into the same type of traps you put out.

Sniping Software

You've probably seen those promotions for sniping software. Perhaps you have even tried such software yourself. Sniping software might be a good idea for the masses, but the Savvy Bidder realizes that sniping software provides minimal tactical advantages and may actually result in a greater number of lost auctions or even overpaying.

Sniping software places a bid on the user's behalf a few seconds before the auction closes. However, that alone does not make for effective snipe bidding, as we discussed. Snipe bidding has much to do with predicting the closing price of an auction in an effort to place the most appropriate snipe bid. The objective is to not bid too high with a snipe bid nor bid too low. This is why the snipe bid amount is best determined near the auction's close (See law #30: *The Closing Price is Best Surmised Near the End*).

If you enter a bid amount into the sniping software early in the auction's period, then you risk not setting the snipe bid amount appropriate to the auction's estimated closing price. It simply doesn't make any sense to snipe an auction with a bid amount that is not based on a good estimate of the auction's probable closing price – your bid amount may be much too high leaving you exposed to overpaying for the item. Or, your bid amount may be too low leaving you vulnerable to loosing the auction.

Let's assume, for example, that an auction will close in 3 days at 20:22:04, eBay time. The auction's current price is $150.00 with no reserve. Your research indicates a typical closing price of $190.00 in the eBay community. You then enter a snipe bid price of $180.00 in the sniping software and set the software's timer to bid in this example auction a few seconds before the auction is scheduled to end. Now let's consider several different possible outcomes when the sniping software places your snipe bid:

1. The auction's current price has gone to $185.00. You lose since your $180.00 specified bid amount is less that the auction's current price. This may not be an issue for you since you elected to not pay more than $180.00 anyway. But, you also gave yourself little choice than to accept losing the auction in this manner.

2. The auction's current price has gone to $165.00, but there is a proxy bid in place for $190.00. You lose. Even a manually placed snipe bid of $180.00 would have lost this auction. However, by attending to the auction near its end, perhaps you would have been more in touch with the auction.

3. The auction's current price goes to $170.00 and another sniper hits the auction for $190.00. You lose. Once again, even a manually placed snipe bid of $180.00 would have lost this auction to the other snipe. However, perhaps you could have tried a sniper foiling bid tactic prior to a manually placed snipe bid.

4. The auction's current price remains at $150.00 and another sniper hits the auction for $175.00. You win the auction, but *at the other sniper's bid amount*. In other words, you pay almost your specified bid amount because of someone else's snipe bid. A manually placed snipe bid of $180.00 would have resulted in much the same outcome. However, perhaps a sniper foiling tactic could have been utilized prior to your manually placed snipe bid.

5.   The auction's current price remains at $150.00. There are no proxy bids in place and this auction receives no other snipe bids. You win the auction but only by placing a bid that is $30.00 higher than it needed to be or a whopping 12 minimum bid increments ($30.00 / $2.50) – a risky snipe bid indeed.

Scenario five above illustrates why, I believe, eBay does not extend an auction's close when a last minute bid is placed – bidders who place snipe bids that are too high risk a higher closing price if other snipers hit the auction. A similar situation occurs when a high snipe bid amount hits against an existing proxy bid as illustrated in scenario number three above. In effect, snipe bidding is a great way for the auction venue to help auctions close at higher prices.

If you enter a bid amount into the sniping software very close to the auction's close, when you are better able to estimate the auction's closing price, then you have simply introduced a "machine" in your bidding effort. You might as well be in control and manually place the snipe bid. Sniping software that is well designed can provide several benefits such as the collection of data concerning the auction, automation of feedback submission and so on. However, there are auction management software programs that provide these same benefits without the "auto sniping" function.

In summary, I personally never let software do my snipe bidding for these reasons:

♦   It makes little sense to try and decide a snipe bid amount well before the auction's close. The key to effective snipe bidding is to predict at what price the auction is likely to close and therefore what would be the most effective snipe bid amount. There is more to effective snipe bidding than simply placing a bid at the last possible second.

♦   For snipe bidding to be effective, the snipe bidder must be in tune with the auction just prior to the auction's close. This is the time when the auction's participants are examined and when the competitive landscape is best assessed.

♦   It's much more interesting to be personally involved with a snipe bid. I learn more and sharpen my competitive bidding skills – you may find that true for yourself as well.

♦   While the objective in any online auction is to purchase the item, snipe bidding software effectively skips the entire process of price negotiation by driving in a last second bid. The Savvy Bidder recognizes that the best possible purchase price is often realized by good bidding tactics, not just by bidding.

I do not believe that sniping software provides any tactical advantage for the Savvy Bidder and can actually become a liability if the snipe bid amount is specified too far in advance. Sniping software addresses a person's desire to not have to attend to an auction's close to place a snipe bid. It also eases the tension that many feel from the time pressure associated with snipe bidding. I wonder, however, how much more money those conveniences cost users of sniping software. Also, much of the excitement of pulling off a great snipe bid is lost.

Combating Sniper Software

I wish I could hand you a simple way to defeat sniper software. But I can't unless there was a way to deliberately spoof sniping software to operate incorrectly. Since such software sits patiently watching the eBay clock and then submits a bid up to the maximum the software user programmed in, there is not much we can do about it.

However, we can hope that the users of sniper software plug in a snipe bid amount that is too low to win the auction. There is a good chance of this for two reasons:

1. Bidders generally make an effort to pay the lowest possible price for an auction. So, the sniping software user may program in a snipe bid amount that is based on wishful thinking, but not sufficient to win the target auction.

2. Snipe software users may underestimate the auction's closing price by programming in a snipe bid amount too early in the auction. As with all software, garbage in garbage out.

It is also possible that the eBay clock is wrong. At the time of this writing there have been reports of the eBay clock being displayed incorrectly. This would obviously throw the snipe software out of synch with the actual eBay time. Don't count on this as protection against automated sniping. Just be aware of it.

From my own research it is evident that most sniping software applications do not have direct access to the eBay computers. At the time of this writing eBay charges a hefty license and support fee for what eBay calls the eBay API (Application Protocol Interface). The API is a set of commands that gain direct access to eBay's data and command the eBay computer to perform a specific action. Depending on how an application is designed, the API can be used to obtain (read) eBay data or insert (write) data to eBay through a direct command to the eBay servers. An API license could cost the software maker as much as $10,000 per month, depending on the number of API calls into eBay and other factors.

An alternative to the API is to perform what is called "screen scraping". This is where the sniping software pulls out specific bits of information from the HTML stream that is delivered to the user's Internet browser by the eBay server, in this case. Obviously the maker of the sniping software that relies on screen scraping avoids a hefty API fee.

Screen scraping depends on the pattern and position of the data to be pulled out of the HTML. A good software design will look for characters that surround the target data or that comprise the target data itself. Thus, the sniping software has to periodically inspect the HTML from eBay, properly locate the eBay time and date and take action accordingly. Usually the sniping software synchronizes with the user's local computer to keep track of the time and date the auction is scheduled to close. With eBay's propensity to change things around on its screen, sniping software that relies on screen scraping could be rendered useless if eBay where to modify how it displays the auction's closing date and time and other salient information about the auction.

If you would like to view the HTML source of an eBay web page, simply click your <u>right</u> mouse button with the mouse pointer hovering over a web page (but not over a graphic). Click "View Source" with your <u>left</u> mouse button. A new window will display with the HTML content of that web page, i.e., the source code. Try this with an eBay auction listing and look for the date and time that the auction will close.

As I mentioned there is no way I know of to directly defeat sniping software. However I think we can appreciate that the technical complexities of automated sniping may lead to failed snipe bids. More important, however, I think we can safely assume that there will be many sniping software users that misjudge the auction's competitive situation and incorrectly program their sniping software.

Conclusion

We've covered much ground concerning the snipe bid tactic. It is important to remember that there is much more to effective snipe bidding than when you place a snipe bid. You must be observant of the activity in the auction you intend to snipe and be able to make a fairly accurate estimate of the price that the auction will close at. Snipe bidding is interesting and can even get the adrenaline level up. But snipe bidding does present certain risks.

There are a few tactics that you can consider using that might throw a competitive sniper off the mark. By placing two small bids back-to-back, you may cause an opponent sniper to doubt her ability to determine a winning snipe bid. The risk, as mentioned, is that the opponent may place a very high snipe bid. A minimum bid near the auction's end gives the impression that you are not going to be a sniper in that auction. Your objective with a minimum bid is to fool a competitive sniper into complacency.

Sniping is an effective bidding tactic in many eBay auction situations. Develop strong sniping skills, but don't assume that the snipe bid tactic is appropriate in all auctions. In those auctions you intend to snipe, understand the competitive landscape of the auction. Estimate the closing price as best as you can. Position with pre-snipe bidding tactics. Understand the risks associated with snipe bidding and use it only when you feel it is an appropriate bidding tactic.

Notes:

Bidding Techniques

Ultra Fast Bidding

Ultra fast bidding is most valuable in situations where time is limited and you intend to place more than one bid. For instance:

♦ When the auction is about to close with minutes or seconds remaining and you intend to place more than one bid during that time. A Proxy Discovery Run and a "pre-snipe double proxy" bid are examples where ultra fast bidding techniques may come in handy.

♦ When you are working two auctions for identical items and both auctions close within minutes or seconds of one another. In this case, if you lose the first auction to close, you may elect to bid in the second auction to close.

The key to ultra fast bidding is to have a bidding plan. We'll discuss the mechanical aspects of ultra fast bidding in a moment – it is your bidding plan that allows you to move toward your objective without the burden of reconsidering how much you will spend for the item. During the formulation of your plan, you did your research on the item, the seller and your opponents and you decided the target price. You then considered which bidding tactics you might use in the auction. With all of this taken care of, you are best able to bid at the appropriate time without rethinking your approach to the auction.

The target price is important. This is because you do not need to make a purchase decision when it comes time to bid. The vast majority of bidders go through the purchase decision process time and again during an auction. "Now the current price is $350.00. Should I bid $360.00? Maybe I should bid $375.00. Do I even want to pay more than $350.00? Another auction has it for $300.00." And so on. This is time consuming.

However if you had predetermined a target price of $400.00, for instance and the auction's current price is $350.00, the only thought process required is to decide if now is an optimum time to place a bid. You may have determined that sniping the auction would be the best plan, given the potential interest of other bidders and the supply-to-demand ratio for the particular auction item. In that case you need not make any bidding decisions until the end of the auction. If you are working the seller's reserve (by placing a bid just below the seller's reserve), then you are in a waiting mode until another bidder trips the seller's reserve. (Please see *Bidding Tactics in Reserve Auctions* in this chapter.) In that case, there is no need to make a decision to bid until the seller's reserve is tripped.

When sniping an auction, placing just one snipe bid does not require ultra fast bidding skills – it simply requires good planning and good timing. See *The Snipe Bid Tactic* in this chapter for a discussion of the snipe bidding tactic. However, if you want to place pre-snipe bids, ultra fast bidding skills come in very handy.

When two auctions for an identical item (perhaps from the same seller) will end in close proximity to one another, ultra fast bidding skills pay off. Assume, for example, that auction A will end in 30 minutes. You have a bid in that auction and you are the highest bidder. Auction B is for the same item from the same seller and will close in 31 minutes. The majority of bidders interested in this item are bidding in auction A. Your plan is to see if you can keep your costs down for this item by cutting it close in auction A and falling back on auction B if you lose auction A. However, you do not want to bid in both auctions to avoid the risk of winning both auctions. Ultra fast bidding will be used to bid in auction B in the event you lose auction A. In this example, you will have less than one minute to bid in auction B.

Mechanically speaking, ultra fast bidding is facilitated by the following:

1. Be very agile using your Internet browser.

2. Be very familiar with navigation in the eBay web site.

3. Use the double browser bidding method that is discussed next in this chapter.

Ultra fast bidding starts with you knowing how you intend to position to win the auction i.e., have a good bidding plan. You must also be fully committed to the target price to avoid the time consuming process of rethinking what you are willing to pay for the auction. After that, knowing how to navigate the eBay web site is important along with an agility to use your Internet browser.

Notes:

Double Browser Bidding

Double browser bidding is where you use more than one Internet browser to help you with your bidding. The advantage of using more than one browser is that you can monitor certain aspects of an auction with one browser while placing bids with the other browser. An example would be using browser #1 to monitor the bid history of an auction while preparing to place a snipe bid with browser #2. This affords you the ability to quickly view changes in the auction while not losing your place with the browser used for placing your bids.

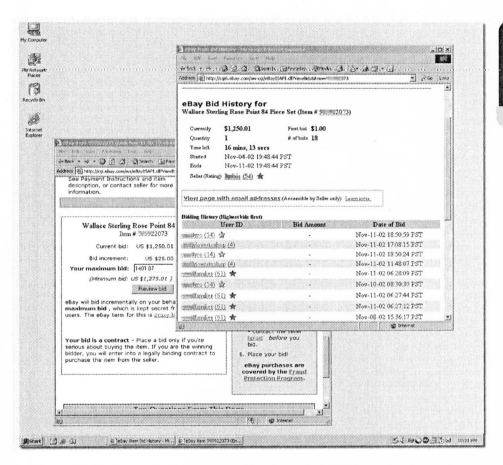

Figure 15 - Two browser windows; one watching the auction's bid history, the other ready to place a bid.

I have always found the double browser technique valuable for performing re-search in an auction. While one browser is set to focus on the auction of interest, the second browser is used to drill down the various screens as I research the seller and the opponents of the auction I am currently working with.

Another very good use for a double browser setup is to enable you to be prepared for a double proxy bid. With one browser, you place the first of the two proxy bids while the second browser is ready to place the second proxy bid. If a second proxy bid is needed, a simple mouse click finishes placing the second proxy bid via browser #2.

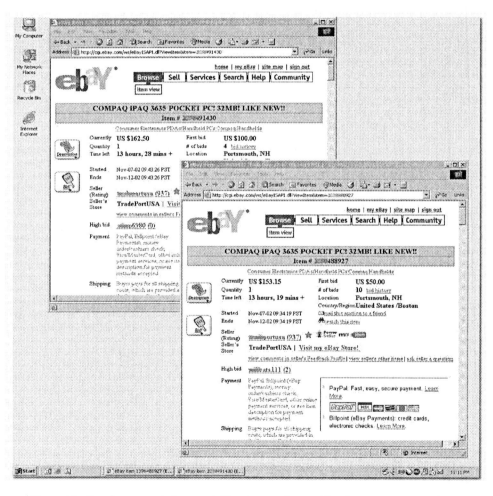

Figure 16 - Two browser windows watching two auctions selling the exact same product.

When two auctions are running for the same item by the same seller, but will close within a few minutes of each other, I use the double browser configuration to prepare a bid for the second auction. The objective is to bid in the first auction and if I lose that auction, I am set and ready to bid in the next auction. When I have this opportunity, I will often bid as low as my tactic allows on the first auction knowing that I'll have another chance with the second auction.

If I have an opponent who also intends to bid in the second auction in the event that he also loses the first auction, I am banking on him not being as quick to bid in the second auction as I. My opponent bidder will likely need to run a search, select the auction from the search result, go to the bottom of the auction listing page, enter a bid amount and click submit and then confirm that bid. With the loading of the browser pages, all this navigation takes time. Meanwhile, I am already there with my second browser and I can place a bid with just a few mouse clicks.

To be able to bid with more than one browser, *you must be signed in on each browser and each browser must be running on the same computer*. It might seem a bit strange, but your eBay sign in is browser specific. That is, with the aid of a "cookie" it is the browser that remembers that you are signed in, not the eBay web site. Each browser that you launch has a cookie associated with the browser instance. Thus, you can sign in with two or more browsers on the same computer. Being signed in on each browser, you can then bid from each browser. It is important to remember than just because you signed in with one browser, does not mean that you will be able to bid from other browser instances – each browser must be signed in.

You won't be able to sign into eBay using the same sign in ID and password from two different computers. This is because the eBay web site expects to see the same IP address as that of the first browser that signed in. While this serves as a form of security to help eliminate the fraudulent use of a person's sign in ID and password (at least at the same time as when you are signed in from your computer), I expect it is simply a side benefit of the sign in mechanism.

Remember that a browser loses its sign in to eBay after a period of no activity from a particular browser (my experiments indicates 40 minutes, but the time may be changed by eBay at any time). I check to ensure I am still signed in by clicking the *My eBay* link at the top of each eBay page. If I am taken directly to the *My eBay* page with no sign in request, then I know that I am still signed in. Of course, I click the Back button of my browser to go back to the page I was on before testing the sign on. If my sign in has expired, I complete the sign in page and navigate back to the page I was originally viewing, ready to bid.

Using more than two browser windows, you could be watching other auctions, perhaps for the same or similar items. Browser windows that are not being used for actual bidding do not need to be signed in. However, you will have to manually refresh each of the other browser windows to view any changes made to those auctions. Using multiple browsers enables you to monitor the progress of other auctions for identical or similar items.

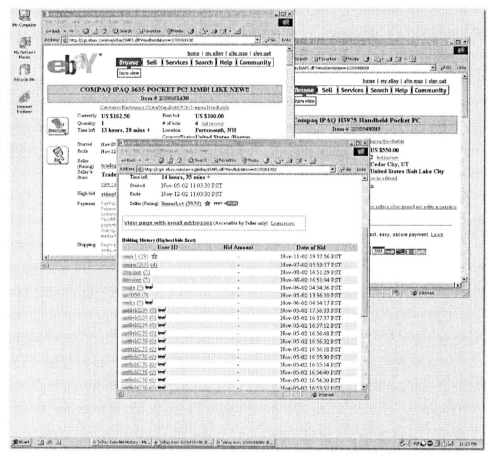

Figure 17 - Three browser windows; two windows watching two auctions selling the same item and the third (foreground) being used to research opponents in another auction.

The preceding screen shots illustrating multiple browser windows were captured from a computer monitor running at a 1600 x 1200 pixel resolution. Lower screen resolutions will not accommodate as much screen content as illustrated here.

Using multiple browsers may give you a competitive edge because you are prepared to move quickly should you need to. It also allows you to monitor other aspects of an auction you are participating in to avoid the rather lengthy navigation required when using a single browser window. It has been my experience that novice computer users often overlook the fact that their computer is capable of running much more than a single program at a time. I have encountered many people who sit and wait while one program processes something, not realizing that they could be working in another program at the same time (this is called "multitasking"). I think Microsoft got it right by naming its operating system "Windows" which implies a multiple task operating system. Microsoft did not name its operating system "Window". So take advantage of having two or more browsers running at the same time. Be prepared to navigate and bid with speed as the occasion requires.

Notes:

TACTICS AND
TECHNIQUES

Conclusion

Strategic bidding requires more than simply being a buyer. To be competitive you must determine a target price from which you establish a bidding budget and manage it for maximum competitive leverage. You must create a bidding plan, yet be able to adjust your plan quickly as needed. You must know what bidding tactics to deploy and then deploy them decisively. These are what help make you a formidable opponent.

You must take a closer look at an auction's landscape. You must try to understand what motivates your opponents. Certainly, you must thoroughly know the rules and the mechanisms of the eBay auction venue so that you can work well within them.

Ironically, making the additional effort to be a strategic bidder is not that much harder when you consider the effort that your opponents likely expend. It is more difficult, I believe, to go through the process of reassessing your personal valuation each time the current price increases. It is harder to try and win auctions with that nagging fear and avoidance of overpaying. It is harder to participate in an auction without a clear strategy and have the auction toss you here and there as its landscape changes. It is harder to participate in an auction when you have little understanding of what is motivating your opponents because you didn't take the time to try and understand their bidding patterns.

While being a strategic bidder does take effort, the objective is for that effort to yield a competitive strength that your opponents may not have. By being more competitive it is quite likely that winning eBay auctions will be much easier and rely less on luck. Sure, there will always be the unknown element of what your opponents might be willing to pay for the auction. You'll never be quite sure if snipers lie in wait to bid in the final seconds. There will always be auctions with undisclosed reserve prices. You'll even have unexpected situations such as when the auction market's demand for the item suddenly drives the closing price much higher that the typical market price. These unknowns disturb those who take a buyer's approach. The Savvy Bidder views these unknowns as challenges that make winning eBay auctions rewarding.

My Journey

In my early days of bidding on eBay I found it disconcerting to compete in an environment where there was so much I couldn't know. I found myself wishing I had the inside scoop so I could have a decisive competitive edge. But, I realized that it is the variables, unknowns and uncertainties that make winning online auctions rewarding. But, these challenges got in my way when I ignored the fact that eBay is actually a competitive purchase environment. I eventually realized that when I think like a strategist, I actually have a better chance at winning eBay auctions.

So there came a time when I stopped being a buyer and started being a strategist in eBay auctions. When I began thinking in terms of strategy, I lost very few auctions. And that's when the fun really began. When I was a buyer, the irrationality of the other participants in the auction seemed confusing. When I became a strategist, I saw how to leverage the habits and even the irrationality of my opponents to help *me* win the auction. I realized that there is more information available to me than I had thought and came to appreciate the competitive power of information.

When I thought as a buyer I thought of the current price as the purchase price. As the current price gradually increased I found myself able to justify spending a little bit more. Eventually I realized that I was being herded with all of the other sheep, at least in terms of price. So I took control of my own price guideline and developed the concept of the target price. The target price gave me a bidding budget to work with. I learned ways to tactically use my bidding budget to position in the auction.

Your Journey Begins

My journey with strategic bidding started several years ago, yet it doesn't end with this book. It appears as if price-participation buying has caught on and will be with us for some time to come – I'll be ready. Join me on the road if you believe that the eBay experience can hold more rewards for you as a Savvy Bidder.

If you are already a skilled bidder, I hope you have gleaned some bidding tactics that you may not have yet discovered. If you consider yourself a novice bidder then I congratulate you for taking the time to consider the thoughts offered here.

Skilled or novice, I encourage you to try the strategic bidding principles explored in this book. If you don't like them, then don't feel you have to use them. I would much rather you question everything than follow a path you do not accept. If the principles of strategic bidding feel right to you, go on to develop them further. Find a style that suits you personally. Above all, enjoy what eBay and other online auction venues can provide you. Make those benefits the best they can be by thinking deeper than others and by grasping and developing the concepts of strategic bidding.

Thanks for joining me on my journey and best of luck on your own.

Part 3: The Laws of Strategic Bidding

44 Laws of Strategic Bidding

The laws presented in this part encompass the principles of strategic bidding. My hope is that they help you to think like a Savvy Bidder. Use them to that end. Feel free to put aside those laws that don't make sense to you today and patiently wait for a situation where a particular law does apply. Dog-ear the pages of the laws that you want to see an application for one day. Makes copious notes on the pages of those laws that resonate with you.

Some of these laws alert you to the games played by sellers as well as by other bidders. By recognizing these games, you are better able to deal with the confusion the game players create. It is always in your best interest to remain highly focused on your objective. If you want to tinker in online auctions, then do so. If you want to win auctions, then remain clear about your objective. I think you'll find that several of the laws presented here will help you keep your objective clear despite the often noisy environment.

Several of these laws help you think like an aggressive competitor. By aggressive I mean getting into the fray as a strong competitor. While I don't recommend breaking the rules, you must not be a fearful or timid bidder. I do not suggest that you bid with abandon. Rather, take decisive steps to position in the auctions of your choice using strong bidding tactics within your bidding budget for that auction. Don't be shy about it. Get in there and work the auction, fully expecting that you will win it. Don't just try to be a winner during the auction – be a winner at the auction's close.

There are also several laws that warn of the nastier aspects of the eBay community. Any online auction community, not just eBay, is a rich environment for the con artist. This is made possible by two factors; the Internet affords anonymity and where many gather, there will be a relatively small percentage that will be dishonest. But, don't let your fear of this element spoil your fun. It is much easier to fool the unobservant – the Savvy Bidder is much more aware of the landscape in which she plays. Remain alert and never suspend your belief.

Above all, these laws help you preserve the fun of participating in eBay auctions. It's fun to launch stealth bids; to clearly see the traps laid for the unsuspecting; to inspect and analyze the auction landscape before you. And of course it's fun to win auctions, especially when you win at the lowest price possible.

And finally, there are several laws that spare no punches as it concerns eBay itself. My intent is not to taint your image of eBay. Rather, the Savvy Bidder prefers to know the problem areas so they don't become a trip point. eBay was never a perfect environment and never will be. The laws that deal with eBay's imperfections are presented to help you maintain your perspective.

Laws Table of Contents

THE LAWS OF STRATEGIC BIDDING

Law 1: Understand the Premise of Auctions

To be a Savvy Bidder it is important to understand the premises on which eBay auctions are based.

Some of the following premise statements are obvious while others are not. The important thing is that you have a deeper understanding of what eBay auctions are attempting to accomplish for the various players.

Premise #1: Pertaining to single-unit auctions, every auction article (a tangible good) has five possible types of value that can be attributed to it:

1. The perceived value that the <u>seller</u> (the current owner) assigns to the auction article. The seller's value does not necessarily match the market's perceived value.

2. A bidder's personal valuation, i.e., what a bidder believes the item is worth to her personally. Initially, this value is derived from a personal need or desire to own the item but is often increased as a result of competition in the auction.

3. The eBay auction market value can usually be determined by reviewing recently closed auctions for the same or similar item. Recently closed auctions reflect the end result of previous competitive situations for the same or comparable items.

4. An value external to the online auction environment can usually be determined by pricing structures of the manufacturer, a merchant, or a distributor. For instance, MSRP (Manufacturers Suggested Retail Price) or street prices.

5. An appraisal value as determined by certification, appraisal or expert opinion.

Premise #2: No bidder can know for certain the personal valuation of the other bidders or their motives for participating in an auction. However, all bidders can make observations about the bidding methods and patterns of opponents.

Premise #3: An auction is a price negotiation venue where the final price is determined by the participating bidders (within the constraints set by the seller). The seller offers an item at a starting price (a First Bid price) and perhaps sets a "not lower than" price (a reserve price). From there, bidders state what they are willing to pay, doing so with bids. Thus, the bidders negotiate the final price and this negotiation occurs among the bidders without the seller's involvement. If the final negotiated price meets or exceeds the seller's price terms (for instance, a reserve price), then the right to purchase the item is awarded to the highest bidder upon the auction's close.

Premise #4: The seller's objective is to sell the auction article at the highest possible price. Generally, bidders attempt to purchase an item at the *lowest* possible price. In typical single-unit eBay auctions the closing price is kept down by a lack of bids and low bids while pulled up by higher bids. The closing price reflects the price that the immediate market justified.

Premise #5: eBay auctions are specifically designed to induce competition among those interested in purchasing the item being auctioned. Competition is key to the success of eBay auctions. Because a new bid must be at least one bid increment higher than the current price to be accepted, each new bid increases the current price, and ultimately the auction's closing price. If an auction receives no bids at all, this price escalation process cannot occur. The greater the number of bids in the auction, the higher the closing price will be.

Premise #6: Mechanically, the single-unit eBay auction is designed to eliminate bidders. This may seem a strange concept, but it is key to the success of a single-unit auction. The premise is to create competition by posing the current price as a purchase price and hiding information that would otherwise help a bidder know if his bid will take the lead if placed. Only after a bid is placed does the bidder discover if he has placed the highest bid or not. If there is an existing proxy bid, the bidder is informed at that time that he did not achieve the highest bid position and he is effectively eliminated at that bid, *even though his bid is used to increase the current price.* If he does achieve the highest bidder position, new bids are enticed for the purpose of displacing him. This elimination process is important because it allows competing bidders a chance to take the highest bid position, which is a reward to most in its own right.

Premise #7: Sellers in eBay auctions hope that competition in the auction will drive up the closing price. The seller further hopes that the actual closing price will be higher than the seller's own perceived value or actual investment in the item.

Premise #8: Knowledge of the item improves a bidder's competitiveness in that auction. The more a bidder knows about an auction item that contributes to ownership desire, the more aggressive that bidder tends to be with his bidding. Such bidders tend to be risk neutral, i.e., not overly concerned about overpaying for the item. Conversely, when a bidder is less informed about an item she tends to be risk averse (avoids the risk of overpaying).

The informed bidder tends to place a more accurate personal valuation on the item while the uninformed bidder is often not sure of an appropriate personal valuation. When personal valuation is justifiable in relation to actual value, there is less bidding apprehension. It stands to reason that if a bidder has knowledge that other bidders do not have, that bidder's competitive position in the auction can be leveraged considerably.

Knowledge of an item also helps reduce losses. An informed bidder recognizes when an item has a lower actual value than what is implied by actual bidding in the auction, by the seller's First Bid, reserve price or the seller's description itself. Active bidding tends to increase the personal valuation perception among bidders who have become caught up in the competition itself. And finally a well-informed bidder recognizes that bidding activity does not necessarily correspond to the item's actual value.

Premise #9: Supply and demand applies in eBay auctions.

♦ When an item is plentiful in the auction environment, bidders can be more selective about which auctions they will participate in. In addition, bidders tend to bid low knowing that there are or will be other auctions for the same article. Sellers of plentiful items must eventually conform to the price that the market dictates for such items.

♦ When an item is in short supply and high demand within the auction environment, bidding tends to be more competitive. Sellers are in a better position to press the auction market's price tolerance.

♦ When an item is scarce or in very short supply, and when there is a high demand for that item, bidding tends to be more active and bids tend to be more aggressive. Sellers are still subject to selling at what the market will pay, but can typically expect a better closing price on such auctions.

♦ When an item has a known value external to the auction venue, such as when a retail price is published and readily available, bidders have a pricing point of reference but still attempt to purchase at the lowest possible cost. Auction sellers typically must conform to such external pricing and usually must provide or allow a discount (the eBay auction environment is still thought of as a discount environment for new merchandise).

THE LAWS OF STRATEGIC BIDDING

Premise #10: While the vast majority of online auction sellers are honest there exists the potential for misrepresentation (accidental or intentional) as well as fraud. Every online auction can be manipulated, both by sellers and by bidders. Manipulation by sellers usually attempts to artificially increase the auction's closing price while bidder manipulation tends to strive for obtaining the item at a very low price.

Keep these premises in mind. They will help you understand the concepts of strategic bidding.

Notes:

Law 2: Negotiate, Don't Buy

The Savvy Bidder regards the online auction process as price negotiation. As a negotiator the Savvy Bidder always remembers that the current price will not necessarily be the actual purchase price. This frees him from the spell of the current price mirage.

It is not hard to understand why eBay auctions are thought of as simply a means to purchase articles of interest. There is a format by which to search for items, there is a seller behind each auction, there is at least one article to be purchased per auction and there are instructions for completing the purchase. It is little wonder that most bidders view eBay as simply a place to make purchases. But, except in the case of *Buy It Now* auctions, there is a sequence of events that must always be completed before an eBay auction purchase can occur. This is, of course, the bidding that establishes the final selling price.

The auction format is a mechanical process of establishing a selling price of a tangible good (and sometimes services or information). The actual purchase can occur only after the final price is established. In single-unit eBay auctions, the person who has the highest bid at the auction's close (equal to or greater than the seller's reserve price) almost always becomes the person who earns the right to make the purchase. However, all non-winning bidders contributed to establishing the final selling price even though such bidders did not earn the right to make the purchase.

Knowing that the auction format is actually a process to establish a selling price, the Savvy Bidder understands the importance of being a price negotiator first and a buyer last.

The Negotiator vs. the Buyer

The objective of a negotiator-minded bidder is to influence the purchase price while the objective of a buyer-minded bidder is to make a purchase. The negotiator works toward being positioned in the auction for the win while the buyer works toward the purchase. For example, a buyer-minded auction participant may look at the $50.00 current price of an auction that typically sells on eBay for $100.00 and falls for the current price hook thinking "I could buy that for half of the going price". The negotiator looks at the same auction and thinks, "How can I position myself in this auction to win at the lowest possible price?" The negotiator is aware of the probability that the $50.00 current price will not be the closing price of the auction. Essentially, the negotiator is considering the entire auction process while the buyer takes a snapshot view of the auction.

THE LAWS OF STRATEGIC BIDDING

The current price, being the most obvious price indicator concerning the auction, indicates to the buyer-minded bidder the price he would pay if the auction were to close at that point. In fact, this is how the current price of an online auction is explained. However, the auction is not going to close until a specified time, so this logic is not valid and serves to pull people into auctions as buyer-minded bidders.

The buyer-minded bidder tends to not consider where the price negotiation may go and therefore remains in a reactionary mode as the clock works closer and closer to the auction's close. He focuses on the current price, which is the one element of an auction that cannot be relied on (except in *Buy It Now* auctions). Because the current price is presented much like the purchase price we have become so familiar with in retail, the current price is reacted to like an actual purchase price.

Being able to see the auction as a whole enables the negotiator-minded bidder to plan for and expect the current price to increase. The negotiator works to be in a position to influence the final closing price and uses specific bidding tactics to that end.

Perhaps the most important aspect of being a negotiator in eBay auctions is that the negotiator is freed from taking a fear-based approach to auctions. A buyer wants to purchase the item but also tries to minimize the price he might have to pay. This puts a constraint on the buyer rooted in price avoidance. The negotiator, on the other hand, takes a realistic approach and acknowledges that the final closing price may well reach up to the typical closing price for the item (for the same or comparable items). The negotiator therefore makes an effort to plan for a *probable* closing price in advance of actual participation in the auction. This enables him to bid within the full price spread (the difference between the current price and the typical closing price).

From eBay's and the seller's standpoint, it is preferable to have auction participants who are buyers rather than negotiators. This is because buyers react to events in an auction. An event, such as a bid that increases the current price, is perceived as an obstacle to the buyer's ability to make the purchase. How does the typical bidder react to this obstacle? By either bidding a bit higher or abandoning the auction. Those who continue to bid are those who drive up the auction's current price, creating a higher closing price. This in turn means a higher final sales fee to eBay and a happier seller.

The buyer-minded bidder tends to continuously reassess if he will pay the current price. And, human nature being as it is, the mind can accept a slightly higher price easier than a much higher price. Since small increments in the current price are much easier to accept and respond to, it is the activity in the auction itself that establishes the value of the item in the mind of the buyer. The negotiator doesn't see it this way. Rather, she has a preconceived personal valuation of the item and is therefore freed from a continual reassessment of value as the current price escalates. For strategic purposes, the negotiator establishes a target price that is referred to independently of the events in the auction.

The challenge for the Savvy Bidder is that she is attempting to negotiate with opponents who are usually trying to purchase. It is often difficult to determine, or even understand, what motivates certain participants to bid in a particular auction. However, the Savvy Bidder tries to understand how the buyer-minded bidder might think in an auction. The following table compares the thought processes of the buyer-minded bidder to those of the negotiator-minded bidder.

The Buyer-Minded Bidder	The Negotiator-Minded Bidder
"I want to purchase this item, but I don't know how much I'll have to pay when the auction closes. I'll bid just the minimum and see what happens. I can always bid again."	"I want to purchase this item, but I don't know how much I'll have to pay when the auction closes. I'll establish the target price and work my resulting bidding budget."
"I've always wanted one of these but I don't want to spend any more than $100.00.	"I've always wanted one of these but I don't want to spend any more than $100.00. I'll bid 50% of my budget and check the auction near its close."
"I don't have time to research this auction. I'll place a small bid and see what happens."	"This auction typically sells for $250.00 on eBay. I'll place a proxy bid at half of that amount now to conserve my bidding budget for later in the auction."
"That current price is a great price! I know that item usually sells for much more. I'll place a bid just over the current price."	"That current price is a great price! However, I expect that bidders will take the auction's price up to something more typical of the market price. I'll place a moderate proxy bid now and be prepared to place a higher proxy bid later".
"I don't know what the seller's reserve is so I'll just place a small bid and see what happens."	"I don't know what the seller's reserve is so I'll e-mail the seller and ask for his reserve price. Then I'll decide if I'll participant in the auction."
"The current price looks reasonable. I'll bid just above the current price."	"According to the current price the participants have not yet brought the price up to the typical closing price. I'll develop a bidding plan based upon the probable closing price of this auction and jump in when the time is appropriate."

Table 2 - Comparison between Buyer and Negotiator thinking.

The negotiator thinks of the current price as the current state of the price negotiation. The negotiator uses the current price to help determine a bidding strategy, not as a purchase price. As the auction draws to a close, the current price provides more of an indication of the purchase price, but is still subject to change. Except in *Buy It Now* auctions that have not received bids, the current price can be misleading during the auction when regarded as the purchase price.

By taking a negotiator approach, the Savvy Bidder is participating in the auction consistent with its purpose and intent – to establish the selling price. The Savvy Bidder understands that the final price is not determined until the auction closes and therefore does not treat the current price as a purchase price.

Also see laws *#8: Don't Focus on the Current Price, #5: Know the Target Price, #12: Understand Current Price Escalation*

Notes:

Law 3: Never Think of Yourself as "Winning"

> A Savvy Bidder knows that there are no "winners" until the
> auction closes and all bids are reconciled. The Savvy Bidder
> understands that thinking of herself as "winning" while an
> auction is running is not only erroneous, but may cause her to
> lose her competitive edge.

The Savvy Bidder realizes that the only win in an auction that matters is the win
that occurs when the auction closes. Until then, the process is one of price negotiation among persons interested in purchasing the item. When the Savvy Bidder
elects to participate in the price negotiation during mid-auction, she enters a bid
appropriate to her strategy in the auction. But to achieve her primary objective, it is
not always necessarily to take the highest bidder's seat during the auction; rather to
position herself so that a win can be captured at the auction's close.

From a tactical point of view it makes sense to allow an opponent to believe he is
winning the auction. By not taking the auction away from the current highest bidder (the bidder "winning" the auction), that bidder has a tendency to relax, feeling
no need to do anything more for the moment. *The highest bidder is effectively out
of the negotiation process for as long as he holds the highest bid position.* On the
other hand, if he is outbid, then there is a need to respond if he has any interest in
purchasing the item.

By not considering yourself as "winning" an auction, you have a higher probability of maintaining a strong competitive stance. In fact, the management of your
bidding budget is based on *not* expecting to maintain a highest bidder position. For
strategic purposes, the Savvy Bidder never thinks in terms of being the highest
bidder, i.e., as "winning" the auction – the win comes only when the auction closes
and she is the highest bidder.

Notes:

Law 4: Know What You are Bidding On

Becoming informed about an auction item is important for the Savvy Bidder. This allows the Savvy Bidder to bid confidently, free of having to continuously reevaluate the purchase.

At first glance online auctions seem to be battlegrounds of money where money determines who wins and who loses. However, while running, auctions are actually battlegrounds of knowledge. This is because it is the degree of knowledge about an item that ultimately determines the perceived value of each bidder in the auction.

The more informed a bidder, the more likely he is to place strong bids in the auction if that knowledge bolsters his desire for ownership. Naturally his bids pull up the closing price of the auction.

If a bidder lacks knowledge of the item, he contributes to keeping the closing price of the auction down. He is not certain of its value and favors a cautious approach. Smaller bids have a lower impact on the current price. Such a bidder tends to look to other bidders in the auction as a price guide, or more often, tends to become focused on the current price. The bidder who lacks knowledge tends to be fearful of paying more than might be necessary. Please see Law *#33: Take Heed the Winner's Curse.*

Bidders who are knowledgeable of the item are in a position to take a competitive advantage. The reason for this is fairly obvious – the informed bidder works the auction armed with a personal valuation that is not as dependent on his opponent's bidding actions. He is more confident and is less afraid of over bidding.

In assessing the value of an item, the Savvy Bidder goes beyond simple (and often easy to obtain) pricing information and learns more about the item itself. By understanding the item's attributes, negative as well as positive, she is better able to set a personal valuation and bid accordingly. Meanwhile, bidders who do not take the time to learn about the item effectively allow the auction itself to establish their personal valuation.

If you know that an item has a typical market value of $350.00 for example, and that value is acceptable to you, then you are mentally prepared to bid up to $350.00. This does not mean that you will actually bid up to that amount. Rather it allows you to place strong bids as you see fit or place stealth bids that an opponent might never consider. Because you are knowledgeable of the item, you are not throttled by fearful bidding.

You also have a wider array of bidding tactics available to you. This is because you have a wider bidding budget to use for strategic purposes. This allows you to bid with stealth or strength, as you deem necessary. Meanwhile, opponents who are less certain about their personal valuation are more likely to place weak bids that have a minimal competitive value.

Of course, knowledge of an auction item can protect you as well. If you know that a particular item is not worth the seller's *Buy It Now* or the reserve price or even the current price, you can avoid the auction. If you see that an auction has received bids that have brought the current price beyond what you know as the actual value, then you can abandon the auction. Once again, your knowledge of the item has allowed you to not become focused on the current price as an indicator of value. In addition, you are spared from being led by the competition.

As a Savvy Bidder you understand that the more informed you are about an auction item, the more realistic your personal valuation will be for that item. Armed with better information, you are less likely to be influenced by the very opponents you seek to defeat. You are far less likely to place significance on the personal valuation that other bidders seem to express through their bids. You are also spared the relentless pursuit of the current price, which less informed bidders use as their value guideline.

See Law #33: *Take Heed the Winner's Curse*

Notes:

Law 5: Know the Target Price

A target price frees the Savvy Bidder from regarding the current price as a purchase price. A target price provides a stable price guide that is not subject to change as competition enters the auction. This allows maximum strategic use of the Savvy Bidder's money.

Much discussion has been provided concerning the importance of having a target price when participating in eBay auctions. Please refer to the chapter *The Target Price* in the *Foundations* part of this book. However, because a target price is so important to strategic bidding let's summarize the primary advantages here:

♦ A target price frees you from the shackles of current price focused bidding. At any time in the auction you can quickly determine where the current price is *in relation to the typical market price*. This better enables you to select bidding tactics that are consistent with the market value of the item.

♦ With a target price you have a stable price goal that is not subject to change as competition enters the auction. You are effectively isolated from the influence of individual opponents.

♦ With a target price you know when to abandon the auction. Not only have you accepted a target price (which is based on recent market performance) but you know when continued bidding will create a situation where you may over pay.

A target price is an important element of strategic bidding. I encourage you to always establish a target price before bidding in any auction.

Also see laws *#2: Negotiate, Don't Buy, #8: Don't Focus on the Current Price* and *#12: Understand Current Price Escalation*

Notes:

Law 6: Manage Your Bidding Budget

> **The Savvy Bidder knows that the strategic use of his bidding budget will help him leverage his money in an auction, not just spend it.**

For strategic purposes, the Savvy Bidder works with a bidding budget which is used throughout the auction to gain position for the win. But having a bidding budget is one thing. It is quite another to know how to manage that bidding budget and to leverage it competitively.

If you were to place a single bid at the maximum you are willing to pay for the item, you may find that another bidder has deeper pockets or a higher personal assessment of the item's value. Thus, you have no other choice but to let the item go or spend more than you originally intended. If you were to place a bid that is much lower than what you would pay for the item, you may find that another bidder easily takes the item away with a higher bid. As with expending your bidding budget too soon, under utilizing it does not serve you well. Consider these examples:

1. An auction's current price is at $50.00. You have established a target price of $100.00. With several days to go in the auction, you bid your full $100.00 as a proxy bid. Another bidder then bids $110.00. You must either let the auction go or bid at least $112.50. And the bid/outbid cycle may continue, with you having already run through your allocation of money for the auction.

2. An auction's current price is at $50.00. You have established a target price of $100.00. With several days to go, you bid $55.00 to conserve your bidding allocation. Another bidder outbids that, you outbid him, he outbids you and so on. Soon, the current price has reached your $100.00 maximum target price, or higher.

In the first example, you made it harder for another bidding to outbid you, but you had no budget left when you were outbid. Your bid set up a target for other bidders to reach. In the second example, you had plenty of bidding budget left, but it was easier for another bidder to outbid you and a bidding battle ensued. Your small bid made it easier for another to simply justify a few additional dollars and bid. Now consider this example:

♦   An auction's current price is at $50.00. You have established a target price of $100.00. With several days to go in the auction, you bid $75.00 to make it a harder for another bidder to outbid you while conserving some of your bidding budget. But, another bidder does indeed outbid you, so now the current price is $80.00. But, you don't bid too soon. Rather, you wait until near the close of the auction and use the remaining $20.00 of your bidding budget to discover the highest bidder's proxy amount if one exists, double proxy bid or perhaps snipe the auction (see part *Bidding Tactics and Techniques*). In this case, you managed your bidding budget with the expectation of additional competition in the auction. A side benefit is that if your original $75.00 bid was not outbid, you win the auction at less than your target price.

In the above example you spread your bidding budget out to cover strategic maneuvers at the most opportune times during the auction. You must decide in each auction how you will time the outlay of your bidding budget. You always want to avoid expending too much of your budget too soon which weakens your staying power in the auction, or to expend too little so as to not be competitively strong enough. You strive to not create a target for other bidders with a high proxy bid, yet avoid placing easily outbid minimum bids.

A good rule of thumb for optimizing your bidding budget is to always conserve a portion of your bidding budget for the final moments of the auction. This is the time when aggressive opponents "go for the win" because near the end of an auction is when the auction's closing price is most predictable. In addition, the impending close of the auction demands immediate action. One must also consider that it is very close to the auction's close when snipers might hit the auction. You'll want to conserve as much of your bidding budget as practical to remain competitive in the critical minutes just before the auction closes.

It will be up to you to judge how much of your bidding budget to conserve. Here are some suggestions:

- Conserve more of your bidding budget for the final moments in auctions that have many bidders actively participating. With many bidders competing for the same item, you'll need more of your budget to gain a competitive position, to outbid with a sufficiently high proxy bid or even to snipe the auction.

- In auctions with low bidder participation but with a few aggressive bidders, conserve enough to be able to place a strong proxy bid near the end of the auction. Also, bear in mind that snipers may strike. Placing a higher than normal proxy bid near the auction's end has a greater chance of unseating an aggressive bidder.

- A strong proxy bid near the auction's close helps protect against snipe bids. Snipe bidders make an effort to predict at what price the auction will close. This improves the chances of a sniper placing a bid that is high enough to win the auction, but not too high to create a risky bid. A high snipe bid is risky because if the auction is hit with another snipe bid, the auction mechanism will reconcile (in milliseconds) all bids and award the auction to the highest bidder. And, because the auction closes, multiple snipe bidders have no option but to accept the consequences. Thus, too high of a bid could work against the snipe bidder. By placing a proxy bid just before the auction closes, you may reduce the success of an opponent's snipe bid because the closing price of the auction is less predictable, causing snipe bidders to bid apprehensively Please see Law #30: *The Closing price is Best Surmised Near the End*.

♦ In auctions where there is initially low participation, but where the item has a high potential market value, you may want to conserve some of your bidding budget for when bidders discover the auction and become active.

♦ Another notable situation is when a seller posts two simultaneous auctions for an identical item. When the first auction closes, one or more losing bidders may revert to the second auction and bid aggressively in that auction. While the first auction was running it took activity away from the second auction. But, on the first auction's close, losing bidders reverted to the second auction creating a sudden increase in activity. Because the first auction had helped create demand for the auction item, the losing bidders in the first auction may go to the second with more determination to win it.

♦ In auctions where the item has low potential market value with low bidder participation, still conserve your bidding budget for the period near the auction's close. It may be best to wait and see who enters the auction. Of course, in this type of auction it might be better to place a proxy bid of say 50% to 75% of your bidding budget and let the bid stand for awhile. Bear in mind that you can never know for sure what activity an auction will receive nor do you know for certain *when* an auction will receive activity. A good rule is to always assume that aggressive bidding activity will occur.

Your bidding budget is an important asset. You will want to manage its use throughout the auction so that you gain the most effective use of the money you have allocated to winning the auction.

Notes:

_____

Law 7: Assess the Seller

> The Savvy Bidder knows that until she actually receives the item won at auction, the performance of the seller remains uncertain. The Savvy Bidder proceeds with all reasonable caution and researches not only what is being sold, but also who is doing the selling. The Savvy Bidder avoids becoming entangled in a poor transaction by refraining from bidding in suspect auctions.

Nearly every bidder knows something about what they are bidding on. This knowledge is gleaned from the seller's description, by referring to other auctions (running or recently closed) and information from outside of the auction community. In addition, information often comes from personal, professional or collector familiarity. However, it is more difficult to know the seller. How do you know if the seller is representing the auction item fully and truthfully? How do you know if the seller will ship the item? These are questions that are important to your decision to participate in an auction if you are to have a positive experience with the seller.

What motivates a seller to list her item in an eBay auction? The obvious answer is that the seller desires to sell the item. But, it would be worthwhile to explore motivations for selling via eBay auctions. Let's do something perhaps a bit controversial and type cast sellers into categories for the purpose of our discussion. (The following statements are numbered for reference, not to imply priority).

1. The seller prefers the money more so than the item itself. She has gone "closet mining" and has found some possessions that could be turned into cash for use in pursuing other interests.

2. The seller has an item that he no longer has need for and offers it for sale, not really being all that concerned with the amount of money received for it. There is more interest in getting rid of it without throwing it away.

3. The seller is selling at eBay auctions primarily as a hobby and is interested in the auction process as a means to buy and sell as an interesting past time, in other words as a means of trade.

4. The seller has acquired new merchandise specifically for resale and thus has a financial investment in the item. The seller wishes to move new (or semi-new) merchandise at a profit. This seller is a retailer.

I pose these questions:

Which seller type do you feel <u>safest</u> buying from?

Which seller type do you feel would provide the best follow through once you win the auction?

If there is a dispute upon receipt of the auction item, which seller type would likely resolve that dispute even if he took a financial loss?

Which seller type do you think is most likely to put the time and effort into her auction listing to present it well and to assure content accuracy?

Which seller type is more likely to "pad" the auction with a higher than normal shipping fee or even a handling fee?

And here's a very tough question: if fraud were involved, such as shilling, which seller type is most likely to participate in it? (Pick a seller type even if you aren't sure of the answer. No one's looking.)

We come across many auctions where it is obvious that the seller does not really know what he is selling. Some sellers often do not know the item's market value and do not put forth the effort to present the item well. Such listings often contain very sparse descriptions, often with the bulk of the listing discussing shipping and payment terms. Photos are poor, if they are provided at all. Or the photo is excellent, but is the manufacturer's photo, not a photo of the actual auction item. However, the item itself may have real value to the auction community, even though the seller may promote it poorly. The seller may have a valuable treasure from your prospective, yet thinks of the item as just something to get rid of.

Are you comfortable buying from this type of seller? Your discomfort may be confirmed by the auction community placing fewer bids or placing small low risk bids. The fact is that a seller often advertises her own disbelief in the value of an item by posting a low quality listing. I can only imagine the cumulative loss of auction dollars because so many sellers list poorly.

Let's turn our attention to the category of seller that puts forth a good effort to present an item in an eBay auction. The item is described well and the photos do the item visual justice. Shipping and payment terms come after the item has been presented, that is, after the potential bidder has had a chance to learn about the item. The seller's terms treat all bidders with respect and do not indicate a deep lack of trust of the bidder community. The auction listing shows that care was taken to explain the item and its current condition. These sellers are likely to get a better closing price for their auctions because bidders have more confidence buying from them.

Statistically speaking, a small percentage of eBay auctions are posted by sellers with fraudulent intentions. Of course, remain ever vigilant of fraud and even misrepresentation while keeping things in perspective.

By assessing the seller before bidding you may save your time, your money and aggravation. It is disheartening to have expended an effort to research an item and place bids only to receive something other than what you believed you had purchased. Try to assess what motivates the seller. By doing so, you will get a better appreciation of the person from whom you intend to purchase.

Also see Law *#21: Seller Ratings Can Mislead*

Notes:

Law 8: Don't Focus on the Current Price

> **The Savvy Bidder makes a concerted effort to not focus on the current price. This is because he understands that the current price entices bidders to continue bidding which serves to maximize the auction's closing price.**

The primary function of the single-unit auction format is to increase the current price as bidding proceeds. In fact the word auction stems from the Latin word *auctio*, which means to increase. As you know, when a bid is placed in a single-unit eBay auction the current price is increased according to a specific formula:

♦ If a bid is placed that is <u>equal to</u> the required minimum bid, then the current price is increased to the bid amount. The eBay mechanism then sets the requirement for the next minimum bid amount according to eBay's bid increment scale. (See *Minimum Bid Increment* in the Glossary.)

♦ If a bid is placed that is <u>greater than</u> the required minimum bid, the current price is increased to the next minimum required bid and the remainder of the bid becomes a proxy bid.

♦ If a bid is placed that is <u>greater than</u> a reserve price, should one exist, the current price is immediately increased to the reserve price. The remainder of the bid (the amount greater than the reserve price) becomes a proxy bid.

♦ If a bid is placed that is <u>greater than</u> an existing proxy bid the current price is immediately increased to the amount of the outbid proxy plus one minimum bid increment and the remainder of the new bid becomes a proxy bid.

Thus with each bid in a single-unit eBay auction, the eBay mechanism keeps raising the current price and requires that the next bid be equal to or greater than the next minimum bid increment. The current price is increased with each new bid whether or not the bidder becomes the highest bidder or the seller's reserve is met, should one exist. Because bids cause the current price to increase, most bidders will make an effort to minimize the impact their bids have on the current price. Naturally, bidders are going to pay close attention to the current price.

Certain buying dynamics occur when a bidder is current price focused. The first dynamic is that it is much easier for a bidder to accept a small increase of the current price than a large increase. The IRS has been raising federal taxes in relatively small increments for years because it understands that people are more willing to accept (or tolerate) a relatively small increase than a large one. Relating this concept to online auctions, a $5.00 increase in the current price is much easier to accept than a $50.00 increase. So, when the highest bidder is outbid, it is not usually a leap to simply accept a slightly higher price and bid again – at the next minimum bid increment or higher, of course. Specific bidders eventually reach a point where the cumulative price exceeds their personal value of the item (or their budget) and bidding stops for them. The bidder who survives the longest (or perhaps I should say, tolerates the highest price) wins the auction.

The second dynamic is that the current price *implies* what the market is willing to pay for the item at any given time. If the current price is below what a bidder is willing to pay, her mind reasons "You mean I could buy this for half of what I'm willing to pay?" However, the current price is not an accurate indicator of the market's interest – the current price is simply the current state of the price negotiation among the participating bidders. Until the auction closes, the current price provides no definitive indication of the true personal valuation of the participants. Of course, the current price provides no indication of the interest in the item of persons who have not yet bid.

The current price not only capitalizes on people's willingness to accept small price increases, it also implies that the participants are willing to pay at that price, when in fact they may be willing to pay much more. Thus, bidders who are current price focused often lose perspective of their own personal valuation, and in fact may never completely form a valuation that is independent of the current price. When all bidders in an auction are current price focused, bidding generally becomes a cyclic process that serves to steadily raise the auctions closing price. This is because each bidder continuously raises his personal valuation in relatively small amounts based on the current price. In a very real sense, the current price dupes bidders into believing that the auction item could be purchased at approximately the current price.

The Savvy Bidder understands that the current price is not necessarily an indicator of what participating bidders are willing to pay. Rather she understands that the current price is only the current state of the price negotiation process, helped along by the auction mechanism itself. Also, the Savvy Bidder does not fall into the trap of adjusting her personal valuation based on what it appears she *might* be able to purchase the item for, as indicated by the current price. Rather, she established a target price before participating in the auction and works the auction against that price guideline.

One benefit of the target price is that it keeps you from placing too much importance on the current price. With a target price you are able to establish a bidding budget for strategic purposes. With a target price you can avoid chasing the current price under the assumption that bidding at or near the next minimum bid requirement is actually winning the auction. In fact, by chasing the current price bidders are actually playing into the process of raising the closing price of the auction.

So the next time you are poised to place a bid in an online auction, think about the importance you may be assigning to the current price. Always keep in mind that the current price serves to entice bidders to bid just a little bit more. Also, remember that the current price is not necessarily what a specific bidder would be willing to pay for the item – he may actually be willing to pay much more.

Also see laws *#2: Negotiate, Don't Buy, #5: Know the Target Price* and *#12: Understand Current Price Escalation*

Notes:

Law 9: Eliminate Luck

Luck does play a role in winning eBay auctions. However the Savvy Bidder works to eliminate as much of the luck as possible. Luck plays a lesser role in winning auctions when a strategic approach is taken.

Luck is a factor in all eBay auctions. This is because you cannot predict what other bidders will do. This makes online auctions a game of chance. However, your objective is to eliminate as much of the luck factor as you can. Do this by preparing for your participation, by gathering information, by exploring the auction's landscape, by understanding the dynamics of online auctions and by using sound tactical bidding.

There are telltale signs that you are thinking in terms of luck playing a major role in your ability to win eBay auctions. Here are a few examples:

"I'm winning the auction." – As discussed in Law *#3: Never Think of Yourself as "Winning"*, you risk lowering your competitive strength.

"I hope I'm not outbid." – Expect to be outbid. Prepare in advance for being outbid and manage your bidding budget accordingly.

"I hope this bid meets the seller's reserve price." – Find out what the seller's reserve price is <u>before</u> bidding. If the seller will not tell you her reserve, then consider holding your bids until another bidder meets the reserve.

"I hope this snipe bid is enough." – Before placing a snipe bid do all you can to estimate what the probable closing price of the auction will be.

Many, if not most of your opponents, will consider luck a major factor in their ability to win auctions. By making an effort to eliminate luck, you separate yourself from your opponents, competitively speaking.

The premise of this law is to think in terms of strategy, not luck. Acknowledge that luck may play a role in your auction participation, but do not rely on it as a way to win auctions.

Also see Law *#3: Never Think of Yourself as "Winning"*

Notes:

Law 10: Bid Begets Bid

> **Each bid in an auction expresses an interest in purchasing the item. This is turn encourages others to bid. The Savvy Bidder understands the competitive significance of bids.**

Before the first bid is placed, an auction can be considered only on the merits of the item itself. This is because prospective bidders have no indication of any other person's actual interest in the auction. The longer an auction continues with no bids, the lower the probability that a market exists for that auction or will develop for it. As can be seen by simple observation, there are many such auctions on eBay at any given time. Many sellers, knowing that an auction may get off to a slow start will set a very low First Bid price in the hope that a few bidders will regard the auction as a potential bargain and place a bid.

The first bid to be placed in an auction initiates price negotiation. The first bid is also the first public indication that there is a market for the item, or at the very least one interested buyer. At the moment of the first bid, a market begins to manifest itself for the auction item potentially establishing a level of confidence in other persons who are also interested in that item.

After a second bidder places a bid, a third interested person may feel even more confident that the auction is worth negotiating for. The manifestation of the market for the item further develops with each new bid. Bid begets bid because each new bid raises the confidence level of others who are considering the auction. Bids also suggest that a prospective bidder should become active in the auction to carve out a chance to win it.

As the market develops for the item, the activity among the competing bidders tends to generate a stronger sense of value. This in turn promotes competition among the participants. This also encourages bidders-in-the-wing to get involved. Of course, as the bidders compete with one another the current price increases. The escalating current price serves to weed out bidders by eliminating those who are unwilling to pay more than their peers. However, the escalating current price also indicates that the item has a value of at least the current price. In this manner, the current price serves to both eliminate individuals from the auction as well as entice others to join in.

There are other factors that help a market develop for an auction item. For instance the knowledge that the interested persons have of the item's purpose, functions, feature set or brand name helps a market develop. A demand in the auction community may already exist for the item or the demand could be external to the auction market. Also, the seller's description, First Bid price and terms of sale help develop the auction's market. What is of interest to us at this time is how bids in an auction help substantiate the belief that the auction is worth pursuing.

By understanding that a market for a particular item is nurtured, in part, by the bidding activity in that auction, you can understand how your own participation will also help the development of the market for the item. If you bid in the auction, you help increase the auction's market because your bid indicates interest.

If you were to place a high bid, your bid will tend to pull the market up to the new price level you set with your bid. In effect, your high bid states that you believe that the item has a value of at least the amount of your bid if and when your high bid becomes known by another bidder outbidding it. In this case, your bid not only indicates your interest in the auction, but also implies a particular personal valuation.

If you were to place a minimum bid (a bid that is one minimum bid increment above the current price) you indicate less confidence in the value of the item. However, your bid increases the bid count in that auction, which is also an indicator of interest. It is interesting how some bidders will place several or many minimum bids in an auction thinking that it makes the auction appear highly competitive. But, a higher bid count actually implies a greater interest in the auction. Only those bidders who look closely at the bid history will realize that there are actually less unique participants than the bid count indicates.

Remain aware that your participation in the auction helps build a market interest. As each bidder expresses an increasing level of confidence through new bids, the current price escalates, resulting in a higher closing price. The Savvy Bidder aims to avoid competition, not create it. As such, she often decides to withhold participation during certain periods in the auction, depending on the circumstances in the auction. More important, she is aware of the possible impact her bids will have in terms of increasing the interest others may develop in the auction.

Also see Law #20: *Bid Activity Does Not Necessarily Mean Value*

Notes:
_____

Law 11: This Is Not Retail

> The Savvy Bidder uses care to eliminate retail buying habits
> and expectations from his online auction experience. The Sav-
> vy Bidder knows that being retail-minded in online auctions
> reduces his competitive effectiveness.

As a Savvy Bidder you need to understand that the eBay auction environment is different in many ways to the more familiar traditional retail environment. Understanding the differences is key to your bidding success for two reasons. First, the greatest danger is that you may approach eBay auctions in the same manner and with the same expectations as in a retail purchase. Second, if you recognize when your opponents are taking a retail-like approach to an auction, you will be better positioned to compete against those opponents. Before we get into this interesting subject, let's briefly compare the retail and eBay environments.

Traditional Retail	Online Auctions
The purchase price is determined by the merchant.	The purchase price is determined by the bidders collectively (above the seller's First Bid and/or reserve price).
Price negotiation is uncommon in retail.	Bidding is a process of price negotiation.
Established physical presence, i.e., the storefront.	No observable physical presence – a virtual presence.
You perform transactions with people.	You perform transactions with "entities", i.e., Membership ID's. In-person and phone contact is uncommon.
You are not anonymous.	You are anonymous to a large extent.
You can handle, inspect and often "test drive" merchandise you are considering purchasing.	You cannot usually handle, inspect or "test drive" merchandise you are bidding on.
Time limitations to purchase are not a primary consideration. A sale about to end is about the worst time pressure you will feel (at the merchant level).	eBay auctions have a very specific time limit. The auction ends at a precise time without regard to your being ready.
Since you know the price, you can make a purchase decision based on the price.	In the typical single-unit online auction, you do not know the final price until the auction closes (except Buy It Now auctions). A final purchase decision (based on price) cannot be made during the auction.

THE LAWS OF STRATEGIC BIDDING

Traditional Retail - cont.	Online Auctions - cont.
Competition with other buyers is not a primary concern.	Competition with other buyers is a fundamental aspect of the auction format.
You know how much another person will need to pay to purchase the merchandise item. In fact, that price happens to be the exact same price you will pay (at the same retail establishment).	You do not know the price other bidders (or persons not yet bidding) are willing to pay.
Retail caters to the product needs of the current market. There must be a certain demand for retailers to justify the product continuing to occupy shelf space.	Because the seller bears the burden of stocking the merchandise, the online auction environment acts as a venue for a wide range of market needs.
Ownership is quick. Once you decide to purchase, you need only complete the process of paying at the checkout counter, which virtually all retailers try to make as easy as possible.	Ownership is delayed while others are given a chance to bid. You must wait for the auction to end. You then have to wait for shipment.
There are a wide variety of payment methods available to at in retail; cash, check, credit card, debit (bank) card, etc. The method of payment is not normally an obstacle to ownership.	When buying via an eBay auction, you often have deal with restrictive payment methods. Sellers generally do not trust personal and business checks. It is unwise to send cash through the mail. Use of credit and debit cards is only available if seller is registered with an Internet payment service or credit card service provider.
Most retail establishments do not operate 24 hours per day, 7 days a week.	While running, you can participate in an online auction 24 hrs per day, 7 days per week, including minor and major holidays.
The merchant is not normally in a monopolistic position (the product is usually available from other merchants as well).	The auction seller is in a monopolistic position, at least with respect to his own auction. If there happens to be no other auction for the same auction item, the seller temporarily "owns" the market in the auction community.
Because of well-defined and enforced regulations by local and state authorities, fear of fraudulent activities by retail establishments is not a primary concern.	Due largely to the ability for dishonest sellers to remain anonymous, the large number of unsuspecting bidders and other factors, fraud in online auctions is a perceived risk.

Table 3 - A comparison between retail and online auctions.

Interesting comparison wouldn't you agree? Traditional retail is a predictable, tangible and very familiar purchasing environment; eBay auctions are not predictable, are competitive and the price is not normally determined until the auction ends. Retail provides a physical closeness to the product during the purchase decision while eBay auctions necessitate a physical separation from the product during the auction. But, eBay auctions permit 24/7 purchase activity and provides limited anonymity.

Because retail is so familiar to nearly every person and is a dominant method of acquiring merchandise, we tend to approach every purchase situation just as we have learned in our retail experience, and with similar expectations. But, just glancing at the above comparison between retail and eBay, we see that there are several significant differences. With eBay auctions there is competition, you often do not know the final purchase price during the auction, you are not able to touch and handle the merchandise prior to purchasing it and you have to wait to posses the merchandise if you win the auction. But the attraction of eBay auctions is that you can make a play to save money on purchases, you have access to merchandise that retailers long ago dropped or that ran their course in terms of the distributors marketing and profit objective. Also, you get to engage in an exhilarating game of competition, staking your claim using a valuable asset – your money.

In retail we do not normally negotiate the price because the price is predetermined. Retail has made an effort to minimize waiting to receive the merchandise. In retail, we can be as mechanical as we wish, making purchases as just part of a normal day. Or we can comparison shop for as long as we want. So, it is natural that we might take these same expectations into the online auction world.

But, online auctions present us with different challenges. Consider:

♦ Having to negotiate a purchase price can be intimidating for many. How do you know what is an appropriate price? It would be much simpler to purchase an eBay item without having to deal with competing buyers. Perhaps this is why eBay's *Buy It Now* feature is popular (eBay evidently recognizes that its membership is retail oriented).

♦ Perhaps in some of us there is a reluctance to offer a price that is lower than what we think is a "fair" price, or at least what we are willing to pay for the merchandise. Is it possible that we might prefer to bid all the way up to the price we think is fair and reasonable?

Don't Take this Wrong. But...

If someone were to offer you $1.00 for your $300.00 watch, you would likely be insulted and would certainly turn down such an offer. We are uncomfortable being the receivers of ridiculous offers and we don't want to be givers of such offers either. Yet, "ridiculous" offers are fine in eBay auctions! Because that's the way the online auction game is played and because of anonymity, bids can be ridiculously low without insulting the seller. Nevertheless, the ability to make ridiculously low offers in eBay auctions is somewhat foreign compared to how we typically buy merchandise in the traditional predetermined-price retail market.

The social norms we have been well taught are dutifully carried into the online auction environment. It is far easier to pay a predetermined price – we need not put forth an effort to suggest a price, we don't risk sounding financially challenged and we take no risk insulting the merchant. The UPC (Uniform Product Code) label is telling you at the retail store – "this is the price, take it or leave it". If you make the purchase you do not feel that you have taken advantage of the merchant – you feel you have made a fair exchange albeit at the merchant's terms. If you didn't make the purchase, there's no problem because the merchant expects a percentage of non-buyers.

If you haven't already gathered, the eBay auction proxy bid system enables you to carry over to eBay what you have learned from the retail world. With a simple proxy bid, you are able to dispense with often frustrating and time consuming competitive bidding. The proxy bid system affords you a low effort method of purchasing – just what you have come to expect from your favorite local retail merchant. Of course, you may not win the auction with your proxy bid, but to many the effort saved is often worth the possible loss of the purchase. In the part *Bidding Tactics and Techniques* we discuss using proxy bidding for competitive positioning rather than simply as a way to purchase an auction item.

Hey. That's Mine!

Winning the right to purchase a product is not something we are accustomed to having to do. In the common single-unit eBay auction format, we cannot purchase the product unless we are the highest bidder when the auction closes. Even if we are the highest bidder a "winning" position can be snatched from us at any time while the auction is running. While this is normal in online auctions, it would anger us if another customer at the retail store came up to us, removed a product from our cart and claimed it for herself on the premise that she is willing to pay more for it.

By everyday retail commerce etiquette, such behavior is offensive and would keep people from using the store. One can imagine the scene if retail shopping was based on who was willing to pay the most. (Perhaps the salvation of online auctions is that no one has the immediate ability to shout at one another.) You would likely snatch the product back from another's shopping cart, proclaiming that you are willing to pay more than they so you'll be taking the product back, thank you. In eBay auctions, this same scenario plays out all the time through the process of bid, be outbid, and bid again. It is a frustrating game for those who simply want to make a purchase from an eBay auction.

While we understand the online auction game, it nevertheless rubs against the grain of what we have grown accustomed to it in terms of purchasing at retail. And, since the only obvious way to retain a claim in a single-unit eBay auction is to outbid another, that's the common response.

Once outbid, the only ability to reclaim the item in a single-unit auction is to commit to spending more money for it. It is in this way that bidders become increasingly vested in the auction. That's the hook that retail stores don't have. By having to defend the right to make the purchase, a bidder becomes increasingly determined to own the item, to a point.

Don't Make Me Work

A great many bidders who participate in eBay auctions do so as if it were retail. Since the eBay membership is drawn from the consumer population, it is natural for them to bring with them retail buying habits and expectations. Understanding this, the Savvy Bidder is much better equipped to compete in auctions. This is because he understands the inefficiencies of competing in eBay auctions as a retail-minded buyer. Such a buyer is simply not "tuned in" to the competitive approach to purchasing.

Over the past years eBay has shifted from being an auction-based swap meet in its early days to a profit-conscience business. It comes as no surprise why eBay has increasingly facilitated retail-like buying – there's good money in it. The irony is that the price negotiation model (auctioning) is in contrast with the predetermined price model (retail). The result is that retail-minded buyers must go through a price negotiation process while auction-minded buyers must contend with retail-like constraints.

To illustrate retail-like constraints, sellers very often set the First Bid up to the typical closing price of the same or comparable item. Or the seller may set a reserve price that corresponds to the item's retail price. eBay's *Buy It Now* feature certainly caters to retail-like buying. With these price constraining methods, the seller pushes up the auction's price to effectively predetermine the price, just as does a retail merchant. This defeats the intent and purpose of the auction format. In such auctions, there is limited opportunity for bidders to negotiate the price since a "floor price" exists, determined by the seller. In contrast to retail's "take it or leave it" approach, auctions with a floor price create a "take it or pay more" situation.

There is little anyone can do about this retail/auction hybrid format on eBay. In fact it is likely that eBay will continue to migrate toward retail. There may actually come a day when eBay will become the largest virtual department store in the world. However, it is also likely that there will always be independent sellers on eBay who provide the products (and who bear the burden of stocking, selling, handling, taxes and so on). Sadly, I predict that sellers will adopt the predetermined price model more and more. This should come as no surprise since it is the retail price model (predetermined pricing) that has the greatest potential for the seller to extract the maximum profit from each sale. If the seller remains in control of the selling price, the seller is sure to set pricing for a profit.

One factor that will contribute to sellers' migration toward the predetermined price model is the erosion of the seller's profit by the continual increases in listing, sales and promotional fees imposed on the seller by eBay. In other words, by continuing to squeeze the seller's profit, the natural reaction by sellers will be to push up the floor price of the auction (by setting higher First Bid and reserve prices). In my opinion, the price negotiation process is the best process for an auction environment. If both eBay and eBay sellers were to remain focused on the price negotiation model they may actually fair much better over the long term.

So what does this mean for the Savvy Bidder? First, since eBay's membership is comprised mainly of retail-minded buyers and eBay is mixing the retail model with the auction model, the Savvy Bidder is more likely to have retail minded opponents. Second, the Savvy Bidder can remain aware of his own purchasing habits and make an effort to avoid bringing retail buying habits to eBay auctions. Third, he is better able to select appropriate bidding tactics, given a better understanding of the seller's chosen price model (predetermined or negotiable).

Notes:

Law 12: Understand Current Price Escalation

Because the Savvy Bidder remains aware of how price escalation occurs in eBay auctions, he is in a much better position to remain free of the current price chase.

This law serves to point out one basic concept; auctions are designed to maximize the closing price. To accomplish this, in part, the auction mechanism parades the current price as a purchase price. Since the bid amounts of other bidders are hidden in eBay auctions, individuals become current price focused by default. As shown in Figure 18, the auction mechanism then enables, even encourages, individual bidders to place a small bid at the minimum bid increment. The end result is a gradual acclimation to the auctions final closing price.

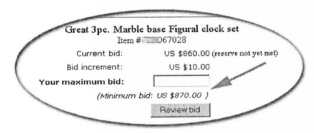

Figure 18 - An eBay screen portion showing the required minimum bid amount.

Small Increases Add Up

By taking a closer look at eBay's minimum bid increment scale we can better understand that, on a bid-by-bid basis, the scale has a relatively small impact on the current price. However, over the life of the auction, such small increases add up with the objective of closing the auction at the highest possible price.

The following table is eBay's minimum bid increment scale (as of this writing). I have added the column labeled "Percent Increase" to illustrate the percentage of increase *within* each level of the scale. For instance, in the $100.00 to $249.99 level, a Bid Increment of $2.50 would equate to a percent increase of 2.5% to 1%. This percentage increase is calculated by dividing the bid increment by the current price. For example, to get the percentage for the lower end of the $100.00 to $249.99 level: $2.50/$100.00=.025 or 2.5%. To get the percentage for the upper end of this level: $2.50/$249.99=.0100004 or 1%.

Current Price	Bid Increment	Percent Increase
$.01 - .99	$.05	500% - 5%
1.00 - 4.99	.25	25 - 5
5.00 - 24.99	.50	10 - 2
25.00 - 99.99	1.00	4 - 1
100.00 - 249.99	2.50	2.5 - 1
250.00 - 499.99	5.00	2 - 1
500.00 - 999.99	10.00	2 - 1
1000.00 - 2499.99	25.00	2.5 - 1
2500.00 - 4999.99	50.00	2 - 1
5000.00 and up	100.00	2 and down

Table 4 - Table listing eBay's Minimum Bid Increment scale (in U.S. dollars). Table includes the author's calculations to show the percentage increase within each level.

The above information was accurate at this time this book was published. For the latest eBay bid increment information, please refer to the help pages at www.ebay.com.

Now that we have percentages within each minimum bid increment level, we see that with levels beginning at $100.00-$249.99 a bid will not increase the current price more than 2.5% at the lower end of each level. And, at the higher end of each level, the increase is never larger than 1%. Thus, in these levels, the most an individual bidder ever has to accept is 2.5% over the current price. (Of course if there is a proxy bid in place, a bidder who bids at the minimum bid increment will not attain the highest bidder position).

These relatively low minimum bid increments help reduce "current price shock" because the minimum bid increment is not a significant amount in terms of a percentage increase. If you were considering purchasing an item with a current price of $556.00, for example, you would be required only to increase your willingness to pay 1.7% more than the current price ($10.00/$556.00=.017 or 1.7%). Ten bucks is not a significant increase to ask of interested buyers who are already willing to spend $556.00. Thus, the minimum bid increment scale works to increase the auction's current price in relatively small and palatable increments.

It's the Competition

So far we have been speaking on a bid-by-bid basis. In other words, when a bidder considers the auction as it stands at any given moment, it is relatively easy to justify just a percentage or two to remain in the auction. Of course, there are often several or many bidders that cumulatively serve to increase an auction's current price. This illustrates that individual bidders, when focused on the current price, often do not recognize the effect that competition has on the auction. Rather they find it relatively easy to bid just a little bit more in an effort to purchase the item.

The Savvy Bidder recognizes that competition in the auction is what really matters. It is the competition, or the collective bidding, that ultimately sets the auction's closing price. When individual bidders weigh their continued participation based on relatively small increases to the current price, they tend to loose sight of the cumulative effect small price increases have over the duration of the auction.

The Savvy Bidder makes an effort to not get caught up in the price escalation syndrome by accepting relatively small increases over the current price. Rather, he considers the probability of the auction reaching it's full potential market value and thus is more interested in positioning during the auction rather than simply trying to purchase the item during the auction.

So, the next time you are poised to place a bid in an online auction, think in terms of the competition in the auction and how it may affect the auction's closing price. Resist bidding simply because it's easy to justify the minimum required bid amount. The objective is to not get caught up in a current price chase. One way the Savvy Bidder avoids this is to keep in mind the probable price the auction will close at based on research done to establish a target price. The target price helps you remain focused on the competitive landscape, not the current price.

Also see laws #2: Negotiate, Don't Buy, #5: Know the Target Price and #12: Don't Focus on the Current Price

Notes:

Law 13: Bidding Is Not Buying

The Savvy Bidder recognizes that bidding does not carry the same realism as paying. She therefore makes an effort to not get ensnared into placing easily justifiable new bids.

When you hand over payment at the store, you see the representation of value (your money) actually being traded for the merchandise. This reminds you of the resources required to complete the transaction. In auctions persons negotiate for the right to make the purchase – actually making the purchase comes only after winning that right which comes only by meeting the requirements of the auction, which is being the highest bidder in a single-unit auction. During such negotiation there is not the same level of realism as when making payment at the time of purchase. In other words it is easy to bid – payment is off in the future a bit and may not even be necessary since the auction may be lost anyway.

Since bidding is separated from paying in auctions there is less resistance in justifying a new, higher bid if necessary. Even a new bid does not trigger the emotions associated with actually making the payment. Granted the bidder is aware that he will be obligated to pay the amount of the closing price *if* he wins the auction, but that awareness does not carry the same weight as actually making the payment.

I wonder how many people would bid in an online auction if they had to actually make a payment in the amount of each bid. Of course, if the auction was lost, the money would be refunded. Handing over the money to back up each bid would bring a sense of realism to bidding. But this won't happen on eBay because this would cause an association between bidding and payment (and would be a difficult accounting task). Bidders would surely curtail bidding if they actually had to post money to back up each bid.

Nevertheless auctions work, in part, because the auction process pushes the realism of the actual payment away from the bidding process. This, in conjunction with palatable increases in the current price as discussed in Law #12, makes it easy to bid. Due to the ease of bidding bidders who take a purchasing approach will often forfeit competitive strategies. The Savvy Bidder is aware that some of his opponents may not be fully aware that they are not actually purchasing when they are bidding. This may allow the Savvy Bidder to leverage the relatively weak competitive position of such opponents. For the Savvy Bidder this opens up the possibility of himself using strategy as a means of positioning in the auction. The Savvy Bidder remains ever aware that bidding is actually negotiating for the right to purchase the auction item and proceeds accordingly.

Notes:

Law 14: Leverage Your Money

> **The Savvy Bidder recognizes that winning eBay auctions is not just how much money he is willing to spend, but how well he leverages it.**

I recently had a conversation with an avid traditional auction buyer. We were discussing bidding strategy. Well, actually I was discussing bidding strategy – he was completely disinterested. He explained rather abruptly, "The only strategy is to be the highest bidder." I then asked, "Isn't there anything you could do on the auction floor to be a more competitive bidder?" He simply answered "Bid higher." That was the end of our conversation.

I believe the thinking of this person represents the majority of eBay bidders; that it is the *amount* of money alone that wins auctions. It's easy to understand why people think this way. In fact, this is how auction sellers prefer people think. It is important to understand, however, that how one leverages his money in eBay auctions is as important as how much he spends.

A prospective bidder may survey an auction; see that it has a current price of $500.00, and decide that he is willing to pay that amount and bid accordingly. This is a buying approach where the primary focus is on the amount of money that it appears one will spend on the auction. The Savvy Bidder will look at this same auction scenario in light of its probable market price, set a target price, establish a bidding budget, formulate a bidding strategy and then bid. She seeks to use her money to position in the auction.

So how does one leverage his money in an auction? The underlying principle is to not think like a buyer. Rather to think like a negotiator. Ask yourself how you can most effectively use your bidding budget (the difference between the current price and the target price). Perhaps it would be best utilized with one or two strong proxy bids in an effort to suppress competition. Perhaps several minimum bids would be appropriate to ferret out competition. Or perhaps the full amount held for a snipe bid. Or your bidding budget could be used in a combination of bidding tactics, depending on the situation at hand. The objective is to look for ways to use your bidding budget to own the best competitive position in the auction at the moment the auction closes.

As discussed in Law #3: *Never Think of Yourself as "Winning"* the buyer-minded bidder thinks that being the highest bidder is winning the auction. The Savvy Bidder understands that being the highest bidder is not necessarily the best position to be in (except at the instant the auction closes). In fact, the Savvy Bidder recognizes that not bidding at certain times is a viable tactic. In this way, you leverage your money by *not* bidding at times where your money would not yield an immediate competitive advantage or would not contribute to positioning you as the highest bidder at the instant the auction closes.

Money leveraging is possible because opponents will typically take a buyer approach. Because opponents make an effort to keep bids small, it affords the Savvy Bidder opportunities to use his bidding budget for stealth and positioning bids as well as for competitively strong bids. While opponents are placing apprehensive bids, the Savvy Bidder is negotiating for position.

The Savvy Bidder recognizes that competitive strength does not necessarily come from high bid amounts. Rather stems from carefully selected and skillfully implemented bidding tactics. He also recognizes that buyer-minded bidders forfeit competitive strength when they fail to recognize that auctions are won by the skillful use of money, not just how much money is used.

Also see Law #15: *Bid to Win*

Notes:

Law 15: Bid To Win

The Savvy Bidder never bids in any auction she does not fully intend to win.

The Savvy Bidder has the skills to increase his probability of winning auctions. Before he places his first bid, he has become knowledgeable of the item, the seller and the participating bidders. He has determined a target price and has decided which bidding tactics to use to position for the win.

The Savvy Bidder does not need to reassess his participation in the auction with each increment of the current price. He understands the auction's probable closing price and has only to negotiate a winning position upon the auction's close. Certainly there is an interest in keeping his actual cost of the auction to a minimum, but he understands that this is best accomplished by utilizing sound bidding tactics.

The fear of overspending is not an issue with the Savvy Bidder. Since he has a bidding budget, he can bid aggressively or stealthily within that budget as appropriate. *A bidder who is fearful of spending money within a predetermined budget will not be an effective bidder.*

The Savvy Bidder never invests herself in the ownership of an item to the point where she will pay more than the target price. If the target price is inconsistent with her personal valuation, then she will adjust her personal valuation to avoid expending an effort to an auction at an improbably low closing price. However, this personal valuation adjustment is performed *before* participating in the auction. A personal valuation is never made based simply on the valuation of another bidder and certainly is not based on an auction's current price alone. The reason for this is that she cannot know what is motivating each individual opponent. In addition, the current price does not necessarily represent the actual final purchase price.

The Savvy Bidder pre-allocates funds for a particular auction and thereby avoids continuous reassessment of what she will pay for the item. The Savvy Bidder allows herself the use of the full amount of her bidding budget for a particular auction if necessary, thereby eliminating fear-based bidding. The Savvy Bidder also knows when to let the auction go and therefore is able to bid free of the fear of overpaying. The end result is that a Savvy Bidder has a good foundation by which to win auctions.

Also see Law #16: *Be Highly Competitive*

Notes:

Law 16: Be Highly Competitive

The Savvy Bidder is a smart competitor.

Since the eBay environment is specifically designed to create competition, participating in eBay auctions requires that your competitive prowess be finely tuned. Also, in my opinion, eBay provides the highest competitive online auction environment that exists at the time of this writing. This makes it essential to be highly competitive.

Several factors create this highly competitive milieu. First, the large number of eBay members means that there is a higher probability of encountering competition. Any competition (bidding) in a single-unit auction always escalates the auction's current price. Second, a great many sellers have had enough experience to know how to "push" pricing. (To push pricing is to set the First Bid and/or reserve price up to the typical market value of the auction item). This means buyers don't carry away as many bargains as they once could. Third, and most basic, the auction format is a commerce method with built-in scarcity, presenting only one item per single-unit auction. Since there can only be one winner of a single-unit auction, artificial scarcity is created which fosters competition.

The eBay environment provides bidders with just enough information to encourage competitive bidding, but not enough to place a bid that is an absolute sure win. This causes a semi-blind competitive approach. In this semi-blind environment, bidders tend to revert to simple buyers and play a game of chance to see who becomes the lucky winner.

From time to time you'll participate in auctions with few or no other opponents and those may turn out to be easy wins. There the lack of information will have less impact. But don't expect every auction to be easy to win. When you encounter opponents that are very determined buyers, or highly skilled as bidders, or even extremely irrational, you'll find that strong bidding skills will serve you well.

Being a bidding strategist is an excellent way to remain alert, aware and focused on your objective. You'll be ready for highly competitive situations. You'll be less prone to reverting to a simple buyer approach. You'll recognize tactical opportunities. Best, you'll enjoy the eBay experience more. Always be ready to turn on the competitive valve.

Notes:

Law 17: See the Unseen

> **A fundamental element of strategic bidding is to "see" that which is not clearly seen. Information analysis is key for the Savvy Bidder.**

One way that the typical bidder deals with a lack of information is to bid the lowest practical amount. I call this "safe bidding". After all, it would seem that bidding low is a way to minimize the risk of overpaying for the item. Rarely can an online auction item be physically inspected. Thus a risk is always present that the item will not be as described or what the buyer expected. Bidders who lack confidence in the value of the item tend to bid low so as to manage their risk.

Lack of Information

Many, many auctions are posted that lack important information about the item. Consider some reasons why information might be lacking:

- ◆ The seller has acquired the item from a source where information about the product was not important to the sale. In other words, due to a low selling price, the previous seller (on or off eBay) did not extend the effort to provide any more information than what was essential to transfer ownership quickly. Examples might be estate sales, tag sales and other eBay auctions. As an item is passed from one owner to another under such circumstances, information available about that item often becomes diluted until a seller finally takes the time to research the item in her auction listing and convey better information about it to the next buyer.

- ◆ The seller does not feel it is necessary to "educate" the buyer beyond describing the item and its current condition. Here the seller relies on a small fraction of eBay members discovering the auction who already know enough about the item to compensate for the seller's abbreviated description.

- ◆ The seller may simply not know all of the facts about her item and wisely chooses to not offer information that may be inaccurate. Avoiding inaccurate information is to the benefit of the bidders. It is also to the benefit of the seller since she does not run the risk of misrepresenting the auction item.

- ◆ The seller may not put forth the effort to inform bidders about the item in his auction listing even though he has the knowledge. Why bother? After all it is possible that the item will not sell or will not sell at a price that

justifies an additional effort in the listing. So why take 30 minutes to prepare the auction listing? I believe that a very large number of auctions are
listed by sellers who do not believe that the final price will justify their
time and energy. In fact, you can quickly find hundreds of auctions where
there are indications that the seller has put forth minimum effort. Often it
indicates the seller's belief that the auction may not yield a return on his
effort. Ironically, the seller's lack of confidence may actually reduce the
closing price of the auction because the confidence of the bidders is corre-
spondingly reduced.

♦ The seller may feel that offering information about an auction item may be
superfluous to bidders who are already knowledgeable of the item, and so
again, why bother? It is true that eBay auctions often do attract knowledgeable buyers. However, we cannot know for sure how much auction
purchasing is done by the truly serious collector who may have much better sources.

It is reasonable to expect sellers to want to sell their merchandise with reasonable
effort and, of course, at the highest sale price. This is simply a matter of the seller
balancing his investment of time with the potential closing price. In standard commercial systems, all participants in the manufacture and distribution chain seek to
be paid commensurate with their labor and the value they provide to the product.
This is one reason why we are sometimes shocked to learn the markup of retail
merchandise. For example, new clothing can have a markup of several thousand
percent by the time it reaches the consumer.

When supply and demand is factored in, the markup can be aggressive on merchandise where demand is high or exceeds supply. We find that in the eBay auction
environment there is just as much interest in maximizing profits and capitalizing
on supply and demand than in other structured commercial environments. However, since auction bidders collectively have a bit more control over what the final
selling price will be, the seller has less confidence in the final outcome in terms of
a selling price. Naturally, until the seller has good experience with a particular
product in auctions, there may be a tendency to put less effort into the sales mechanism, i.e., the auction listing.

I commend eBay sellers who do a superb job listing their auction items. Perhaps
these sellers know that auction buyers have a greater need for product knowledge
compared to other commercial medium. Perhaps they know that buyers respond
favorably to merchants who know their product and who, through generously con-
veying information about the auction item, help the buyer to assuage fears. Perhaps
these sellers also know that buyers in eBay auctions have an inherent distrust of
buying sight unseen and from persons unknown to them.

Whatever the justification for information lacking in an auction listing, you still have to contend with the missing information. One way to compensate for lacking information is to make assumptions from what you already know about the item. But there's a risk when filling in what you think you know as we'll explore next.

Assumptions

The human mind has an amazing ability to "fill in the blanks". The mind replaces missing information with "best fit" information based on personal experience. Perhaps you have written something and left out a word, such as "a". But you never saw the mistake when you proofread your material. Your mind may automatically fill in the missing "a". Have you ever written and proofread a sentence only to find later that it contained two "the" words back to back? Our mind corrects the picture for us as it assists us in perceiving what we expect.

Early in my eBay experience, I purchased a radar detector from an eBay seller. What a great deal I thought. A brand name radar detector could be purchased for much lower than the $230.00 retail price. I read the auction listing carefully, researched the model on the manufacture's web site and then employed good bidding skills. Yes, I won the auction at a low price of $89.00. When the radar detector arrived (after 8 days in transit), things didn't look so bright anymore. I had received a repaired unit in a generic box with a poorly rendered ink-jet printed replica of the retail box cover. To top it off, the manufacturer's one year warranty statement was rubber stamped with a juicy and drippy red "VOID". I did find a little yellow slip of paper in the box that gave me a 90 day warranty from some obscure repair shop in New York city. It's a good thing I don't speed – the radar detector spontaneously goes into "test mode" every once in a while, which is probably why the retail customer returned it in the first place.

So what had I missed? I went back to the auction listing and confirmed that the seller did indeed do a fantastic job presenting the radar detector, complete with a great photo albeit the manufacturers photo, detailed specifications and even a warranty statement (which did not specify a length). What the seller did not tell me was that the unit was repaired. I *assumed* the unit was new because a lifetime of retail purchase experience has conditioned me to accept new as the norm *unless* I am told otherwise. Since I wasn't specifically told that the unit was anything but new, it never occurred to me to assume anything different. And, because I had suspended my belief, I didn't question why I might be able to purchase a new radar detector for less than half of its retail price.

But then I found what I had missed. When I examined the listing more closely I finally understood an obscure statement that read:

THIS IS A QUALITY RENEWED PRODUCT WITH WARRANTY

My mind might have recognized the word "reconditioned" or the word "refurbished". But I had missed the word "renewed". My mind saw the good words "quality" and "warranty" and heard "new" rather than "renewed". My mind signaled that all was well. The statement might as well have been written

THIS IS A QUALITY NEW PRODUCT WITH WARRANTY

And I thought I was good at this auction stuff.

Was the seller misrepresenting his merchandise? No. But he may have been attempting to mask information that he knew would cause bidders to be wary of the auction. I then knew what they mean by *Caveat Emptor*.

The irony of my radar detector purchase was that my mind was functioning perfectly. It did exactly what it has been conditioned to do for many years – it filled in missing information for me automatically. In this case, I was disappointed that it functioned a bit too well. But in most activities in our daily life such "auto correction" is essential and helps us cope with very complex circumstances and activities.

The mind has a tendency to fill in missing information with more familiar data or with what it would like to beleive. You must remain aware of those situations in which your perception will deceive you. The propensity for sellers to simply omit information, or carefully mask negative information is enough to make purchasing at auction disconcerting. When the occasional seller masks information which is then misunderstood by the prospective bidder, things get a bit tricky. Listen to what the seller is *not* telling you, stop when a seller has coined as new word or term (such as "renewed") and proceed with all due caution.

Also see Law #22: *Expect the Unexpected*

Notes:

THE LAWS OF STRATEGIC BIDDING

Law 18: Turn Data into Competitive Strength

> eBay auction listings consist entirely of data. These small elements of facts that, when viewed in the proper manner, reveal information can be used to bid effectively. The Savvy Bidder uses auction data to bolster his competitive strength.

We make decisions based on information. When we do not have all of the facts our decision making ability is impaired and we tend to substitute the missing facts with suppositions. Obviously, it is always in our best interest to have as much information as possible to avoid coming to erroneous conclusions.

By collecting and analyzing data on a subject of interest, you assemble a picture you can use to make informed decisions. When bits of data are arranged into a familiar "view", the data becomes much more meaningful. Data such as Twelfth, Downs, 1955, Pete, December is almost useless until the data is arranged into a recognizable pattern. Pete Downs December Twelfth 1955 is meaningful because its view complies with patterns that we are familiar with, in this case a name and birth date. Thus data becomes most useful when arranged in recognizable patterns.

Let's discuss how the auction data could reveal information that may not be obvious if we simply happened into an auction and started bidding.

What is your primary goal when bidding in an auction of interest to you? Of course, it's to win the auction with the least expenditure on your part. So, what kind of data do you need to formulate an effective bidding strategy? Let's list the data you might need:

1. The target price for the auction (See chapter *The Target Price* in part *Foundations*)

2. The current price to provide the status of the negotiated price to date.

3. The auction's closing date and time to indicate how much time is remaining to position in the auction.

4. The current highest bidder.

5. The bid history (which reveals the auction's participants).

Now let's see the actual details such dates, times and prices.

1. The seller is **selleronebay** (fictitious).

2. The current price is **$33.50**

3. The auction close date is in **5** days at **10:52 PM** (eBay time)

4. The current high bidder is **ebaybidder** (fictitious).

5. The bid history lists **ebaybidder** having placed **3** bids, with **6** other bidders having each placed 1 bid.

Let's think out loud to see how this data might be used to formulate a strategic bidding plan. The data is in bold type. Don't worry about understanding the terminology, just focus on how the data is fashioned into a "view".

"Based on my research, the target price for this item is **$50.00**. Since there is a current price of **$33.50**, I have a bidding budget of $16.50. Since **ebaybidder** is active in this auction with **3** bids in the bid history and is currently the highest bidder, if I were to jump in now I may create a bidding war, which my $16.50 bidding budget may not be able to handle. Since I have **5** days until the auction closes, I have plenty of time to monitor the auction. So I'll let **ebaybidder** remain content that he is "winning" the auction. Of course, I don't know where **ebaybidder's** maximum proxy bid amount currently stands, but if I attempt to discover that amount now, with **5** days remaining, there will be more opportunity for **ebaybidder** to take the auction back again or for the other **6** bidders to take the auction." (Now for the bidding plan): "Considering this data, I'll enter the auction in the last 5 minutes of the auction if the current price hasn't exceeded the target price. Then I'll perform a Proxy Discovery Run and then lay in a snipe bid in the last seconds of the auction."

There are a number of possible variations to how this particular auction example could play out. However, the point here is to emphasis how you can make strategic bidding decisions based on available data. You want to fashion available data into a "view" to help you achieve your objective of winning the auction for the least expenditure possible. Also see Law #19: *Leverage the Bid History*

Notes:

Law 19: Leverage the Bid History

> **The Savvy Bidder never just glances at the bid history of an auction. Rather he digs deeper to glean valuable information his opponents don't see.**

Once you unlock its secrets, the bid history is a powerful tool to help you understand your opponents. Within it lies valuable information that will help you assess the players and the general direction of the auction. The key to unlocking the bid history is to understand how to extract more information than meets the eye. What we'll do in this law is discuss how to "see" into the bid history in such a way that you can better set your strategic direction for that auction.

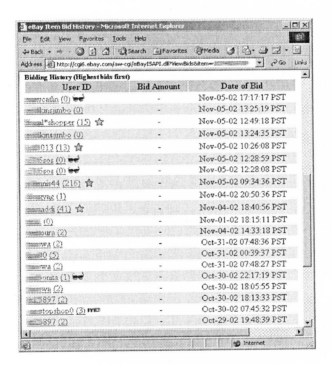

Figure 19 - An eBay screen portion showing a typical eBay auction bid history listing.

The Obvious

First let's list the obvious information revealed by the bid history. Then we'll delve into the not so obvious. By simply glancing at the bid history of an auction that has not yet closed, you clearly see the following information:

♦ The date and time, to the second, of each successful bid placed in the auction (Pacific Standard Time, PST)

♦ The eBay ID of each bidder. The presence of a bidder's ID indicates that she placed a bid at a particular date and time. A bidder's ID can appear multiple times, depending on how many bids she has placed in that auction thus far.

♦ The profile points of each bidder in that auction.

With just this surface information we glean the following:

♦ The frequency of bids by certain opponents is very important. If a particular bidder has made multiple bids in the auction, it often indicates one of the following:

  ♦ The bidder has been placing minimum bids and may be apprehensive about what to spend in the auction. The bidder often finds it necessary to keep taking back the auction by bidding higher each time.

  ♦ Several or many bids in an auction often indicate that the bidder has been adjusting his personal valuation as the auction's current price increased.

  ♦ When several or many bids occur one after another close in time, it usually indicates that the bidder performed a Proxy Discovery Run against an existing proxy bid.

♦ Since we can also see from the bid history the date and time when each of the bids were placed, we know when the auction began receiving activity. We can easily determine if the auction's activity began soon after opening, or ramped up during the mid point of the auction. This helps judge the market interest. The number of bids from unique bidders *may* also be an indication of the market demand for the item.

The Not So Obvious

Let's look at the information that isn't so obvious in the bid history:

♦ Of course, the actual bid amount of each bid is unknown during the auction.

♦ The bid history doesn't make it obvious which bidder has a proxy bid in place. But, once you know what to look for, the existence of a proxy bid becomes evident.

♦ The bid history will not forewarn you of specific snipers. However, if an opponent with a propensity to snipe auctions reveals himself during the auction, you may be able to pick up a sign of a potential sniper. At the very least you might be able to predict if the auction is "snipe worthy".

♦ The bid history, being a historical log of all bids accepted by the auction venue, won't tell you if the seller will cancel the auction. However, the bid history can provide clues that the auction is off track, which might prompt the seller to cancel the auction.

♦ The bid history doesn't make detecting fraud a sure bet. However, since bidder IDs and bid times are recorded you may be able to detect if a person is manipulating the auction.

Next we'll discuss what information in the bid history can be useful for strategic purposes. We'll start our discussion by first reordering the bid history.

Reordering the Bid History

Looking closely at a typical bid history list, we see that it is generally in reverse chronological order, that is, the more recent bids are higher in the list with the older bids being further down the list. Look even closer and you will see an occasional bid that is out of place in terms of its true chronological order. This is important because this indicates the current highest bidder.

So, while the list is generally in reverse chronological order, there are exceptions. By reordering the bid history, we are able to put all bids in order by the date the bids were placed.

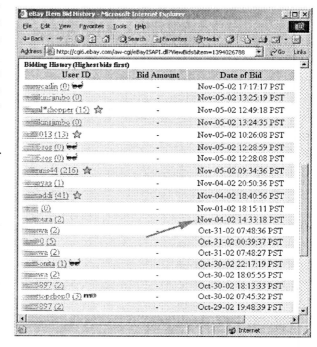

Figure 20 - An eBay screen portion showing a proxy bid in the Bid History.

Reordering the bid history is valuable when analyzing the bid history. The reordering process puts all bids into a chronological sequence by the date and time each bid was placed. The objective is to make the bid history easier to decipher. While you do not have to reorder the bid history, doing so may help for certain types of analysis.

The way I reorder a bid history list is to capture the bid history text into Microsoft Excel and then sort by date and time. To capture and reorder a bid history list, perform the following steps:

1. Select the auction bid history you want to capture.

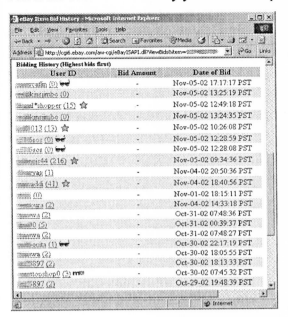

2. Using your mouse, highlight *just the list portion* of an auction's bid history screen. Do this by sweeping your mouse from the lower right of the history list up to the upper left of the list *while pressing the left mouse button*. Release the mouse button and copy the text using CTRL C (hold down the control key and press the C key). Avoid highlighting anything but the actual list.

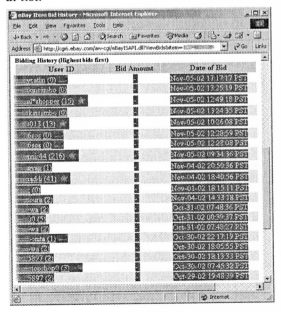

3. Start Excel and create a new blank worksheet. Paste the copied bid history list into the blank Excel worksheet using the "Special Paste" option under Excel's "Edit" menu. Make sure that you select "Text" from the options window as shown below. Also make sure you have selected the top left cell in Excel, which is cell A 1.

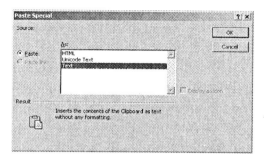

4. Now that the bid history text is pasted into Excel, you'll note that all of the text was pasted into one Excel column. Beginning with the next step, you'll separate the text into columns so you can sort the list.

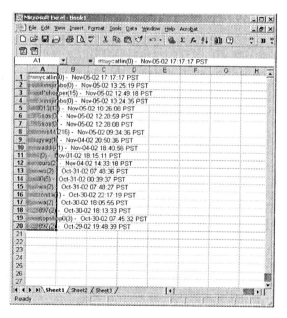

5. To convert the pasted text into columns select "Text to Columns" option under Excel's "Data" menu. Click "Next" on the first window. Then, in the second window, make sure to check the "Space" checkbox. Click next and then click the "Finish" button.

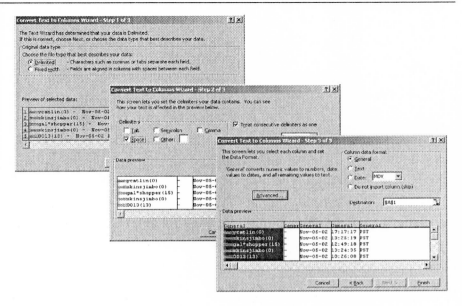

6. The text-to-column feature converted the bid history text into separate columns. This will allow you to sort the data.

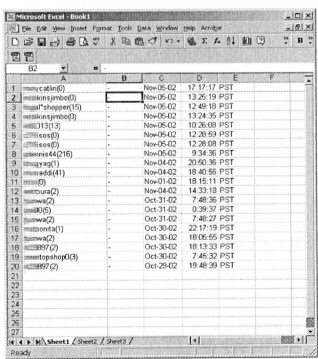

7. Select the "Sort" option under Excel's "Data" menu. Be sure to select column C (the bid date column) and column D (the bid time) as shown below. Leave the sort direction setting for column C on "Ascending" but change the sort direction setting for column D to "Descending". Click the "OK" button to perform the sort.

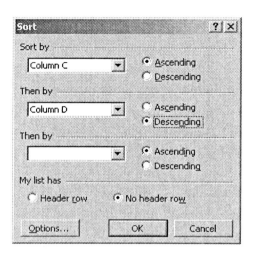

8. You now have a reordered bid history! Save your Excel worksheet and begin your analysis.

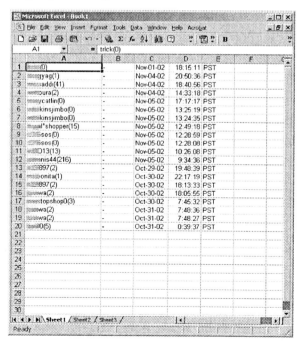

Whew! Now that we have the bid history list in Excel, let's see what information we can glean from it. We'll be alternating between our reordered bid history list and normal bid history lists, depending on what information we wish to glean.

Minimum Bidders

Looking through our sample reordered bid history list, we see that one bidder has bid several times but was outbid each time. Can we assume that this person is a minimum bidder? Can we surmise that such a bidder is likely to be easily defeated since he is obviously focused on the current price? In your own auctions, look for bidders that bid repeatedly but are always outbid – the more bids placed and outbid, the more likely the bidder is placing minimum bids. For more on this subject please see Law #8: *Don't Focus on the Current Price.*

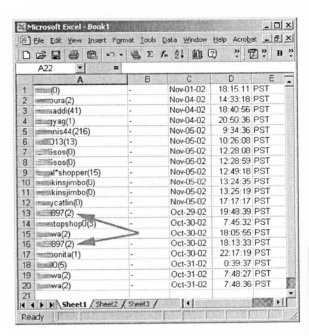

Figure 21 - The re-ordered bid history in the Excel spreadsheet showing a bidder having placed several minimum bids.

Determined Bidders

How do you know a determined bidder when you see one? Simply by looking at his bid activity you can often tell if a bidder is determined to win the auction. His member ID shows up in the bid history throughout the auction. He is often outbid, but is rarely discouraged. He repeatedly takes back the highest bidder position. Don't underestimate the competitive capabilities of the determined bidder. Such a bidder may even bid beyond the current market value of the item.

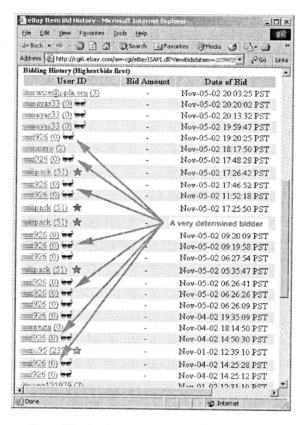

Figure 22 - An eBay screen portion showing a determined bidder in an auction's Bid History.

Proxy Bidders

Bidders who had placed a proxy bid are often easily identified in the bid history. You'll recognize proxy bids by the fact that it often took several bids before the proxy amount was outbid.

In Figure 23 you see a proxy bid that took several bids before it was exceeded. While you can't know the actual amount of the proxy bid until the auction ends, you can detect that this player is not a timid bidder. Bidders who use proxy bids are often aware of the auction item's market value and are not hesitant to spend up to the market value if necessary. They are often strong bidders because they do not get caught up into thinking they can win auctions on the cheap. When faced with an opponent who uses proxy bids don't underestimate his ability to win auctions.

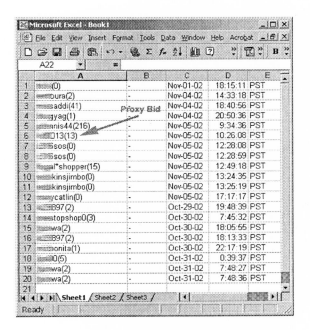

Figure 23 - The re-ordered bid history in the Excel spreadsheet showing a proxy bid.

Proxy Discovery Runs

As discussed in the chapter *Bidding Tactics*, we are aware of the objective of those who perform Proxy Discovery Runs. Such bidders are often trying to outbid another bidder who has a proxy bid in place and without bidding too far over that proxy bid. Once an opponent who made the Proxy Discovery Run is revealed, we can surmise that he relies on this bidding tactic. You may then decide that placing a stiff proxy bid in the auction yourself may not be a suitable bidding tactic. If, however, such a bidder continues to show a propensity for the Proxy Discovery Run, it may be possible to leverage that against him by placing a small proxy bid just prior to sniping the auction (if you choose to snipe the auction). In this case, the bidder may actually become so occupied with your small proxy bid that he runs out of time in the auction.

The Highest Bidder

You don't need a reordered bid history to determine which bidder is currently the highest bidder. The bid history provides that information by placing the current highest bidder at the top of the list.

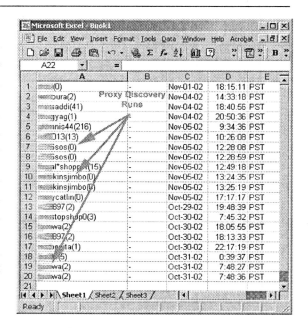

Figure 24 - The re-ordered bid history in the Excel spreadsheet showing several Proxy Discovery

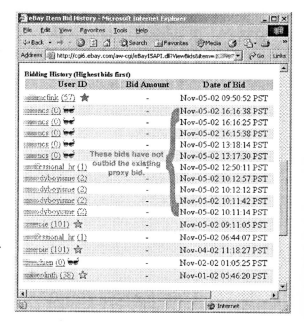

Figure 25 - An eBay screen portion of an auction's Bid History where several bids did not outbid an existing proxy bid.

If the current highest bidder had placed a proxy bid, we sure would like to know what the proxy bid amount was. Since this is not something we can know, we'll have to settle for getting a feeling of how significant the existing proxy bid might be. Figure 25 illustrates a situation where 3 bidders have been trying to outbid the current highest bidder for at least 6 hours. This is clear by the fact that there have been multiple bids *after* that of the current highest bidder. When you encounter a situation like this, you can quickly surmise that the bidder with the existing proxy bid may have placed a rather healthy proxy bid.

Bidding Wars

Getting in the middle of a bidding war can be nasty and costly. In a bidding war, two or more players are dueling it out, each trying to keep the highest bidder position. Often the bids of each are minimum or small proxy bids which test where the other's price pain point is without risking overpaying for the auction. Very serious bid warriors place strong proxy bids. In either case, the auction's current price escalates. You can spot a bidding war without reordering the bid history.

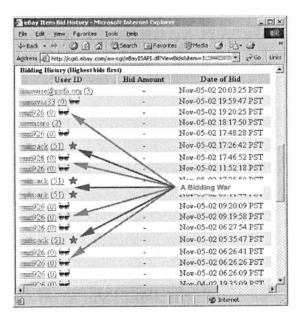

Figure 26 - An eBay screen portion of an auction's Bid History in which several bidders were engaged in a bidding war.

Detecting Shill Bidding

Shill bidding occurs when bids are placed with the intention of pulling up the auction's current price by a bidder who has no intention of winning the auction. At one time, shill bidders would simply retract a bid that held the highest bidder seat near the close of the auction. That would leave the second highest bidder the winner. But these days bid retractions have become synonymous with shill bidding. Shill bidders now take the less obvious route by repeatedly placing proxy bids that are relatively easy to outbid. They usually do not place minimum bids because bids at the minimum bid increment do not raise the auction's current price as quickly as a relatively small proxy bid.

With the bid history is its reordered state, you can better detect multiple proxy bids by a single bidder. If a bidder has repeatedly bid throughout the auction, but discontinued bidding near the end the auction, could this indicate shill bidding? Using the bid history, you are able to spot bidding patterns to help identify situations that may be suspicious.

It is not easy to detect shill bidding simply using the bid history. There are other indications that must be considered. However, an extensive probing of online auction fraud is outside the scope of this book. Suffice it to say that the bid history *may* provide an early warning of shill bidding. Please see Law #40: *Catch Fraud Before It Catches You* for a brief look into the online auction fraud subject.

Spotting Bidding Patterns

Even though we can't see the actual bid amounts during a running auction, we can detect bidding tactics. We can glean if a particular bidder seems to prefer minimum bids or proxy bids. We can see if a bidder prefers to bid early or late in the auction or if she performs Proxy Discovery Runs. These are all bidding tactics.

Since we can easily review the bid history of auctions that have closed, we can investigate specific opponents to see if they used similar bidding tactics in those auctions. It is important that you do not assume a specific bidder favors a certain bidding tactic simply by looking at his bidding activity in one auction. Rather you want to investigate multiple auctions.

Discerning the patterns of your opponents is a worthwhile endeavor. Of course, remember that other bidders can run the same pattern analysis on you. Please see Law #31: *Leverage Bidding Habits* for more on this subject.

The Type of Bidder

Look at the bid history of any auction that has received bids and you will likely see a wide range of profile points among the bidders. You'll see plenty of zero point eBay members and will often run across eBay members with profile points in the thousands. As discussed in Law #24: *Never Underestimate Your Opponents*, do not mislead yourself by thinking that zero point members are inept at winning auctions. In fact, zero point, or very low point members are often very determined to win. Such bidders may not have highly tuned bidding skills, but they are often tenacious about holding onto the highest bidder position, believing that being the highest bidder is "winning" the auction.

High point members are usually skilled at winning auctions, but skilled bidders often do not need to win a particular auction. Because they move around the auction venue they frequently uncover better auction candidates. In fact, high profile members may actually be sellers mining for bargains in their quest of the buy-low-sell-high formula. Follow a member's trail to help you determine if he is predominantly a seller.

The bid history serves to illustrate the mixture of bidders in the auction. The mixture has no meaning in terms of your bidding strategy in the auction. In other words, do not assume such things as:

♦ "Since all of the bidders have very low profile counts, I can easily win this auction", or

♦ "Since all of the bidders have very high profile counts, I am going to have a rough time winning this auction", or

♦ "Since some of the bidders have very low profile counts, they will probably be weak bidders", and so on.

You would do well to not assume that a particular auction only attracts bidders of certain bidding skill levels. Also, avoid assigning any particular value to a bidder's profile point count. Please see Law #24: *Never Underestimate Your Opponents* and well as Law #35: *Respect "The Mark"*.

The Seller's Reserve

We have no way of knowing the amount of a seller's reserve price simply by looking at the bid history. If the seller does not disclose his reserve price in his auction listing, bidders are blinded with respect to the reserve. However, we can often tell if an auction is progressing slowly because of an undisclosed reserve. This is often evident by multiple bids that are obviously very low or minimum bids.

If you examine an auction's bid history after the seller's reserve has been met, you might see how the bidding dynamics in the auction have shifted. As discussed in the section *Bidding Tactics in Reserve Auctions* of the chapter *Bidding Tactics,* the bidders no longer have the seller's reserve price to contend with and bidding may become more active. You can use the bid history to help clarify if bidding dynamics have changed so that you can determine your own bidding tactics.

Gauging Activity

You can use the bid history as a way to assess activity and competitive jockeying within the auction. However, first scan the bid history to identify repeat bidders who are increasing the auction's bid count. You will often find that a particular auction is receiving the attention of just a few bidders. Look for Proxy Discovery Runs that increase the bid count rapidly. These bidding actions do not necessarily indicate that the bidders are highly competitive. They may be actively bidding in an auction, but their tactics are not necessarily competitive.

The Bid History As Feedback

With an understanding that the bid history is best utilized as a means to understand your opponents, it provides an excellent resource to examine once an auction has closed. It is helpful to review the bid history of every auction you win or lose. By doing so you can fine tune your ability to predict the behaviors of opponents in future auctions. Since you can never trust that opponents will behave consistently, it is wise to return to the auction to examine if your assumptions were close.

The thrill of online auctions is that no one can accurately predict who will do what. However, people will often adhere to a favorite pattern if it seems to work for them consistently. As a Savvy Bidder, your challenge is to do your best to understand the behaviors of your opponents so you can meet the challenges of your opponents.

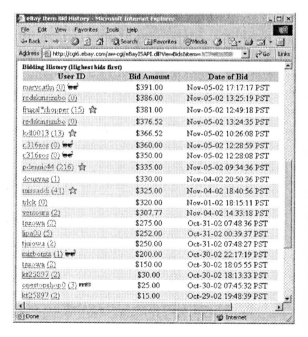

Figure 27 - An eBay screen portion showing the Bid History of a completed (closed) auction.

Fun With Charts

You can obtain some interesting information from the bid history by creating a chart using Excel as we discussed earlier in this law. Figure 28 is the bid history data from a closed auction which has been brought into an Excel spreadsheet. The date and time rows are each sorted in ascending order. Figure 29 shows an Excel chart that plots the bid amounts over the duration of the auction. Notice how the plot line dips in two places. These are bids that were outbid by an existing proxy. You can perform other types of analysis with charting such as bid activity, the activity by bidder and so on.

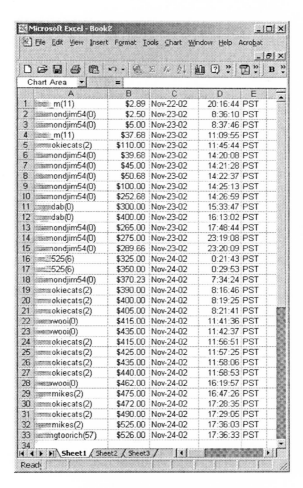

Figure 28 – The bid history data from a closed eBay auction placed into an Excel spreadsheet.

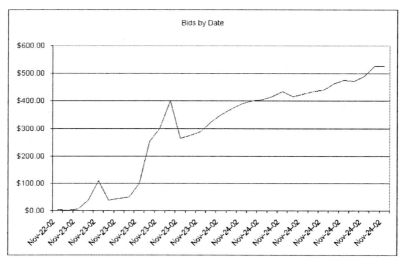

Figure 29 – A Microsoft Excel line chart showing how bid amounts increased during the auction. The peak in the line at Nov-23-02 was a $400.00 proxy bid (see Figure 28).

Keep an "Opponents List"

Since you are examining the bid histories of some or all of your auctions, you might wish to maintain a private list of opponents who have presented you with a competitive challenge. Of course, such a list is most valuable when you repeatedly encounter the same opponents who are interested in the same type of auctions as you are. For instance, if you are an avid comic book collector and scout eBay for issues, you are likely to encounter certain opponents within that circle. By keeping an "Opponents List" you can record private notes concerning the attributes you have observed of certain bidders from one auction to the next.

Conclusion

Analyzing the bid history helps you predict if a particular opponent may be formidable. While you must never underestimate the competitive capability of any opponent, you may be able to leverage weak bidding skills to your advantage. Remember that a zero or low profile count does not necessary indicate weak bidding skills – it's actual performance that matters. When faced with apparently strong opponents, you can alter your own bidding tactics to not encourage such opponents to take an even stronger stance in the auction. Remember that an opponent with high profile points may even perform poorly.

Yes, much of the information you extract from the bid history is speculative. You must remain fully aware that the predictions you make based on the bid history may not actually come to pass. The bid history is designed to keep bidders guessing. However, analyzing the bid history is only a part of strategic bidding – a part that helps you determine who your opponents are and how to competitively deal with those opponents.

I can assure you of this; if you do not try to extract information from the bid history, you will forfeit a potentially valuable element of being a Savvy Bidder.

Also see Law #18: *Turn Data into Competitive Strength*

Notes:

Law 20: Bid Activity Does Not Necessarily Mean Value

The Savvy Bidder is not lulled into believing that an auction has a higher value simply based on the number of bids the auction has received. By looking deeper she often discovers that the bid count resulted from just a few bidders.

You've seen them, auctions that have high bid activity. At first glance, it seems to imply that the item is in high demand and that bidders are "fighting" over the item. But, this assumption might not be accurate – one must always look at the auction more closely. Consider some factors other than high demand that might contribute to high bid activity:

♦ Some sellers encourage bidding activity by listing an item that has a potentially strong market value by setting a low or very low First Bid price and perhaps with no reserve. This promotes bidding activity because of the stark contrast between the opening price and the potential market price. The fact that the auction has no reserve is appealing because the seller has not placed a price constraint on the auction. When I sell on eBay I often list items with an extremely low First Bid and no reserve because I know this helps create higher bid activity. This is simply tapping into people's desire to own an item of interest at the lowest possible price.

♦ When an item appeals to a large number of bidders yet is in short supply in the auction community, the seller has an opportunity to capitalize on the situation. Because demand is higher than the supply there is the possibility of more competition. This increases bid activity that in turn increases the current price.

♦ Bid activity itself promotes additional bidding. The fact that 30 bids from 30 unique bidders, for instance, have been placed on an item implies that it is desirable to own. This desirability is, in part, influenced by the desire that the bidders expressed in the form of bids. Bidders continuously outbid one another and new bidders enter the auction to get in on the action. Bidding activity typically creates yet more bidding activity. See Law #10: Bid Begets Bid.

♦ A single bidder may place multiple bids at the minimum bid increment in an effort to discover the current proxy bid of the highest bidder. The objective is to bid just over the current highest bidder's proxy bid and avoid placing a proxy bid that may be too high.

◆ And then there is the bidder who submits many small bids with the specific intention of making the auction look very busy. Such a bidder may think he is making a statement that he intends to win the auction, thus dissuading other bidders. This is clever, but is a poor tactic. Such bidding actually creates the potential of attracting even more competition because the increased bid count causes the auction to stand out in eBay's search results page – naturally a person interested in the item being auctioned is going to want to take a look at the auction.

◆ Bidding activity can be artificially induced by a shill bidder. A bidder who is in collusion with the seller (the shill bidder) places multiple bids with the intention of increasing the auction's apparent activity. The higher bid activity encourages yet more bid activity. Often the shill bidder doesn't even need to do much more than bolster the bid count and then simply disappear, having completed his devious mission.

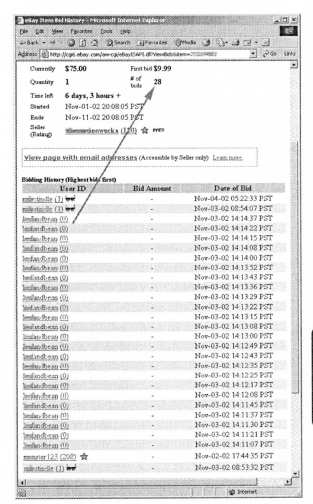

Figure 30 - An eBay screen portion of an auction's Bid History showing the effect of a single bidder placing multiple bids.

As can be seen by the above points, the number of bids placed in an auction does not necessarily mean that the item is actually worth more. Rather, the *perception* of value is often created by the very bidding activity itself. Since the only way to win the single-unit eBay auction is to bid a higher price than all others, the current price continuously escalates as bidders compete with one another. I have seen many auctions where the current price on a newly manufactured product that was readily available in the retail market actually escalated to a price *higher* on eBay. In addition to demand for the product, an important contributor to this situation was the intense bidding activity which itself helped create a higher perception of value.

Ok. You see how bidding activity does not necessarily mean that the item has a market value worthy of the bidding activity. How does this help you formulate bidding strategies?

- First, consider the possibility that your own participation in a highly active auction actually contributes to increasing the auction's bid activity, which of course, leads to a higher closing price. In effect, by your own participation, you may yourself pay a higher price should you win the auction. It is often best to watch the auction and only bid at a strategically opportune time.

- If there are one or two bidders whom you suspect are trying to discover other bidder's proxy bid with a series of multiple minimum bids (a Proxy Discovery Run), avoid giving them any chance to discover your proxy bid amount by not relying on proxy bidding tactics. Rather, stay out of the auction and perhaps participate in the final moments where there is not enough time to perform a Proxy Discovery Run. Of course, you may elect to snipe the auction if the current price has not exceeded the target price.

- If you suspect that the auction is being shilled it is best to stay out of the auction altogether, especially if there are other auctions for a comparable item. If you have very strong suspicion of shilling, report such to eBay's Safe Harbor. Watch the auction to its completion to confirm your suspicion of shilling. By watching suspect auctions you will develop observation skills that will help you detect fraud and manipulation in future auctions.

There are situations where the auction *does* justify high bid activity such as when items are in short supply or the item's real value greatly exceeds the current auction price. If you do decide to participate in such an auction remain determined to:

♦ Drop out of the auction if and when it becomes obvious that you will not win at or below your target price.

♦ Drop out of the auction if and when the auction's current price approaches the retail price if the item is new merchandise. You must be cognizant of factors such as condition, warranty, shipping costs, sales tax, seller reputation and the like to help you determine if another source of the product would be a wiser purchase than the auction item.

The number of bids in an auction does not necessarily indicate an item's market value. You must be aware of conditions that artificially create bidding activity such as a series of minimum increment bids or shill bidding. Participate if you feel that your bidding strategy can be effectively used to win the auction despite the activity and, of course, to win the auction at the lowest price.

Also see Law #10: *Bid Begets Bid*

Notes:

Law 21: Seller Ratings Can Mislead

The Savvy Bidder never allows a seller's feedback profile to influence perception of an item's value. The profile indicates only the seller's past performance – it does not indicate the quality of the item being offered at auction.

We tend to lend credibility to those who have earned credentials; a high profile rating on eBay is a credential since it is not easy to earn. You may think this a minor point, but consider the fact that such a seller's auction may attract more bidders, thereby increasing competition. In addition, you may find that you are willing to pay a higher price in an eBay auction due, in part, to a seller's high profile point count.

The issue here is not whether a seller will live up to his feedback rating – chances are he will. Rather the issue is whether or not a seller's feedback profile influences your perception of value in the item. We can surmise with some confidence that it will influence other bidder's perception of value. This is simply because people extend more trust to those with credentials.

Two scenarios could develop if you place emphasis on a seller's feedback profile in terms of value assessment:

1. You may be willing to bid a higher amount for an item being sold by a seller with a high profile count, or

2. You may be unwilling to pay a fair amount for an item being sold by a seller with a low profile count. This may also be true of your opponents in the auction.

In scenario one, since credibility is lent to the seller based on the positive experiences of past buyers, the item may appear to have a higher value than it actually has. I have, however, purchased merchandise from sellers with over 1,000 profile points, only to find that their merchandise and their service did not measure up to the value I had originally given them because of their rating.

In scenario two, if credibility is withheld from a seller due to low profile points, or a feedback with some negative entries (justified or not), this may lower a value assessment of the item. In fact, the seller may actually have an item up for auction that has very good value.

It is possible that, with scenario one, there may be more competition in the auction. (A seller does not reach 100 or 1,000 or 10,000 profile points without learning something about presentation.) Also a seller may have arrived at a point where, through experience, she can predict the auction's closing price for specific merchandise. As such, the seller lists with a very low opening bid and perhaps no reserve which encourages bidding activity. The end result is that the auction may become highly competitive for other reasons beside the seller's profile.

But you, a Savvy Bidder, can use the perceptions of a seller's feedback rating to your advantage. If the seller's feedback profile point count is low, you may elect to better research and communicate with the seller to assess your risks. In auctions being listed by sellers with high profile points, you may be able to work the auction using more shrewd bidding strategies as discussed throughout this book. Adjust your bidding tactics accordingly, considering a seller's feedback profile count. However, avoid letting a seller's profile count influence your perceived value of the auction item itself.

Please understand that I am not suggesting that you enter into an auction ignoring a feedback profile riddled with negative comments. Use discretion always. But, consider that a large number of potential bidders may refrain from such a seller's auction which may reduce the auction's activity, thereby presenting you with less competition. If a seller's feedback is truly shocking, then don't bid in that seller's auction. However, if the item is attractive to you and you want to bid, consider using the protective measures available to you. For instance, use an escrow service if possible. Pay with your major credit card which almost always has a limit of liability for you. E-mail the seller and express your concern about her profile and see what develops – much is revealed about a person by what they write and how they write it.

Negative Feedback Can Be Removed

There is another factor you must take into consideration concerning a seller's feedback profile. It is possible for a seller to get negative feedback entries removed by leveraging a deficiency in the mediation procedures of Square Trade (http://www.squaretrade.com), a fee-based online merchant dispute resolution service. When a dispute over a transaction arises that involves a Square Trade member, Square Trade has a procedure that is designed to facilitate communication between the trading partners so as to work toward a resolution. While it is not within the scope of this book to discuss Square Trade at length, I have noticed a rising occurrence of sellers contesting negative feedback entries under the Square Trade procedures, and getting those negative feedback entries removed under certain circumstances.

When a person purchases from a Square Trade member and is unable to resolve a dispute with the seller, the buyer has the option of contacting Square Trade to seek resolution assistance. Square Trade then contacts the seller to begin the process. As one would expect if a seller, who is a member of Square Trade, has an issue with a buyer the seller can begin a dispute process as well. A seller may feel that a negative entry was placed in her profile unfairly by the buyer and, for a $20.00 fee, can begin a Square Trade review. Square Trade will then notify the other party in the transaction to seek a reply. If the submitter of the negative feedback replies and reaffirms his original feedback the feedback is normally let stand as originally submitted (unless the feedback entry violates eBay policy). However, if a reply is not forthcoming from the buyer after 14 days, the negative feedback is reviewed by Square Trade who may recommend to eBay that the contested feedback be removed. This permits a seller to contest negative feedback entries with a chance of some entries being removed simply because the trading partner did not respond to Square Trade's inquiry.

Under normal circumstances the Square Trade dispute procedure has undoubtedly helped many resolve disputes that might have otherwise ended in an unresolved situation. However, a large percentage of eBay buyers do not believe that a negative feedback entry must be defended once submitted. This, I believe, stems from being drilled with the message that feedback is not retractable once submitted (unless the feedback violates eBay policy). This strict non-removal stance has been a eBay mainstay since its beginning. Given this, if a seller who is a Square Trade member were to dispute some of all negative feedback entries as a matter of course, there will be a percentage of buyers who will not participate in the feedback dispute process, either because they do not believe they need to defend feedback they felt justified to give or simply do not want to take the time. Those who fail to reply to Square Trade's notification give tacit license for Square Trade system to review and possibly recommend to eBay to clean up the seller's record for the transaction. As you might be able to glean from the discussion of this subject, a Square Trade member could actually have a poorer track record than his or her feedback profile indicates.

As an aside, when purchasing from a Square Trade member, you are tacitly accepting a set of procedures concerning any disputes with that seller. I have not seen any seller yet who states in his auction listing that the winning bidder will be expected to abide by Square Trade procedures in the event of a dispute. It seems that Square Trade members assume everyone just knows that this is the case. This then becomes an implied contract. If you fail to participate in any procedures of this implied contract, the Square Trade system may proceed in favor of its member. Of course, should you require the services and intervention of Square Trade concerning a trading partner who is a Square Trade member, this implied contract can serve you well.

Also see Law #7: *Assess the Seller*

Notes:

Law 22: Expect the Unexpected

The Savvy Bidder is aware that online auctions are full of unknowns. She expects anything and anticipates everything.

The premise of this law is simple – you cannot know for sure what others will do in auctions so you must expect the unexpected. Be prepared for what you cannot predict. Conserve some of your bidding budget for periods of heavy bidding activity. Plan to snipe the auction if that will be an appropriate bidding tactic. Use stealth bidding tactics in an effort to get your opponents to expose their intentions. As appropriate, drive in heavy bids to suppress timid bidders. Bid early or late depending on probable market interest in the auction. Don't be current price focused – that will serve to blindly drag you along with an escalating current price. Research strong opponents in an effort to learn their habits and try to preempt those bidding habits through your own bids. Don't underestimate the tenaciousness of zero-point bidders (see Law #35, *Respect the Mark.*)

Expect to make errors in judgment from time to time. They will result because you do not have access to the kind of information that would give you a definitive competitive advantage – that's the nature of the online auction game. However, if you make an effort to anticipate the events of your auctions and gather information, you will make fewer judgment errors.

Keep in mind that your opponents will also make errors in judgment because they also lack important information. What you want is for your opponents to make big errors in judgment concerning you. Feed in a few minimum bids to help your opponents see you as a non-threat. Place a few seemingly irrational bids (conserving your bidding budget of course) to entice your opponents to believe that you do not know what you are doing. Conserve aggressive bids for the critical points of the auction. Show no pattern so that those opponents who research your recent auction activity are more likely to misjudge you.

Above all, expect that there will be other savvy bidders who will be strong opponents. Never underestimate any opponent regardless of apparent talent or lack of talent. Always expect the unexpected.

Also see Law #17: *See the Unseen*

Notes:

Law 23: Examine What Motivates Your Opponents

> The Savvy Bidder is perceptive about her opponents. She
> watches their actions, analyzes their moves and tries to assess
> their objectives. When she believes she sees their perspective,
> she carries out her bidding plan with new insight.

Single-unit auctions are based on competition. It is competition that causes a continual increase in the price of the item being auctioned. This works as long as there are active bidders. From the perspective of typical bidders, decisions are made throughout the auction based on the actions of the other bidders. Bidders try to outbid another, and the cycle continues until one person demonstrates that he is willing to pay more than anyone else or the auction closes without a winning bidder. For the typical bidder, bid decisions are based on perceived value in relation to the current price.

When a bid is placed, you can't know for sure what motivated the bidder. You don't know what amount he is ultimately be willing to pay. All that is clearly evident is that a bidder is willing, at one particular moment in time, to bid a certain amount. However, the idea is to be perceptive about *why* they have bid. To illustrate this concept, consider just a few of many possible motivations:

- Perhaps an opponent bidder is buying to resell. To help determine this look up the bidder's current and recent auctions. Review both what they have bid on and what they have sold and are currently listing. Are they bidding on similar items to that which they sell in their auctions? If so, it is likely that this bidder has a price limit to ensure a profit should the item be resold at auction. By being perceptive, you can think like this buy-for-resale bidder and deal with his bidding accordingly.

- Review the bid history of the subject auction. Is a particular bidder continuously taking back the highest bidder seat? If so, perhaps the bidder really desires to own the item, perhaps to round out an existing collection. What would you do if you discovered a great article that would add value to your prized collection? You might be eager to win the auction even if it costs a bit more than you would like. Keep in mind that the perceived value of an item can be greater when it is combined with other items.

What do you make of the bidder who placed a bid at the seller's First Bid price, yet hasn't bid since? If you were "auction surfing" and came across an auction with a $10.00 First Bid price on an item you are interested in owning with a worth of potentially $100.00 or even $500.00, would you start the bidding? Your response might be that you would if you needed or wanted the item or intended to resell it at a profit. Yet, it seems somewhat arcane to bid in an auction at an amount that affords you very little chance of winning the auction. So, why would one place an opening bid on an item with a potentially much higher closing price than the First Bid? Considering this may help reveal what is motivating an early bidder. To illustrate:

♦ Perhaps the bidder has placed this auction on her watch list. The *My eBay* page reminds the bidder of an auction of interest. Also, the bidder receives e-mails from eBay as other bidders place their bids in the auction. An early small bid triggers eBay reminder functions to facilitate tracking the auction.

♦ Perhaps the bidder is letting his presence be known in the hopes that other bidders recognize him as an aggressive bidder with whom they should not compete.

♦ It may be possible that the bidder hopes that the auction will be a failure and that the seller will offer to sell privately at the low bid amount out of frustration (even though this is against eBay policy).

Using the bid history, you can see when an opponent participated, but the bid history does not make it clear as to *why* the opponent bid as he did. But you want to try to understand why. The reality is that we will seldom truly understand what motivates individual bidders other than the obvious explanation of "because they want to purchase the item". However, if you limit your understanding to this simple explanation you are likely to miss signs and signals that will help you time your bids more strategically.

Take a football game. Football games are won in part by one team outmaneuvering the other. By blocking better, by out running and outsmarting the other team, one team wins. To be most effective in implementing a winning strategy, each team makes a concerted effort to understand and prepare for the other team's strategy. This is true even though the team can't know for sure the game plays of the other team. Football games are won not by brawn alone, but by implementing a strategy that is carried out while making certain assumptions about the other team's strategy and capability. The objective therefore is to make the best possible assessment concerning the motives of your opponents. This will help you fine tune and implement your own winning strategy.

Notes:

Law 24: Never Underestimate Your Opponents

The Savvy Bidder knows the risks of judging the competitive capabilities of his opponents by their feedback profile rating alone.

Throughout your travels on eBay you will see a wide variety of member profile feedback ratings. Each eBay member has a feedback rating in parentheses to the right of his member ID. For instance the member ID **ebaybidder(128)** (a fictitious ID) has a profile rating of 128. You'll see plenty of zero ratings and even ratings in the thousands.

A natural reaction when you see a zero or very low rating is to assume that the ID owner is new to eBay. In fact, this may not be true. It's eBay's policy to start a feedback profile rating at zero for each new membership ID. At the time of this writing, eBay's policy allows members to change their membership ID after 30 days. Also, in an effort to eliminate the use of e-mail addresses, eBay has been requiring existing membership IDs to be non-email addresses. These are just two examples of situations that result in a new membership ID. These alone should convince you that the person behind a membership ID with a zero rating could be a very competitive eBay bidder, just with a new membership ID. If you assume that a member with a zero rating is a weak opponent, you may be in for a surprise. Please see Law #35: Respect "The Mark".

Turning our attention to high rating member IDs, it is important to note that such persons are not necessarily strong opponents. While it is natural to assume that members with high ratings are more skilled in bidding, they may actually be more interested in winning auctions at a low closing price for resale purposes. Such members are resellers and seek to win auctions at a price that facilitates a profit margin.

There are many eBay members who comb running auctions looking for bargains in an effort to buy low so that they can re-sell at a profit. There are still bargains on eBay, even though they are getting harder to locate. Bargains are often found among sellers who do not know the value of the item they have put up for auction. Often a seller will create a listing title with keywords badly misspelled. To illustrate this try running a search for the keywords "camra" and "cammera" (without the quotes). The last time I ran search on these misspelled keywords I found 128 auctions for "camra" and 17 auctions for "cammera". These poor souls meant "camera" (172,829 auctions). Bargain hunters check all the variations of key words (hint, hint). At any rate, a member with a high profile count could very well be a seller looking to snag auctions at low closing prices. Such bidders may not be strong competitors in auctions that reach the current market value because a good profit margin would no longer be possible.

For competitive purposes never put stock in the profile rating of any eBay member. As mentioned, a zero or low rating may provide no indication of the person's actual online auction experience. It is wise to never underestimate your opponents regardless of what their feedback profile rating seems to imply. Treat all opponents as if they have the potential to be highly competitive. Keep in mind that you cannot know for sure what motivates an opponent to bid. She may desperately need an item to complete her collection in which case the item may have a much higher value to her personally than it does in the current market. She may recognize a future resale value that would exceed even what the eBay market is currently willing to pay. She may simply really want the item for no apparent reason. Since you cannot know the perceived value of another, assume that all opponents will be highly motivated to purchase an auction item.

This law serves to remind to never judge an opponent by his feedback profile alone. If you do you risk misleading yourself into either underestimating some opponents and overestimating others. In fact, I personally disregard the profile ratings of all opponents except the seller of the auction (more on that in Law #7: *Assess the Seller*). I have not yet found a reliable correlation between a person's bidding skills and his profile rating. However, as discussed in Law #34: *Protect Your Feedback Rating*, you want opponents to try to size you up based on your profile points.

And finally you must expect competition in the auction. Expecting competition reminds you to preserve a portion of your bidding budget for those junctures where your money will best serve you in the auction. Expecting competition will help you remain vigilant to the bidding tactics of those active in the auction and others who may enter the auction. By preserving your bidding budget you are able to deploy stealth bidding tactics as the need arises.

Also see laws *#35: Respect "The Mark"* and *#34: Protect Your Feedback Rating*

Notes:

Law 25: Keep Your Opponents Off Guard

The Savvy Bidder bids when no one expects him to bid and refrains from bidding when he is expected to bid. The Savvy Bidder keeps 'em worried and off guard.

The premise of this law is to deliberately vary your bidding tactics from auction-to-auction and within an auction itself. This helps keep opponents off their guard by varying your bidding style. The strategy is to have no discernible pattern that could be used to anticipate your moves.

Let's review some typical patterns and how opponents may react to them:

♦ When you immediately take back the highest bidder seat if another outbids you, you demonstrate a propensity to react in a certain way. This makes you appear predictable. An observant opponent could use this against you by placing minimum bids, expecting you to reciprocate thereby exposing your interest in the auction.

♦ You always bid with your favorite cents such as 1 or 3 cent values. Such a favorite bidding pattern can easily be discovered by opponents who take the time to research your bidding activity in recently closed auctions in which you have participated (even if you did not win those auctions).

♦ You always snipe your auctions. There's not much anyone can do about it in an auction you intend to snipe, but you could become known as one who prefers snipe bidding. Even if previous snipe bids did not win the target auction your bid, as logged into the bid history of that auction, indicates that you attempted a snipe bid. Observant opponents may be ready for you if they think you have an interest in the item.

The key to keeping your opponents off guard is to not develop bidding patterns. Following are a few examples:

♦ Bid when you are ready according to your bidding plan, not in response to an event during the auction, such as being outbid by an opponent.

♦ When you are outbid, hold off to give the appearance that an opponent's bid knocked you out of the auction. See Law *#28: Show No Interest.* Resume participation in the auction only when the timing is right per your bidding plan.

◆ Avoid a favorite cents value in your bids. In fact, avoid cents in your bids entirely except for tactical bidding. (See *Bidding Tactics with Cents* in part *Tactics and Techniques*.)

◆ Avoid minimum bids unless you have a specific tactical purpose for placing them. A minimum bid is equal to the minimum required bid increment. For instance if an eBay auction's current price is $250.00, the required bid would be $255.00. By bidding at the minimum required bid you demonstrate a tendency to follow the current price. In other words your personal valuation is tracking the current price. Of lesser consequence, you demonstrate that you are easily led by the eBay bidding sequence that defaults a new bid to the minimum required bid increment.

◆ Open the auction at the First Bid amount. Give other bidders cause to ponder why you would waste your time on an auction you probably couldn't win with such a low bid. Let them know you are aware of the auction and that you intend to participate. If some of the bidders in the auction know you and know you are good at eBay auction bidding, they may feel intimidated by your presence.

Be a stealth bidder by varying your bidding pattern. This applies to the amount of your bids as well as how and when you bid. Keep opponents off guard by making it difficult for them to predict your bidding tactics. Meanwhile, always try to understand the bidding patterns of your opponents.

Also see laws *#31: Leverage Bidding Habits*, *#29: Be Unpredictable in Your Bid Amounts* and *#28: Show No Interest*

Notes:

Law 26: Use Deception to Confuse Your Opponents

The Savvy Bidder knows that competitive deception is often useful. She uses it to help her opponents feel unconcerned about her participation while working to gain a winning position in the auction.

In the context of competitive bidding in online auctions, using deception means that your bidding actions (or lack of) can serve to throw your opponents off. In other words, try and cause your opponents to *not* properly respond to your bidding actions. I am are speaking of competitive deception here, not fraudulent deception. Deceptive bidding does not mean that you violate any of the rules of the auction venue (or any law external to the auction venue) or take an unfair advantage of any party in the auction. See Law #43: *Don't Break the Rules*.

Examples of deceptive bidding are:

♦ Placing a minimum bid is a way to imply that you are an unsure bidder – unsure bidders are not normally regarded as competitive.

♦ You do not quickly respond if another outbids a proxy that you had placed. If you are still capable of winning the auction within your bidding budget, not responding too soon implies, for a while, that the auction has actually exceeded your ability and interest to win it. This may also help quiet competition in the auction.

♦ You may elect to make a short Proxy Discovery Run (see part *Bidding Tactics and Techniques*). Your objective is to imply that you are following another bidder's valuation. Opponents may regard you as one who does not know the potential market value of the item and thus not a strong competitive bidder.

♦ In an undisclosed reserve auction, a few minimum bids may make you appear as a bidder who does not know the seller's reserve price. Of course, you have e-mailed and asked the seller what her reserve price is. If it is provided you, your tactic is to bid giving the appearance that you don't know the reservse. See part *Bidding Tactics and Techniques* for more about bidding in reserve auctions.

♦ *Not* bidding is a form of deception, especially if you have previously bid in the auction. By refraining from bidding, you imply that you are no longer interested or the auction or it has exceeded your personal valuation.

Deceptive bidding tactics can help your opponents disregard you as a competitive threat or to take the wrong course of action in response to your bidding actions. To accomplish this, you take bidding actions that do not appear to be competitively strong. Yet, those actions provide you with benefits in your effort to position for the win. Of course your bidding actions must always remain within the rules of the auction venue and the laws external to the auction venue.

Also see laws *#43: Don't Break the Rules* and *#27: The FUD Factor*

Notes:

Law 27: The FUD Factor

The Savvy Bidder creates fear, uncertainly and doubt in the minds of her opponents to shape how they respond to her bidding actions.

FUD is an acronym for fear, uncertainty and doubt. Fear is elicited when your opponents become concerned they will lose the auction to you. Uncertainty is raised when your opponents are unsure how to compete with you. Doubt surfaces when your opponents have lost confidence in their own ability to win a particular auction given your participation.

Fear

When you participate in an auction, your opponents will either regard your participation as inconsequential or what they will have to contend with. At times, you will want your opponents to fear your participation. At other times, you will want them to pay you no mind. Which stance you wish your opponents to adopt will depend on your tactical objective at the time.

An eBay member with a 1,000 point profile appears to be better at the auction game than a member with 10 profile points. This may not actually be true, but it's often the perception. In addition to your profile points, opponent bidders can explore your recent auction activity and get a sense of how aggressive a bidder you have been. They can discover what bidding methods you seem to favor, i.e., minimum bidding, proxy bidding, sniping, or other. Just a strong profile point rating alone can cause your opponents to fear your participation. When opponents research you, they can glean information about you that may cause them to worry about competing against you.

You can also cause opponents to fear your participation by selecting appropriate bidding tactics during the auction. You may want your opponents to believe that they cannot win the auction unless they exceed what they are willing to pay. Most bidders will make an effort to avoid overpaying and indeed may get caught up trying to save as much money as possible. There are several bidding tactics that might help create this overpayment fear. One is to place a strong proxy bid, but one that conserves your bidding budget. Another tactic, a double proxy bid, implies that you are a highly motivated bidder. (But it may also imply that you are an uncertain bidder.) Bear in mind that minimum bids do not normally solicit fear. Minimum bids imply that you are uncertain of what you are willing to pay for the auction and that you are a cautious bidder. Minimum bids are easily overcome and may draw you into bidding war. You want your opponents to fear taking you on as a competitive bidder, not play cat and mouse with you.

Alternately, being feared as a strong opponent is not always in your best interest. Fear is not always something you want to create since that could lead an opponent to become too aggressive with his bidding. Keep in mind that, during mid auction, most bidders will assume that bidding a higher amount than anyone else is the road to winning the auction. When a very determined opponent considers you a strong competitor, the result may be that he places a high proxy bid in an effort to compete against your bidding. Also, it is possible for an opponent to simply place a proxy bid at the maximum he is willing to pay for the auction and let luck take it from there – a simple way of dealing with competition. In this case, the bidder takes little notice of your bidding, or anyone else's for that matter.

If you feel that your participation in an auction might create a highly competitive reaction among your opponents, consider placing several minimum bids. When those minimum bids are outbid, do not respond right away. Ideally, opponents will consider you a weak bidder or, at least, a bidder who is not going to pose a competitive challenge in the auction. This is one way to *not* create fear of your participation. Of course, when you are ready, bid in the auction to win it.

When appropriate look for opportunities to create fear of your participation in an effort to stifle your opponent's competitive strength. Your objective is to get opponents to believe they cannot win the auction within their price comfort. When appropriate, appear to be a weak bidder to help your opponents not reciprocate strongly. Each auction will be different so select bidding tactics appropriate to the auction.

Uncertainty

A great many participants in single-unit eBay auctions feel uncertain that they will win an auction in which they participate. This is because no one can know for sure what any present or future participant is ultimately willing to pay to win the auction. In addition, no participant of single-unit auctions can view the dollar amounts of previously placed bids while the auction is running. The single-unit eBay auction is based almost entirely on uncertainty induced by a lack of information.

In theory, this uncertainly is what drives up the auction's closing price. The premise is that a participant who is highly motivated to purchase the item will use his money to compensate for the unknown elements in the auction. In practice, it doesn't always play out that way. Many participants in single-unit eBay auctions make a concerted effort to place the smallest possible bid to compensate for the lack of knowledge of the competition, i.e., they place "safe bids". But such safe bids are also valuable to the auction process, so the auction venue and sellers gain from that practice as well.

You can actually augment the uncertainty inherent in single-unit auctions by not taking certain actions that may otherwise bring a level of certainty to the auction. You'll want to avoid patterns in your bidding methods (see Law #29: *Be Unpredictable in Your Bid Amounts*). This makes it harder for your opponents to predict what action you will take in the auction. Another way to perpetuate uncertainty is to bid when you are not expected to bid and not bid when it seems that you should.

In terms of having access to information such as bid amounts, you have no special advantage over your opponents. However, as a Savvy Bidder you take the time to glean information concerning the auction's landscape and make an effort to deduce the probable actions of your opponents. You enter each auction with the target price, bringing a level of personal certainty to the auction. By managing your bidding budget, you plan for uncertainties as new participants enter the auction, including snipe bidders. Such planning often provides a competitive edge that others simply do not have.

Doubt

There is an overriding shadow of doubt that most bidders have pertaining to their chances of winning auctions. This doubt is heightened when a bidder makes little or no effort to determine the probable closing price of the auction based on recently closed auctions for the same or comparable auction item. This interferes with a person's ability to be competitive because he does not have a reliable price guide.

The Savvy Bidder prefers that all of his opponents in an auction doubt their ability to win the auction. Doubt keeps opponents apprehensive. It causes bidders to exercise care to avoid overspending. Of course the most common way to avoid overspending in an auction is to bid low. Bidding low does not usually serve to control the auction.

You may be able to accentuate doubt in your opponents by utilizing certain bidding tactics. The double proxy bid tactic might serve to imply that you are a very determined bidder with a higher personal valuation than the opponent. A high proxy early in an auction might serve to set the stage for opponents to "get serious or get out" (but a high proxy may also present a competitive target as discussed in part *Bidding Tactics and Techniques*). If you are an avid snipe bidder, any opponent bidder who takes the time to investigate your bid activity in recently closed auctions will see that you are quite capable of snipe bidding the current auction as well. Let your past bidding activity help create doubt. What's one way to get researched by your opponents? Get your membership ID on the auction's bid history list with a simple minimum bid.

Consider the FUD factor when you select your bidding tactics. FUD often causes timid bidders to make irrational choices and interferes with their ability to be competitive. It's a powerful addition to your competitive arsenal.

A final word on this subject; use care to not yourself fall victim to the FUD created by your opponents. You will encounter other savvy bidders and you will encounter irrational bidders – both, intentionally or not, may create fear, uncertainty and doubt in your mind.

Also see laws #26: *Use Deception to Confuse Your Opponents* and #29: *Be Unpredictable in Your Bid Amounts*

Notes:

Law 28: Show No Interest

> **The Savvy Bidder helps her opponents disregard her as a competitive threat by not quickly responding to their bidding. The Savvy Bidder takes the auction only when *she* is in the best position to do so.**

At traditional (non-Internet) auctions, there are physical attendees. Each can safely assume that all present are potential bidders for at least one item being auctioned. Not only can the demeanor of the attendees be observed, but also the number of attendees. This provides visual feedback of the potential competition that exists. Of course, the actual bidding by the attendees is what really matters.

In an eBay auction each interested person is completely anonymous until they actually place a bid. I always remind myself that there could be several or even hundreds of interested persons reviewing the exact same eBay auction as I. Keeping this in mind helps me realize the importance of planning my strategic approach in the auction. (I love it when a seller adds a visit counter to her auction listing because it provides me an indication of the potential interest in the auction.)

Naturally auction participants consider a bid by another person an indication of interest in the auction. While bidders cannot see the actual bid amount, they do see the bidder's identification in the bid history list. Bidders typically assume that if a bidder placed one bid, there is a probability that she will bid again. Further, the more bids that a particular person places, it is assumed that she has a greater interest in winning the auction. It follows that if your membership ID is logged into the bid history after having placed a bid, *you* are a competitor. The more bids you place, the more competitive you are presumed to be.

If you have placed no bids in the auction, then you are not considered a competitor in the auction. In fact, you are not considered at all because there is no visible indication in the auction's bid history of your participation. But, if you had placed a bid several days ago in the auction, and have not bid since, then you may be presumed a lower competitive risk. For example, if you have placed only one bid on day one of a seven day auction, who's all that worried about you on day seven?

However, since a Savvy Bidder is generally not concerned about being the highest bidder until the auction closes, suppose you place a minimum bid early in the auction and simply fade away for a while. The notation of your membership ID in the bid history grows older each day of the auction. The conclusion you want your opponents to make are one or more of the following:

1. That bidder has forgotten about the auction.

2. That bidder is no longer interested in the auction.

3. That bidder is no longer a competitor.

Refraining from bidding unless it serves a specific tactical purpose helps keep the auction's closing price down. It also serves to discourage other bidders from entering into direct competition with you. You could stake a claim early in the auction, allow some time for your competitive threat to subside and then reenter the auction when you feel the time is right to do so.

Not responding when outbid may also serve you well by implying that you are no longer interested in the auction. In eBay auctions, if you do not bid you do not pose an immediate competitive threat (except if you have a proxy bid in place that has not been outbid). I employ this tactic frequently. After having taken a position in the auction, I rarely reciprocate to another's bid, even if she outbids me. I temporary show no interest to reduce the appearance that I will continue to be competitive. In other words, I prefer to position to win the auction, not create more competition. Of course, I take a strong position in the auction when I feel doing so will give me the greatest tactial advantage.

Also see Law #25: *Keep Your Opponents Off Guard*

Notes:

Law 29: Be Unpredictable in Your Bid Amounts

The Savvy Bidder is unpredictable in the amounts he bids. This makes it more difficult for opponents to identify favorite bid amounts and habits.

It is easy to review the bidding activity of selected opponents in the auction you are currently participating in. But eBay has provisions for its members to review the auction-related activity of its members in running auctions as well as recently closed auctions. Of course, your opponents can review your bid activity as well. Here's a brief list of the kind of information available concerning all eBay members:

♦ The bidder's current profile points.

♦ All of the bidder's feedback statements including positive, neutral and negative (unless the member has made his feedback private).

♦ The date and the exact time, to the second, of each bid placed in a particular auction (viewable whether or not the auction has closed).

♦ The exact amount, to the penny, of each bid placed in a particular auction (viewable immediately after the auction closes in which the bidder participated).

♦ Retracted bids.

Obviously, this information is important to help you assess the seller in a particular auction. However information about your opponent bidders can also be very helpful in understanding their bidding patterns. Let's focus on one particular aspect of opponent information – the bid amounts.

You will observe that a great many bidders tend to bid in whole dollar amounts. For instance, they tend to bid $10.00, $23.00 or $106.00. You may find 50 cent values such as $10.50 or $50.50, but there is a tendency to bid in nice, round, whole dollars.

However, more experienced bidders will use cents in their bids, for example $10.01, $45.03 or $123.51. These bidders realize that an auction can be won by just a single cent. More important, these bidders know that a very large number of players bid whole dollars. Thus, using cents in a bid can yield competitive benefits when used at the appropriate time.

You can review the bid history of closed auctions to determine if your opponent bidders have "bidding habits" such as a favorite cents value, if they use cents in their bids. If an opponent seems to favor 3 cents in their bids of previously closed auctions, this suggests that she may use cents in her bidding in the current auction as well. Of course, there is no assurance that an opponent will follow any past bidding patterns. But if you are alert to the possibility you are better prepared to contend with such a bidder.

It is easy to review the bid history of your opponents, including the values they may favor for their bids. You may be able to defeat a bidder simply by knowing his or her favorite cents value.

As you know, your opponents can also review *your* bidding activity, including any favorite cent amounts you may use. Therefore, *it is important to not have favorite bid amounts*. This is one trap you never want to fall into. Other bidders who take the time to learn more about you will see if you have a favorite bid cent amount and could use that knowledge to your disadvantage. For instance if you favor the 1 cent amount in your bidding, an alert opponent bidder could be prepared for you and bid $50.03 against your $50.01 bid, quite possibly winning the auction by this narrow margin. If your typical cents value is in the range from .01 to .03, an opponent bidder could easy outbid you with .11 or .33 cent values in his bid, assuming the same dollar amount. So, it is wise to never bid the same cent amount.

I avoid using cents in my bids at all during mid-auction. But when I do use cents, I vary the cent value from bid-to-bid and auction-to-auction as widely as possible. In one auction it might be .34, in another .59 and yet in another it might even be .91. I have two objectives for varying the use of cents in my bids:

1. I don't want to leave evidence of or imply any favorite cent amount that could be used against me, and

2. I vary my use of cents to make opponent bidders work a little harder. This gives opponent bidders who research me one more thing to keep track of and adjust to.

I have won several auctions solely by putting my cent value higher in my proxy bids near the end of the auction. In one auction, a sniper had bid $43.50 while I had a proxy bid amount of $43.51. (I determined the .51 by placing a proxy bid amount equal to 5 bid increments over the current price plus 1 cent. My opponent evidently set his bid at exactly 5 bid increments.) The 5 increments gave me good sniper protection margin and the 1 cent gave me additional protection (which paid off). In this case the sniper worked hard only to lose by one penny. This could have backfired on me if the sniper used the same logic, adding a penny on his bid for safe measure. In that case, the bid that reached the eBay computers first would have won the auction. I would have been safer had I bid $50.53.

Consider not using cents in your bids at all *during* the main period of the auction. Reserve the use of cents for your bidding in the last minutes of the auction and certainly use cents if you snipe the auction. The reason for this is that *you want other bidders to bid with whole dollar values and no cents.* By helping to perpetuate the whole value bid habits of your opponents, you have a higher chance of the cents being more effective in the final moments of the auction should you place a bid at that time.

Another important reason to avoid cents in bids during the auction's main period is because the minimum bid increment is thrown off the whole dollar value and the auction bid mechanism causes the cent value to be carried forward. The following example illustrates this:

1. The current price of the auction is $62.00.

2. The minimum bid increment is $1.00, so the next bidder will need to bid at least $63.00.

3. You or another bidder come along and bid $63.01 (for whatever reason).

4. The current price goes to $63.01.

5. The minimum bid increment is still $1.00 so the next bidder needs to bid at least $64.01 ($63.01 plus the $1.00 minimum bid increment). The cent value reminds all remaining bidders that 1 cent matters and could make a difference in the outcome of the auction.

What could you do to fix a situation where the current price has a cents value? That is, what bid could you place to get the current price back onto the whole dollar? A bid of $1.99 would put the current price to $65.00 – a nice round dollar amount. I call this an Adjustment Bid (see *The Adjustment Bid* in part *Bidding Tactics and Techniques*). Assuming no other bidder throws the current price back into having a cent amount, the use of cents in your final bidding may have a tactical benefit for you and may even win the auction. By the way, this price adjustment tactic will work whether or not you take the highest bidder seat. Since the cent values of your "adjustment" bids will vary (assuming you don't over use Adjustment Bid tactic), you do not expose yourself as having any particular bid habit involving cents.

Also avoid the use of cents in proxy bids that are placed during the main period of the auction. The use of cents in proxy bids provide very little competitive value. If you were to place a $250.03 proxy bid in an auction with a $200.00 current price, for instance, the .03 on your proxy bid does not afford you any more protection against other bids than a $250.00 proxy bid would. More important, should your proxy bid be outbid, the cents value in the proxy bid will cause the current price to have a cents value – which you want to avoid.

Avoid using cent values in your normal bidding during the auction; it throws the auction off of the more comfortable whole dollar value and spoils the benefit of using cents near the close of the auction. Consider an occasional Adjustment Bid to bring the current price back to a whole dollar value. Reserve cent values for last minute proxy bid and for snipe bids. If you favor .01 in your bids, especially if you snipe auctions, competing snipers who take the time to research you will glean your favorite cents value. Always randomly vary the cent values you use from one auction to another and during an auction (please see Law #31: *Leverage Bidding Habits*).

Also see laws *#31: Leverage Bidding Habits* and *#25: Keep Your Opponents Off Guard*

Notes:

Law 30: The Closing Price is Best Surmised Near the End

The Savvy Bidder knows that the closing price of an auction is best estimated near its close. She bids wisely so that she is able to remain in the competition during this critical period.

As you know single-unit eBay auctions have a predetermined end time. The practical reason for a precise end time is so that the auction process can be automated, eliminating human intervention. With millions of eBay auctions running, the requirement for human intervention would be impractical. However, a precise ending time also has the effect of requiring persons interested in the auction to act within the auction's period. Thus a predetermined ending time creates a sense of urgency.

Early in the auction's period this urgency doesn't play as important a role as it does near the end of the auction. Early in the auction there is still time for interested persons to watch to see what bidding activity occurs and to ponder actual participation. However as the end of the auction draws near, persons interested in purchasing the item must act if there is to be any possibility of winning. It is for this reason that active bidding often increases near an auction's end. Of course, there are exceptions such as when an item is in high demand. But, typically one can expect the activity of most auctions that receive active bidding to ramp up near the closing time.

Not only does bidding activity increase toward the auction's end but the seriousness of bids also tends to increase. Bidders move from watching the auction, and perhaps placing exploratory and safe bids, to thinking in terms of purchasing the item. Because the auction is nearing its end, bidders have less time to study the auction and must act in an effort to secure the right to make the purchase.

Perhaps another reason why bidding ramps up near an auction's close is that many resist being involved with a purchase situation for a protracted period of time. In a retail situation, the process of the purchase occurs in a relatively short period of time. While the anticipatory period may be long, when we are ready and able to buy we don't want lengthy delays. A shorter purchase period allows the buyer to realize the gratification of ownership sooner. Bidding near the close of an auction provides a similarly shortened purchase experience.

A high First Bid price in relation to the typical market price for an item introduces a delay in bidding activity. In this case, the seller has actually eliminated the prospect of cost saving so the incentive is not as great to bid early in the auction. Late in the auction's period, bidders are more likely to accept the fact that the item will have to be purchased at a price that is at least at the current price. Early bidding is also reduced when the seller introduces a reserve price in the auction and keeps that reserve hidden. Once again, there comes a point when bidders must accept the reserve price if they want to win the auction. By specifying a high First Bid and/or a reserve price, compared to the typical market price, the seller very often causes a delay of serious purchase efforts until later in the auction.

The probability of bidding activity increasing near an auction's close is important for the Savvy Bidder to understand. It reminds her to manage her bidding budget so that she still has some of her bidding budget remaining for the period of increased bidding activity. This does not necessarily mean that she should bid only near an auction's close; rather she is prepared for this active period in terms of her bidding budget – it is simply a matter of managing one's bidding budget to have staying power during the active period.

Consider this example of bidding budget management. You place a proxy bid early in the auction that comprises 25% of your bidding budget. This bid positions you in the auction, but you do not expect to win the auction with this proxy bid. Another 25% is then used during the active period later in the auction. With these bids you implement various bidding tactics to position in the auction, place Adjustment Bids, and so forth. Perhaps another 25% is reserved to snipe the auction if necessary or to place a double proxy bid just near the auction's close. So far you have used 75% of your total bidding budget. The remaining 25% is held in reserve in case you underestimated what the participants were actually willing to pay to win the auction. This is one way you can plan for increased bid activity near an auction's close and manage your bidding budget accordingly.

The probability of increased bidding activity late in the auction is one reason why a bid at the maximum you are willing to pay early in an auction's period is ill advised. By placing a maximum bid early, the bidder has used up her entire personal budget for the auction before opponents gear up with a serious intent to win the auction. The maximum bid leaves the bidder's personal valuation exposed to the competition and leaves no room for additional bidding (unless the bidder is willing to exceed her original allocation for the auction).

In contrast to bidding to one's maximum are minimum bids. Minimum bids early in the auction do very little in terms of gaining a position in the auction. Instead they simply erode one's money allocation for the auction and create a disadvantage when bidding ramps up later in the auction.

The Savvy Bidder understands that bid activity is likely to increase near an auction's close. Therefore she seeks to be prepared to bid competitively during that active period. At a more fundamental level, the Savvy Bidder does not view the auction process as a purchase situation. Rather, she understands that bidding is negotiating for a) the final price and b) to be positioned as the winner of the auction

– the purchase comes only after these two conditions are met. Therefore, she does not participate in an auction expecting to purchase quickly. By understanding why bid activity tends to increase near an auction's close, the Savvy Bidder is able to prepare to compete with opponents who think like retail buyers by maintaining a negotiation approach to the auction.

Notes:

Law 31: Leverage Bidding Habits

Except for tactical purposes, the Savvy Bidder reveals no bidding habit that might indicate to his opponents how to compete with him. But, he always looks for the bidding habits of his opponents and fully leverages those habits.

Remain aware that your opponents (and everyone else) can review your bidding activity on eBay. It is therefore easy to discern the type of bidder you are. For instance, if you favor sniping auctions, that will be obvious to others. If you have a favorite cent amount, that too will be obvious. If you are a minimum bidder, your frequent small bids will be easily spotted.

Your bidding habits can be used to preempt you in auctions where opponents have taken the time to investigate your recent bid activity. Understanding your bidding habits may give your opponents a competitive advantage. Therefore, it is wise to make an effort to vary your bidding actions.

So far we have been speaking in terms of habits that may be revealed across multiple auctions. However, there may be situations where you *want* to indicate a bidding pattern in a specific auction. For instance, you may elect to act like a minimum bidder early in an auction with the intention of letting your opponents regard you as an apprehensive bidder. The process might entail placing a minimum bid, being outbid, then placing another minimum bid, which is outbid again. Your strategy might be two-fold: 1) you want your opponents to regard you as a bidder who is easily outbid and 2) you are making an effort to ferret out those opponents who have a strong interest in the auction.

Of course, you have no intention of using this minimum bid tactic for the duration of the auction. As discussed in *Minimum Bidding Tactics* of part *Bidding Tactics and Techniques* you are aware that minimum bidding often has the effect of escalating the current price with little tactical gain. At some point you might deem it appropriate to shift your bidding tactic to the use of proxy bidding or hold and snipe the auction. This is just one example of using patterns in a specific auction to your competitive advantage.

It is far easier for your opponents to understand how you bid in multiple auctions than it is to understand your habits in a specific auction that is currently running. One reason for this is that your bidding patterns are less obvious in a running auction since the competitive situation is not yet completed. In auctions that have closed, your bidding activity becomes historical information that cannot be changed.

Your Opponent's Patterns

Just as your opponents can review your bid activity history, you can review theirs. In the review of your opponents bidding patterns look for habits. Here are a few habits to look for:

- The bidder has a favorite cents value, perhaps ending his bids using 3 cents. Bidders who win auctions often attribute their success to the use of key cent values, which do indeed play a role in winning auctions.

Bidding History (Highest bids first)		
User ID	Bid Amount	D
und@aol.com (48) ☆	$55.05	Sep-02-
8798 (125) ☆ 👓	$55.00	Sep-01-
und@aol.com (48) ☆	$53.00	Sep-02-
und@aol.com (48) ☆	$51.00	Aug-31-
(1838) ☆	$50.00	Aug-30-

Figure 31 - An eBay screen portion of an auction's Bid History showing a bid with a cent value.

- The bidder likes minimum bidding. Minimum bidding seems to be a safe way to bid in auctions. However, it usually demonstrates an attempt to keep the closing price of the auction as low as possible or a bidder is not sure of what he is willing to pay (other than the lowest price possible).

Bidding History (Highest bids first)	
User ID	Bid Amount
8infool (1) Not a registered user	$240.50
8infool (1) Not a registered user	$240.50
onny@netzero.net (54) ★	$238.00
clat@hotmail.com (46) ☆	$238.00
clat@hotmail.com (46) ☆	$230.00
ecast (215) ☆ m👓	$225.00
clat@hotmail.com (46) ☆	$215.00
onny@netzero.net (54) ★	$200.00
8infool (1) Not a registered user	$199.00
vee (100) ☆	$157.50
dytv (289) ☆	$150.50
ro (197) ☆	$150.00
olunt (2)	$120.00

Figure 32 - An eBay screen portion of a completed auction's Bid History showing small bid amounts.

♦ The bidder is a sniper. This is easy to spot when reviewing the bid histories of closed auctions. You will usually see such a bidder's membership name listed in the auction's bid history with a bid time very close to the auction's closing time. This is illustrated in Figure 33. It doesn't matter if the snipe bidder actually won the auction because he has still demonstrated that he attempts snipe bidding. Bidders who are successful with sniping often consider this the best way to win auctions. (But this is not necessarily the case as discussed in section *The Snipe Bidding Tactic* in part *Bidding Tactics and Techniques*). When you spot an opponent that seems to favor sniping, you will be better prepared for that bidder.

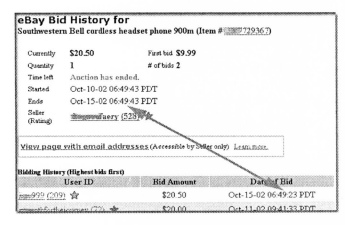

Figure 33 - An eBay screen portion of an auction's Bid History showing a snipe bid with 20 seconds remaining in the auction.

♦ The bidder relies on proxy bidding. Once again this is easy to spot using the bid history of closed auctions and even running auctions. You'll see the bidder's membership name listed earlier in the auction than others who bid after the proxy bid. A bidder may rely on proxy bids as a means to let the auction mechanism do the competitive work. Or such a bidder may simply be prepared to pay what she regards as a fair price for the item. The use of proxy bidding, for strategic bidding purposes, is discussed in part *Bidding Tactics and Techniques* in the section *The Proxy Bidding Tactic*. As is typical of many bidders, once a bidding tactic is discovered that seems to work, they tend to use that tactic repeatedly.

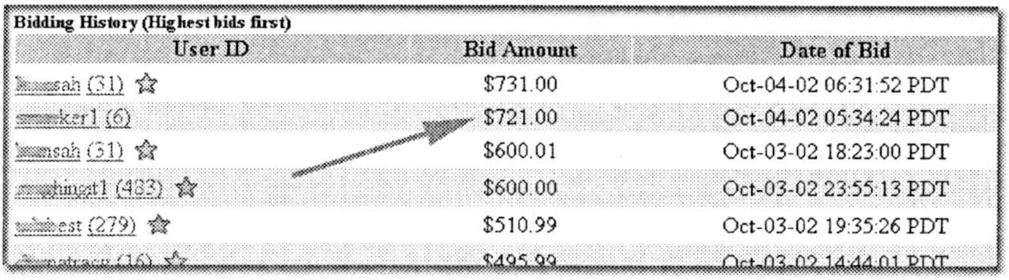

Bidding History (Highest bids first)		
User ID	Bid Amount	Date of Bid
...sah (31) ☆	$731.00	Oct-04-02 06:31:52 PDT
...ker1 (6)	$721.00	Oct-04-02 05:34:24 PDT
...sah (31) ☆	$600.01	Oct-03-02 18:23:00 PDT
...hingt1 (483) ☆	$600.00	Oct-03-02 23:55:13 PDT
...est (279) ☆	$510.99	Oct-03-02 19:35:26 PDT
...tracer (16) ☆	$495.99	Oct-03-02 14:44:01 PDT

Figure 34 - An eBay screen portion of an auction's Bid History showing a significant proxy bid.

There are other patterns that bidders fall into as well. The above examples have highlighted only a few of the types of bidder patterns you will encounter.

Understanding the bidding patterns of your opponent bidders is a fundamental of strategic bidding. When you are able to detect the bidding patterns of your opponents you can better implement a bidding strategy that leverages their patterns to your benefit. This can go a long way to giving you a competitive advantage over specific opponents.

Meanwhile show no pattern in your own bidding activity so your opponents can't predict your competitive strength.

Also see laws *#29: Be Unpredictable in Your Bid Amounts* and *#25: Keep Your Opponents Off Guard*

Notes:

Law 32: Avoid Communication with Opponents

The Savvy Bidder avoids communication with opponents during an auction – she may inadvertently provide an opponent with a competitive advantage.

eBay provides all active members the ability to send e-mail to another eBay member. You can also be the recipient of e-mail from other eBay members. However, it is generally best to avoid communication with opponents in a running auction in which you are participating. This is for the simple reason of not inadvertently giving another a competitive advantage.

If an opponent sends you an e-mail, consider gracefully declining communication during the auction. It is conceivable that a simple answer to an e-mail may be enough to indicate your intentions in the auction. Wait until after the auction to communicate with any opponent.

I adopted this non-communicative policy after receiving e-mails from fellow participants on two separate occasions. One sender suggested that the auction was not worth the seller's reserve price and wanted to know my opinion. On another occasion an e-mail arrived that simply read "Seller X is a fraud." Was it a fraud alert or did the sender hope to scare me away from an auction he wanted for himself?

At this moment I cannot think of any good reason to initiate communication with another bidder during an auction. If you were to send an e-mail with the intention of scaring off another bidder, that is certainly not an appropriate tactic of the Savvy Bidder. If you want an opinion from a fellow bidder, then you expose yourself to being mislead should you receive a reply.

If you want a second opinion regarding the seller, then just feeling that you need to ask for a second opinion may be an indication that you should not continue to participate in the auction. Of course the seller's feedback profile provides some indication of the seller's past performance. However I have never placed too much stock in feedback profiles because they are not a reliable measure of future performance (a subject for another time perhaps).

One method for obtaining opinions about the seller is to e-mail the <u>winning</u> bidders of a few recent auctions of the seller and ask for suggestions. Use caution however as the seller may take offense to you communicating with his customers and eBay may react negatively on the assumption that you are soliciting those customers.

Over recent years eBay has grown distrustful of members who communicat with other members when it doesn't directly relate to bidding in a particular running auction.

While I can appreciate eBay's efforts to curb the unfair advantage gained by scouting for customers or interfering with a seller, I find it unfortunate that there has been a continual clampdown of communication among eBay members. There are good reasons for members to communicate with one another (except, as I mentioned, with your opponents in a particular running auction). But there are those who would abuse more relaxed communication privileges, such as to siphon off bidders or warn bidders away from a seller to damage her auctions. At any rate it is now risky to communicate with other eBay members unless it relates to a running auction. And such could lead to suspension (the stories of this happening abound). While communicating with a seller of an auction you are interested in is acceptable, use your best discretion anytime you communicate with an eBay member for reasons other than concerning a running auction in which you intend to bid.

Notes:

Law 33: Take Heed the Winner's Curse

With a target price, the Savvy Bidder does not fear overpaying in an auction and can bid as aggressively as he deems necessary.

In his book, *The Winner's Curse*, Richard H. Thaler writes: "An increase in the number of other bidders implies that to win the auction you must bid more aggressively, but their presence also increases the chance that if you win, you will have overestimated the value of the object for sale – suggesting that you should bid less aggressively."

Do you see Thaler's logic? The more bidders there are the greater the competition. Competition implies value. The greater the competition the more aggressive you must bid. But this aggressiveness creates a greater chance of you overpaying which in turn prompts you to try to bid less aggressively. If you win the auction, you'll wonder if you paid too much due to your having to bid against the competition. Thus, you may win the auction, but feeling you paid too much. This is the classic Winner's Curse.

What throttles aggressive bidding is "risk aversion" which is a form of self-protection against paying too much. Risk aversion is prevalent among auction participants and is a natural defense mechanism against paying more than necessary. Risk aversion is what keeps auction closing prices down because participants tend to bid as low as they can. However perceived risk is offset by perceived value – the higher the perceived value, the greater one is willing to pay. Thus a normal bidder bids as low as he can under the price he has established according to his perceived value. The problem, as Thaler's logic points out, is that perceived value is influenced by the competition itself – the greater the competition, the greater the perceived value.

The Savvy Bidder has a key that protects him from the Winner's Curse. That key is the target price as discussed in the chapter *The Target Price*. With a target price, which is based on the typical closing prices of recently closed auctions for the same or comparable item, the Savvy Bidder is able to proceed in an auction without the fear of overpaying *and* without being overly cautious.

The fear of overpaying can only occur when you do not know what amount would be too much given the item's typical value in the eBay market or alternately outside of eBay. If you know its typical price, you cannot overpay unless you deliberately bid beyond that price (but that's not the Winner's Curse, there's another term for knowingly overpaying). Because the Savvy Bidder finds out the typical market price before bidding if at all possible, he is relieved of the dilemma of fearing that he is bidding too high and being risk averse to the point of bidding too low.

Armed with a price guideline, the Savvy Bidder does not fear competition because competitive activity cannot pull him into paying too much. More important, he can work his bidding budget as aggressively as he deems necessary without being held back by the fear of overpaying.

Through your own bidding, you can help create the illusion that the competition is strong enough to cause opponents to fear that, if they stay in the auction, they will find themselves the winner at more than they would have preferred, e.g., the Winner's Curse. Some opponents will regard competition as a threat to their ability to win the auction at a price that is comfortable for them. They will likely revert to "safe bids" which is another term for minimum bidding. Because many bidders fear overpaying they revert to less competitive minimum bidding and that puts them on the path to the Winner's Curse.

Notes:

Law 34: Protect Your Feedback Rating

The Savvy Bidder knows that his reputation in the auction community is very important. This is because opponents empower the owner of a stellar profile.

The feedback profile rating is derived from the number of unique feedback statements placed into a member's profile. (Feedback statements from members who have previously submitted a feedback statement for the member are not included in the profile points, but the feedback is still recorded.) One profile point is awarded for each positive feedback remark and one point is deducted for each negative feedback remark. Neutral feedback remarks do not increase or decrease the profile rating but are still recorded.

eBay's feedback system is intended to foster a self-policing environment. The premise is that negative feedback warns others of potential problems with the member. Of course, positive feedback indicates a good experience, presumably indicating that future transactions with the member are likely to go well.

Part of exploring the landscape of an auction is to review the feedback listing of the seller. This is easy to do and smart. However, the Savvy Bidder also checks the feedback of the other bidders in that auction, especially if a particular bidder seems to be a competitive threat. On occasion I explore the feedback profiles of *all* opponents in an auction. I do this to get a complete picture of the auction's landscape in terms of my opponents.

When you encounter an opponent with high profile points, your first reaction might be that the member is skilled in online auctions either as a seller, a buyer or both. You may quickly surmise that the owner of such a profile will be difficult to compete against. This reaction is normal, but the member may not necessarily be a formidable opponent.

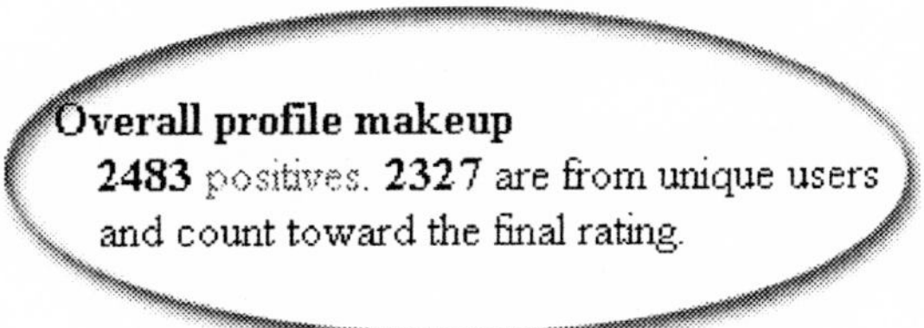

Overall profile makeup
2483 positives. **2327** are from unique users and count toward the final rating.

Figure 35 - An eBay screen portion showing a profile rating.

An eBay member with a high profile count will command more respect. But such may *not* be a skilled bidder. From your perspective, it is a tactical mistake to assume the skill level of any bidder based on their profile rating alone. Regard all opponents as formidable opponents regardless of their profile points. After all, a bidder may totally lack skills in bidding, but be willing to spend more money than other bidders. Money gives any bidder a decisive competitive edge when it comes to winning auctions. Fortunately for the Savvy Bidder, online auction buyers generally make a concerted effort to not spend any more money than necessary.

Even if the higher profile point owner acquired the points by winning many auctions, it still does not mean that the bidder is a significant competitor. It is possible that the feedback points were earned from auctions won over a long period of time in which the bidding was haphazard and completely without strategy.

It is also possible that many of the profile points of another bidder were acquired by selling, which doesn't directly contribute to the ability to win auctions. When you review a member's feedback file, an "S" will be to the right of the feedback remark to indicate that the member was a seller in that transaction. A "B" will indicate that the member was a buyer in the transaction relating to the feedback. You can also view the link to the actual auction listing and jump to that listing if it is still in eBay's database.

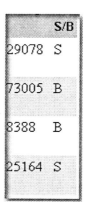

Figure 36 - An eBay screen portion of feedback listing showing the seller ("S") and buyer ("B") indicators.

While the point is clear that you should not assign too much value to one's profile rating, *you want opponent bidders to assign too much value to your profile point rating*. Therefore, you must use care to protect your profile from unnecessary damage. Avoid resolving disputes by giving negative feedback – you may receive negative feedback yourself. (See law #36: *Beware Feedback Leveraging*.) Forget about using negative feedback as a vent for your anger in a not-so-perfect transaction – send an e-mail to the seller directly and speak your mind there. Always seek non-feedback methods for addressing a problem transaction first and leave negative feedback as a means to warn others of a member with whom you had a bad experience.

As much as possible, you want your own feedback profile to intimidate your opponents. Your feedback points do not have to be high to accomplish this. Being free of negatives and neutral entries goes a long way to helping your profile rating give the impression that you are a strong competitor.

Also see laws *#24: Never Underestimate Your Opponents, #43: Don't Break the Rules* and *#42: Ignore Hoax Auctions*

Notes:

Law 35: Respect "The Mark"

The Savvy Bidder assumes, for strategic purposes, that members who wear the Mark are quite capable of being strong opponents.

Figure 37 – An eBay screen portion showing a membership ID with the padlock icon.

A graphic of a padlock is associated with all new eBay membership IDs and is removed after 30 days of retaining the current ID. Being given the padlock is the same thing as being told "We don't have any experience with this membership ID. You could be a crook, here to rip us off and flee. At the very least, you are obviously inexperienced in our elite auction community. Wear this scarlet letter for a while that tells all to use caution dealing with you." One would think that a zero feedback rating would be sufficient to identify a new member and provide a warning to use caution. Yet after providing personal contact information *and* providing credit card information, new members are given "The Mark" and are limited in some activities. What this marking policy does, in effect, is set up new members to be distrusted by their peers and sellers. I have seen auction listings where the seller actually included a statement in the auction warning that the bids of any bidder with a feedback profile count of less than 10 would be summarily cancelled.

> Try this experiment: Using the eBay Basic Search, type in the phrase "zero feedback" (with the quotes). Make sure the "Search Title and Description" option is checked. Click the Search button. When I ran this search, eBay found 18,333 auctions listings that included the phrase "zero feedback". It appears that many eBay sellers distrust those who wear The Mark.

The Mark, I suspect, is intended as a visible warning that the newly registered membership ID may be fraudulent or is, at best, not all that practiced in being a seller or a bidder and therefore may not perform well in transactions. While the logic is flawed, I understand it. But I still do not agree with the method chosen. It might be fairer to the marked member if his or her registration history were made available to concerned sellers, much like a member's contact information is made available in a controlled manner. Such registration history could provide details as to when the member registered and perhaps any other IDs of the member, both currently held and historical.

But the point of this law is not to question this member marking policy, rather to put some perspective on what you might assume about a marked eBay member. The Mark does not necessarily indicate an inexperienced member because The Mark is given to new membership IDs – the member himself could be highly experienced in online auctions as a seller, buyer or both. As such, assume that opponents who wear The Mark are strong competitors and just as worthy of your attention as opponents with a higher profile rating. If you have any preconceived notions that opponents who wear The Mark are in some way incompetent at winning auctions or are easily defeated, get over it. Even if the wearer of The Mark is new to online auctions, such bidders are often tenacious and very determined to win auctions. Don't credit or discredit any opponent's bidding skills based on The Mark or the profile points alone – for strategic purposes, respect the potential competitive strength of those who wear The Mark.

If you wear the Mark, you might choose to see it as an opportunity. When another assumes you are incompetent at bidding in online auctions (as The Mark implies), she may not be prepared for your competitive strength. In fact, it is often best when your opponents assume you are competitively weak as they wont be ready for your moves. Wearing The Mark has absolutely no negative impact on your strategic bidding abilities. In fact, it can prove beneficial because your opponents may make the mistake of underestimating your competitive strength.

However, if you wear The Mark, the sellers of the auctions you participate in may consider you a potential deadbeat. Since the attitude of many eBay sellers is well entrenched by the occasional misfortunes of dealing with actual deadbeats, we are hard pressed to convince many sellers that not all those who wear The Mark are untrustworthy. My best advice in this case is to bid responsibly and avoid putting yourself in any situation that would give a seller any reason to confirm any suspicions.

Also see Law #24: *Never Underestimate Your Opponents*

Notes:

Law 36: Beware Feedback Leveraging

The Savvy Bidder is wary of sellers who refrain from providing her feedback until she has provided them feedback. This puts the Savvy Bidder in a potentially difficult position should the transaction go bad.

I'll go out on a limb here and state that a positive feedback statement may in fact be given to a poor or marginal seller to avoid retaliatory negative feedback. In fact this concern has been voiced throughout the eBay community for some time now. Since feedback statements are public, it is certain that the receiver of a negative statement would feel her eBay reputation was tarnished with a neutral or negative feedback statement. One way to avoid receiving negative feedback is to not give negative feedback. Conversely, one way to get positive feedback is to give positive feedback. This is an unfortunate flaw in eBay's feedback system.

Please note that this law is not addressing feedback extortion. Feedback extortion occurs when an eBay member threatens neutral or negative feedback to coerce his trading partner to perform in a certain manner. Rather this law deals with the less serious issue of leveraging feedback where a member subtly uses his feedback as a control device to obtain favorable feedback.

There seems to be a trend where some sellers refrain from submitting feedback for the buyer until the seller has first received feedback from the buyer. I have encountered many sellers who refrained from submitting positive feedback to my eBay profile even after a fast, trouble-free payment for their auction. I once asked one of these sellers why this was. He explained via e-mail that he does not provide any feedback until the buyer first submits his feedback. He further explained that the buyer is then less likely to forget to submit feedback. (Interestingly, it was obvious by my inquiry that *I* hadn't forgotten about this seller's feedback. Yet the seller still refrained from submitting feedback for me.)

What this seller really wanted was the upper hand in the feedback loop. If the buyer gives the seller a negative feedback, the seller has the option to return like feedback. On a less sinister level, this also effectively encourages the buyer to not forget to leave feedback for the seller, reducing the need for the seller to remind the buyer to leave feedback. If the buyer goes so far as to ignore leaving feedback for the seller, the seller ignores leaving feedback for the buyer. And finally, this "Buyer First" method serves as a reminder system for the seller to leave feedback for the buyer. Any way one slices it, posturing the buyer to leave feedback first is to the benefit of the seller.

wever of greatest concern is the possibility of a seller being retaliatory should buyer feel it necessary to leave negative feedback. Being positioned to be the t to "speak up" may actually jeopardize the bidders own feedback profile. Since dback is made public immediately upon entry, the first to leave feedback has his ition exposed to his trading partner who may take offense to a negative or neu-feedback. I have long been an advocate of keeping the feedback between two ling partners hidden until both submit their feedback. By hiding feedback until h partners submit feedback for the other, neither trading partner could retaliate ause neither would know the rating and content of the other's feedback until h trading partner left feedback. This would most certainly eliminate retaliatory dback. In addition, this "hidden feedback" system would serve to reward each ling partner for leaving feedback in that by doing so the feedback for each is de visible to the public.

a side note concerning the "hidden feedback" system, should one partner fail to mit feedback for the other, the eBay computers could assign a default feedback er 90 days or so. This default feedback (neither positive, neutral or negative) uld serve to give an eBay member acknowledgment for the transaction.

it is now, the eBay feedback system fosters a like-for-like feedback exchange, in, "You say nice things about me and I'll say nice things about you" and visa ·sa, of course. Allowing this to continue, in my opinion, taints the purpose and lue of trading partner feedback. When I review a seller's feedback listing I keep mind that the sellers feedback was likely influenced by the avoidance of the gative-for-negative risk. I can only imagine how many positive feedback ratings ve been entered into the eBay database because of the fear of harming one's own ·dback for speaking honestly about a trading partner.

on't think most sellers that adhere to the "Buyer First" feedback method have a ister motive. All sellers appreciate prompt payment and good communication m the buyer and many sellers submit feedback as a normal part of processing transaction. The mark of a good seller is that when the package goes out the or, all of the details of the transaction have been completed, including feedback the buyer. This is my personal policy when I wear the seller's hat. However, the uyer First" method can easily be taken advantage of. It would be obvious to yone that if a seller receives a negative feedback, the seller's return feedback is ing to be tainted by the receipt of the negative feedback. Negative feedback is ways upsetting and tends to raise emotions that may influence the seller's return edback.

hen the seller leaves feedback shortly after the buyers fulfills all of his obliga-ns in the transaction, such as payment, it indicates to the buyer that the seller w to it that all the details from his end are taken care of promptly and efficiently.

When the buyer reads a positive feedback statement in her profile it sets up a positive attitude for when she receives and opens the parcel. This is important since the buyer may be feeling apprehension whether or not the seller represented her merchandise properly. A positive buyer attitude will help the buyer adjust to minor disappointments concerning the merchandise. (Of course, no amount of positive feedback will undo the damage of misrepresented merchandise, a poor transaction or poor shipping.) Assuming the seller is representing his auction items properly, taking a "Seller First" feedback approach has advantages for the seller because it helps create a more positive experience for the buyer, who may very well seek out that seller the next time he needs an item the seller is offering.

Be wary of sellers who seem to practice feedback leveraging, be it with the subtle "Buyer First" method or the more outright leveraging methods. First, it suggests that the seller may not be entirely sure that you will be a happy customer and second, it may be a method to leverage positive feedback from you for empire building purposes.

Upon paying for an auction, immediately request that the seller provide positive feedback for you and let her know that you will be entering feedback as well upon receipt of the item. (Notice that I didn't say that you will enter "positive" feedback upon receipt of the item). Your objective is to not risk receiving negative feedback yourself if you feel strongly that the seller should receive a neutral or negative feedback from you.

But, how do you know if a seller adheres to the "Buyer First" feedback method? With sellers who you feel the need to use a bit of caution, what you can do is perform a simple analysis of feedback exchanges between the seller and some of his past auctions that closed with winning bidders. Here's how to conduct a feedback analysis:

1. From the seller's auction click on the profile rating that is enclosed in parentheses to the right of the seller's membership ID. Scan down to auctions that closed about 30 to 90 days prior as these auctions are more likely to have both feedbacks left by then.

2. In the seller's feedback statement list locate an auction marked with a 'S'. This indicates the seller was a seller in the auction that pertains to the feedback statement. The feedback statement itself will be from the buyer of that auction.

3. Jot down the auction number and the date/time that the buyer submitted the feedback statement.

4. Now click on the profile link for the buyer of that auction (don't bother going to the actual auction). The profile rating is enclosed in parentheses to the right of the buyer's membership ID.

5. In the buyer's feedback statement list locate the auction number you recorded in step 3 above.

6. Note the date the <u>seller</u> submitted feedback to the buyer.

7. Note if the date of the seller's feedback statement is a later date than the buyer's feedback statement you recorded in step 3 above.

8. Click on the seller's profile rating (in the parentheses) to return to the seller's feedback statement list where you can repeat steps 1 through 7 for other buyers.

Repeat the above sequence several times to determine if there is a pattern that suggests that the seller adheres to the "Buyer First" feedback method.

A word of caution on the subject of feedback leveraging; don't automatically assume the seller is deliberately leveraging feedback if your analysis indicates that the seller consistently provides feedback after the buyer does. It is possible that the seller has developed a work pattern where feedback is left undone for some time after the winning bidder made payment. However, your analysis may indicate if you should be wary of feedback leveraging from a particular seller.

You might want to adopt a policy where you always ask to receive feedback first. When you win an auction be sure to make payment in a timely manner. Then send the seller an e-mail advising that payment was made (or sent) and request that positive feedback be submitted to your profile on satisfaction of the payment. If no feedback has occurred when you receive your item, e-mail the seller and advise him that you will enter feedback *after* he does. This encourages the seller to take the initiative to submit his feedback for you. (It also indicates that you have not forgotten about the seller's feedback). Remind the seller by e-mail every few days. (Remember that on eBay feedback will not be accepted for an auction after 90 days of the auction's close).

Notes:

Law 37: Beware the Hidden Reserve Price

The Savvy Bidder avoids placing large proxy bids in auctions with a hidden reserve price. By doing so the competitive value of the proxy bid may be lost.

You come to an auction for a tchotchke that would enhance your collection quit nicely. You do your research and determine that the item is being accurately represented. You determine that the item has a collectible value of $2,000.00, which you would be willing to pay if necessary. The auction has received a few bids but its still early in the auction. The auction has a reserve price that the seller is not revealing in his auction listing. You write to the seller asking for the reserve price but she doesn't respond to your e-mail. The auction's current price is $450.00.

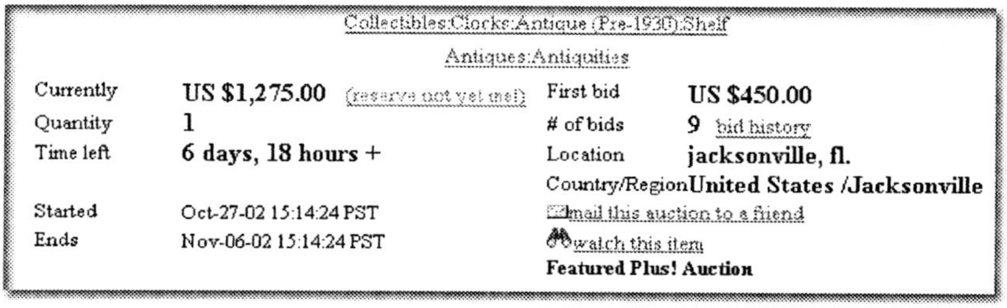

	Collectibles:Clocks:Antique (Pre-1930):Shelf			
	Antiques:Antiquities			
Currently	US $1,275.00 (reserve not yet met)	First bid	US $450.00	
Quantity	1	# of bids	9 bid history	
Time left	6 days, 18 hours +	Location	jacksonville, fl.	
		Country/Region	United States /Jacksonville	
Started	Oct-27-02 15:14:24 PST	Email this auction to a friend		
Ends	Nov-06-02 15:14:24 PST	watch this item		
		Featured Plus! Auction		

Figure 38 - An eBay screen portion showing an auction in which bidding has not yet met or exceeded the seller's reserve price.

You decide to bid $1,500.00 thinking that such a healthy proxy bid leaves you good protection against other bidders. You chose $1,500.00 because it gives you another $500.00 if you have to bid up to $2,000.00 near the end of the auction.

You place your $1,500.00 bid. Then you notice that the current price has been run all the way up to $1,400.00 and you are the highest bidder in the auction. So much for the competitive value of your proxy bid. What happened?

> *On eBay, when a bid is placed that is equal to or higher than the seller's reserve price, the current price is automatically set to the seller's reserve price.*

In our example above, the seller's reserve price was $1,400.00. Since your proxy bid of $1,500.00 was higher than the reserve, the auction's current price was immediately set to the seller's reserve. Your $1,500.00 bid became your proxy bid, albeit with only $100.00 left.

Apparently the assumption is that if a bidder is willing to pay more than the seller's reserve price, then the auction's current price will be set to the reserve price. However, the bidder may not appreciate that the competitive value of his proxy bid may be significantly diminished by this policy. Bidders who are not aware of this will be in for a surprise and may find that they inadvertently caused a large increase to the auction's current price.

Many bidders are blindsided by this bidding mechanism. When you come to an auction that has a reserve price that is hidden and the auction's current price is low with respect to the probable closing price of the auction, consider avoiding placing a large proxy bid. Always ask the seller what her reserve price is and bid accordingly. If the seller will not tell you her reserve price, you might want to consider waiting until other bidders bring the current price up to or over the seller's reserve price. (My personal policy is to not bid in any auction where the seller refuses to provide her reserve price upon request. My stance is that I will not bid blindly with respect to a reserve price.)

As illustrated in this law, consider avoiding having the competitive value of a high proxy bid diminished or destroyed by inadvertently tripping the seller's reserve. The section *Tripping the Reserve* in part *Bidding Tactics and Techniques* discusses how you can strategically utilize the hidden reserve price.

Notes:
_____

Law 38: Bidders are Often Presumed Deadbeats

Some sellers think it necessary to warn bidders of their obligation to follow through when winning the seller's auction. The Savvy Bidder appreciates those sellers who treat *all* bidders as valued prospective customers.

We have all seen those auctions where the seller warns of the consequences of being a non-paying bidder (NPB). Certainly no seller wants winning bidders to ignore payment as it wastes the seller's time and money. But why would any seller choose to spoil the goodwill of his prospective buyers for the sake of warning away a small percentage that may not follow through on a transaction?

Non-paying bidders are a concern for many sellers. Some sellers go so far as to warn away such bidders with terse statements in their auction listings. But they do so by tainting their auctions with indications of distrust. Here are a few seller quotes:

"We participate in Ebay's Deadbeat bidder program.

"We report all No-Paying Bidders to Ebay for possible suspension."

"I'm sorry if I come off like a jerk with all of these rules, but these days, eBay has been overrun by deadbeat bidders and others who have no respect for sellers. It's really a shame that they make it that much more difficult for the rest of us!"

"Deadbeat bidders will be torn asunder by the seller's astral servitors."

"Deadbeat bidders will be visited by Guido and Vito, who will explain reality to them."

"I will send you an email confirming everything and what not. You must reply to this email! This is so I can get your shipping address, payment info, and also cuts down on my paranoia of the evil deadbeat bidder."

"If you deadbeat me: #1 I WILL report you to ebay so I can get a refund of end of auction fees. #2 I WILL leave negative feedback. #3 I WILL post your ebay I.D. and information on usenet newsgroups and other places to let sellers know you are a worthless deadbeat. Don't waste my time or yours."

Because eBay's NPB claim process involves several time consuming steps it is understandable why sellers want to avoid non-paying bidders. Even if the seller is credited the final sales fee for the auction, the seller cannot recoup special feature listing fees and will most certainly have lost the original interested persons. Since eBay forbids off-eBay sales, the seller is required to not contact the second highest bidder and negotiate a sale, leaving the seller little option but to re-list the item. It's understandable why some sellers warn away non-paying bidders in their listing, even if doing so introduces a negative slant to their auctions.

However eBay sellers don't have to remind any bidder that she is obligated to follow through when she wins an auction – such is already specified in eBay's User Agreement which all eBay members accept as a matter of obtaining and maintaining an eBay membership. A bidder is also warned at the time of each bid as shown in Figure 39. When a winning bidder reneges on payment a seller can proceed with any action that is specified by eBay policy without posting additional warnings.

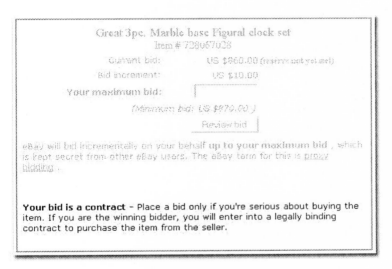

Figure 39 – An eBay screen portion showing the eBay statement to bidders that a bid is a contract.

Some sellers go so far as to threaten to leave negative feedback for a non-paying bidder. However, eBay's Non-Paying-Bidder policy does not include leaving negative feedback as part of the NPB claim process. Perhaps eBay recognizes that there may be good reason for not making payment on an auction. If a seller fires in a negative feedback and the winning bidder meets eBay's criterion for not making payment, what good comes of the seller's personal disciplinarian policy?

> Try this experiment: Using the eBay Basic Search, type in the word "deadbeat" (without the quotes). Make sure the "Search Title and Description" option is checked. Click the Search button. Last time I did this search, the search returned 37,965 auctions listings that included the word "deadbeat". If you think that's a lot of listings, try searching for "negative feedback" (with the quotes). When I ran this search there were more auction listings than eBay could display. It appears that this issue is on the minds of a lot of eBay sellers.

My personal policy is to avoid auctions in which the seller advertises distrust. It matters little if the warning does not apply to me personally. What matters is that the seller is apparently prepared for the winning bidder to be a deadbeat. If I am the winning bidder of such a seller's auction then I am categorically a deadbeat until I make payment. Personally I prefer to purchase from a seller who is more concerned with attracting great customers than protecting himself from the occasional misfit. You must decide for yourself what your own policy will be in this regard.

Unless there is a justifiable reason per eBay's policy, the Savvy Bidder always honors his winning bid. This is not just because of any requirement to do so. Rather, stems from not wasting his time bidding in an auction where he does not intend to complete the transaction, or may be incapable of completing it. Also the Savvy Bidder prefers to not participate in the bad vibes that accompany a seller sending threatening e-mail messages trying to get paid. Being a non-paying bidder is simply not worth the hassle and is not the way of the Savvy Bidder.

Notes:

Law 39: Never Suspend Your Belief

The Savvy Bidder trusts his instincts in all online auctions.

If the auction item looks too good to be true, it probably is.

If the auction looks like a bargain, it probably won't be for long.

If the auction looks suspicious, assume it is.

Need more be said?

Notes:

Law 40: Catch Fraud Before It Catches You

The Savvy Bidder learns to spot danger before becoming ensnared in fraudulent schemes. Nurture your ability to spot a bad auction – it will serve you well.

There are many debates about how well eBay is doing in preventing fraud in its community. Depending on one's viewpoint (and what bones are being picked), eBay is either virtually helpless to stop fraud or eBay is doing all that it should be doing. Such debates are not surprising; on the one hand members look to eBay to prevent fraud while eBay, on the other hand, prefers that its community be self policing. While everyone else does their posturing, the Savvy Bidder acknowledges that he is usually in the best position to spot a fraudulent auction.

Suspicion of fraud in an auction is raised in one of three ways; 1) the auction may be scanned by eBay resident software after it is posted, 2) eBay members alert eBay that the auction may be fraudulent or 3) there is a victim. These are methods of fraud detection, not fraud prevention.

Another reason that online auction venues (not just eBay) are subject to fraud is because of the sheer number of people trafficking the auction venue's web site. Add to this the anonymity of persons in a cyber environment and the possibility of obtaining a great bargain and the online auction environment is ripe for attracting the dishonest and even the criminal. And, because eBay buyers tend to trust the eBay environment, they actually run a higher risk of being caught up in fraudulent situations. To illustrate how trust makes people vulnerable let me relate a story I recently came across.

The San Francisco town counsel needed to solve the problem of pick pocketing in the Bay Market, a problem that was hurting tourist traffic. They hit on an idea to drive out the pickpocket thieves. They placed signs at various locations around the market warning tourists to watch for pick pocketing. Feeling safer, the tourist traffic steadily returned to normal. Then the pickpocket thieves ingeniously posted more of these warning signs and the tourist traffic increased again. What had happened was that the tourists thought they were safer because the thieves in their midst were exposed. What thief would operate in the midst of such forewarned and alert people. But the pickpocket thieves simply capitalized on the tourist's trust. (The story did not state if the signs were eventually taken down. But if they were I wouldn't doubt it if the tourist traffic increased yet again due to a perception that the pickpocket problem had finally been solved.) The moral applies to eBay as well – the safer the eBay community feels, the more susceptible it is to fraudulent activities.

Given the inherent difficulty in preventing fraud by the auction venue, it is important that each eBay member take personal responsibility for his own safety. The Savvy Bidder is in an excellent position to spot and avoid fraud dangers, and even simple misrepresentation. This is because he is alert and aware, constantly seeking and analyzing information that will assist him competitively.

If you approach an auction strategically, you will invariably collect data about the auction and effectively use that data. As you work your bidding plan, you will be looking for signals that alert you when and how to implement the next step in your bidding strategy. As such, you are always postured to interpret the signals you receive. It is this very process of watching for signals with the intent of progressing to the next step in your bidding plan that helps you stay alert to danger signals.

Let's assume for a moment that you are the high bidder of $32.00 in an auction. You are then outbid with a proxy bid with one day left to the auction. Other bidders work up to the current highest bidder's proxy amount and a new bidder takes the auction at $65.00. Your target price was $50.00 (based on your research) and you stuck to your target price and let the auction go. Another bidder comes along and takes the high bidder position with an $80.00 proxy bid, enticing other bidders to outbid the $80.00. Then, with a few hours left to the auction, the $80.00 bidder retracts his bid, moving the second highest bidder to the highest bidder seat. This auction may very well have been hit with shill bidding. But the target price, which is part of your bidding strategy, provided a self-imposed limit to your risks.

Let's look at this same example with slightly different events. You are the high bidder of $32.00 in this auction. You are then outbid with a minimum increment bid of $33.00. Do you take back the auction or do you wait? Let's say you wait, because you see signs of another bidder picking a fight and you prefer to avoid a bidding battle. A third bidder comes along and engages in a bidding battle with another, working the current price up to $55.00, which exceeds your target price. You're out, but you watch the auction anyway. The auction has one day remaining. A few hours before the auction's close, the auction remains at $55.00. That's only $5.00 over the target price – not too much of a stretch. But you come to your senses and refrain from bidding, knowing there will be other auctions. But the two battlers haven't forgotten their need to win this auction and the fight continues. $60.00, then $70.00 and now $90.00. The auction closes and the "lucky winner" gets the item for $90.00.

Was this a case of shilling? Perhaps. What really matters is that you refused to exceed the target price you set and to get into a bidding battle. You resisted justifying a higher price and stuck to your bidding strategy, a decision that may have also protected you from a possibly fraudulent situation. You don't own the item, but you also haven't parted with more than the item was worth to you. As a Savvy Bidder you have built in safeguards against fraud because you are competitively alert in the auctions in which you participate.

One of the greatest benefits of being a Savvy Bidder is that you have a natural self-defense mechanism with which to recognize and quickly reject auctions that might be fraudulent. Consider:

- The target price sets a price limit, thereby automatically providing a measure of protection. This is important since the primary objective of the auction format is to get as much for the item as a person will pay. One type of fraud scheme attempts to raise the auction closing price which is the objective of shill bidding. (Other fraud schemes take payment and never ship the item).

- Also, consider your willingness to research an auction, including the key participants and the seller, as invaluable first steps to spotting a dishonest party. Researching an auction, including the items, the seller and opponents is something that a Savvy Bidder normally does as part of the process, not just when a red flag goes up.

- There is also your ability to analyze the data concerning your auctions. As discussed in the Law #19: Leverage the Bid History, you can see beyond the obvious which may actually help you spot an auction that is being manipulated.

- And finally, by not being the type of person that sees only the current state of the auction, you have a broader vision of the auction's landscape. This helps you spot patterns in the bidding activity. Those who have only a snapshot view of the auction are often the ones who never see manipulation.

This law serves only to point out the importance of being an alert bidder. An in-depth discussion of online auction fraud is outside of the scope of this book. However, there are many excellent web sites, including eBay's help section that will help you understand and avoid online auction fraud. For now, just know that being a savvy bidder is a great start to being a safe bidder.

Notes:

Law 41: Make Payment Super Fast

**The Savvy Bidder knows that sellers appreciate fast payment.
The Savvy Bidder strives to pay quickly and problem free.**

My personal policy is to have money sitting the seller's PayPal account at the earliest possible moment after the auction closes. On several occasions the seller was paid before I received eBay's End of Auction e-mail notice (but I decided that was too fast). There are three primary reasons for this super fast payment policy.

◆ It alleviates me of having to remember that I have an auction to pay for. I get the payment taken care of quickly so that I have one less thing on my mind.

◆ It sends a clear signal to the seller that I am a responsible and prompt buyer. Hopefully the seller is so impressed with the lightning follow through that he will ship the auction item with similar promptness.

◆ It increases the chance the seller will place positive feedback into my profile and without lengthy delay. It is not unusual for me to receive feedback statements that include "fast payment", "lightning payment" and so on. My ultra fast payment is so prominent in the seller's mind that he doesn't forget about me while he holds both my money and the auction item I purchased.

Of course, when paying by a money order, you can't enjoy the potential benefits of super fast payment. I encourage you to seek a means of payment where you are able to fulfill your end of the transaction quickly.

Notes:

Law 42: Ignore Hoax Auctions

The Savvy Bidder never participates in hoax auctions – it's a waste of her talent.

There are people who somehow justify the time and effort to post online auctions that are intended to be funny, make a point or to simply test the system. When you run across such auctions, spend a few minutes being entertained if that's what you want, but my advice is to not place a bid in such auctions.

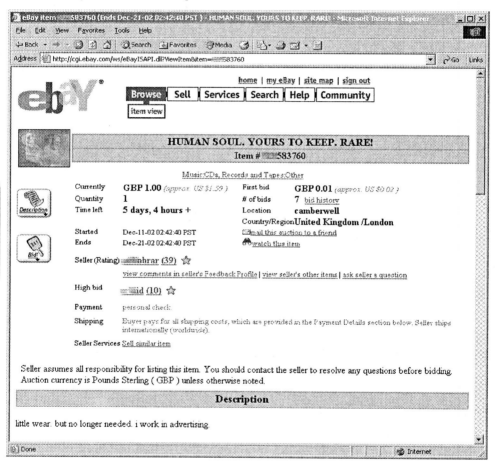

Figure 40 – An eBay hoax auction.

Also see laws *#34: Protect Your Feedback Rating* and *#43: Don't Break the Rules*

Notes:

Law 43: Don't Break the Rules

When playing in someone else's yard by his own choice, the Savvy Bidder follows their rules. Your challenge is to understand the current rules and be ready to adapt to new rules as they are introduced.

Rules exist on eBay to help keep the playing field fair and safe for all (although not all rules accomplish this goal). Rules exist to insure that procedures are followed to enable a smooth transaction once the auction closes. Rules also reduce seller fraud and deliberate misrepresentation, as well as bidder fraud. Many of the current rules resulted from individuals having taken advantage of the system. More rules will follow due to the environment becoming more complex and as clever people discover new ways to exploit existing loopholes.

I am an advocate of well thought out rules. I want the safety they bring me and the time saving they provide me (hassles are time consuming and often expensive). If I am to benefit from rules, I must understand those rules. The Savvy Bidder is especially interested in understanding all of eBay's rules for two reasons: First, he wants to know which actions are permissible so he can operate within the full spectrum of his bidding skills. Second, he wants to avoid inadvertently violating a rule so he can continue enjoying the benefits of the eBay experience. Hassles of any kind waste time and limit freedoms – avoid hassles.

The Savvy Bidder does not necessarily agree with all of the rules and will be outspoken as the opportunity presents itself. However, he makes a concerted effort to not break the rules, even if does not agree with them. Make every effort to follow the rules. If you are not sure if you can take a specific action according to established procedure, do some research or ask for clarification. This is not only in the interest of the community itself, but also in the interest of continuing to obtain the greatest benefit from your eBay experience.

A final thought. Decide for yourself how far you will go to report a rule violator. My personal policy is to report violations if I happen across them. However, I do not use my time policing eBay in search of violators. If you have the time for this, by all means go for it. But I encourage you to use great care that you do not prejudge others by your own definition of how they should conduct themselves. In all cases, be absolutely sure that a rule or policy is actually being violated before turning someone in – I'm sure you would want no less from others.

Also see laws *#34: Protect Your Feedback Rating* and *#42: Ignore Hoax Auctions*

Notes:

Law 44: Know The Playground

The Savvy Bidder strives to understand how the game is played so he can play the game well. eBay will change the game plan when it wills so the Savvy Bidder must also be ready to quickly adapt.

eBay provides a venue for people to buy and sell a bounty of things new and old. It is a great place to test our ability to leverage our money in competitive purchase situations and to browse and participate as our mood suits. eBay provides endless chances to compete and test our will to win the right to purchase as well as our acceptance of losing that right. However, eBay can be place to waste both our time and money. It's an environment where one can get a false sense of purchasing power accompanied by hard hitting let downs.

eBay has reached critical mass in terms of membership. It is now possible to find almost anything you might want to own. There are still great bargains to be had on eBay, but they are getting harder to find and still harder to win the right to purchase. Nevertheless, there is a bounty for all and is still relatively safe for the individual bidder.

The adaptation of the very old auction format to the digital world was a simple concept whose time was just over the horizon when Pierre Omidyar first constructed an electronic auction web site in 1995. I remember visiting the early eBay web site, then called "AuctionWeb" – a humble online auction web site that had few visible indications of having the basis for success. eBay went on to become the world's largest online auction community. Something is right about eBay in the minds of the millions who have been attracted to it.

But eBay is now a big business with business-minded people at the helm. One can only imagine the income generating opportunities that have already been identified by the eBay corporate executives. It comes as no surprise that the eBay landscape is ever changing so it can capitalize on income producing features, not to mention income enhancements realized by functionality enhancements and even policy changes. eBay is truly an incredible money making machine.

For all of the benefits that eBay provides, it is not without its issues. But, as savvy bidders it is important for us to see the picture as it is, not as we would like it to be. The eBay auction environment is not the easiest to work in. There are a myriad of functions to learn with more continuously being added. The eBay screen is getting busier with an increasing array of advertisements and distractions. Change is the word – new features and functions arrive almost as soon as members learn the old ones. As a Savvy Bidder your challenge is to remain focused despite the noise.

Understanding the features and functions of the auction venue is important. You must be aware of them so they don't become obstacles to your competitive strength and your fun. Understanding the functions will also allow you to efficiently perform research and gather information that your opponents may not know how to access.

Many are writing about how to make money selling on eBay. Few are writing about how to save money on eBay. As a Savvy Bidder your challenge is to learn all you can about the eBay playground despite this focus on eBay sellers. There will come a time when the focus will shift to the bidder as a key player in the success of online auctions. By then you will have grown to be an advanced bidder with the insight to recognize emerging opportunities. There will come a day when buyers in a wide array of commerce settings will expect nothing less than to participate in the pricing of a purchase – online auctions are just the precursor to price-participation commerce. And you'll be ready.

There are many eBay rules to learn and follow – things you shouldn't do, can't do and had better not do or else. Winning bidders are often presumed to be deadbeats until they miraculously make payment. New members are given The Mark. There are unilateral policy changes that blindside members that steadily erode all member privileges in an effort to throttle the few who abuse their privileges. As with any gathering of a large number of people, your challenge is to find where you fit and to proceed with both knowledge and reasonable caution.

There is a rigid bidding mechanism to learn. Fortunately the core mechanical process hasn't changed – but it may eventually. As eBay's help area gets larger, it seems to provide less help. Books about how to use eBay are outdated before they make it into the bookstores. The eBay playground will change. You can count on it.

Fraud will always be part of the online auction landscape – the auction format is inherently prone to abuse. It is unavoidable that the eBay playground will be a target of malcontents. However, it is highly probable that eBay will continue to safely serve millions within the scope of its mission. eBay's challenge is to not lose sight of its mission, or at least to adapt new missions after carefully considering the consequences. eBay's challenge is to not break what works. Your challenge is to be an informed and resilient bidder. Your challenge is to be a cautious bidder but not a fearful bidder. Your challenge is to have fun but not at the expense of your budget.

Remain aware of the playground. Adapt to changes. Stay alert. Have fun and be a Savvy Bidder.

Notes:

Glossary of Terms

Absentee Bidder

A bidder who cannot attend an auction. As it relates to Internet auctions, the auction venue places bids on behalf of the absentee bidder if he places a proxy bid. See Proxy Bid.

Absolute Auction

An auction with no reserve. The auction will close at the highest price without being restricted by a reserve price. See Reserve Auction.

Actual Value

The value of an item as it is determined by formal appraisal or other known value measurement criteria. A retail price could also be considered actual value, since such retail price is a price schedule determined by the product manufacturer, distributor or end-seller and as such, the product has a preestablished price structure. Also see Auction Market Value.

Adjustment Bid

This is a bidding tactic with the objective of bringing the auction's current price back to a whole dollar value, i.e., a current price dollar amount with no cents. For example to return the auction's current price to $32.00. The Adjustment Bid tactic is discussed in chapter *Bidding Tactics*.

Auction

Single-unit auction: A sale in which the item being auctioned is sold to the highest bidder. Dutch-based auction: A sale in which a quantity of items being auctions are sold to a certain number of highest bidders. See Dutch Auction.

Auction Close

As it pertains to Internet auctions, the day and time in which bids are no longer accepted in the auction. This close day and time normally corresponds to the ending of the auction period. However, under certain circumstances, an auction may close prior to its initial auction period. See Auction Listing Period.

Auction Item

Usually a tangible good that is offered for sale to the highest bidder in an auction. Services could also be considered an auction item.

Auction Listing

In online auctions, the web page allocated to the presentation of the item being auctioned. A listing may contain text description, images of the item, the seller's rms of sale, the current status of the auction, bidding instructions and functions ld other elements that facilitate the bidder's participation in the auction.

uction Market Value

he value of an auction item as it is determined by the current auction market. The iction market value depends on several factors such as supply and demand within e auction environment, bidding activity, seller pricing structure (opening price, serve price, etc.) and other factors. See Actual Value for comparison.

uction Noise

idding activity in an auction where there currently is no highest bidder who will awarded the auction win. This is often the case in reserve auctions where bid- ng occurs below the seller's reserve price in which case, even the highest bidder ill not win the auction.

uction Listing Period

s it pertains to Internet auctions; the length of time that bids are accepted in the iction. eBay's auction periods are 3, 5, 7 and 10 days.

uction Time Out

s it pertains to Internet auctions; the day and time in which bids are no longer ccepted in the auction due to the auction's listing period ending. See Auction isting Period.

uction Venue

generic term that describes any Internet web site that provides a location for the le of items via an electronic auction format and which receives, processes and lanages bidding in the auctions at that web site.

uto Bidding

he process where the auction venue places bids on your behalf for as long as your id is higher than another bidder's bid amount. See Proxy Bid. Bids are automati- ally placed on your behalf in amounts that are one minimum bid increment higher lan another bidder's amount. Auto Bidding discontinues when another bidder places bid that exceeds the amount of your proxy bid.

ack Bidder

term used in the traditional auction system that refers to the second highest bid- er. Should a sale to the highest bidder be cancelled or nullified, the auction may e awarded to the next highest bidder – the Back Bidder. As it pertains to eBay, nce certain procedures are followed concerning a NPB (Non-Paying-Bidder), the uction seller may elect to offer the auction article to the next highest bidder or lay apply for an eBay fee credit. See Bidder and Non-Paying-Bidder. Also see .nockdown.

GLOSSARY

Bid

An offer in an auction to pay a particular price for the auction item. In Internet auctions, bids must meet certain conditions before they are accepted by the auction venue. Specifically, in the single-unit auction, 1) a bid must be higher than the auction's First Bid and 2) a bid must be higher than the current price plus one minimum bid amount (see *Minimum Bid Amount*). A bid may be less than a seller's reserve if a seller has placed a reserve price on the auction, but bids below the seller's reserve cannot win the auction. When a bid is placed that is of a higher amount than the auction's current price plus one bid increment *and* is higher than any other existing bid, a portion of the bid is retained by the auction venue and used as a proxy bid. See Proxy Bid.

Bid Activity

The activity that pertains to bidding in auctions. Bid activity typically refers to the actual placement of bids. eBay, as do other auction venues, record bids in a bid history. See Bid and Bid History. Also, see Bidder.

Bidder

As it pertains to Internet auctions; any person or entity that is permitted to bid via the auction venue and that places actual bids in an auction. The bidder determines the amount of each bid and the timing of each bid. With some exceptions, the bidder who had placed the highest bid when the auction closes wins the auction and is awarded to the right to purchase the item if the highest bid meets or exceeds the seller's reserve price.

Bidding Budget

The difference between an auction's current price and the target price. Thus, a Bidding Budget is the amount of money a bidder has to leverage in actual bidding. See Target price.

Bidding Plan

The bidding course of action that a bidder intends to take in the auction. The bidding plan will likely consider current bidders as well as potential future bidders. The plan will also consider the remaining time in the auction's period. The objective of a bidding plan is to participate in an auction in such a way as to conserve one's bidding budget. This helps you be an effective bidder up to the auction's close. See Target Price.

Bidding Strategy

The tactics the bidder intends to use in the auction. A bidding strategy attempts to consider the demand for the item, the probable market value, the type bidder likely attracted to the auction as well as those bidder's personal valuation.

Bid History

An historical list of bids in a particular auction. During the auction period eBay does not reveal bid amounts in its single-unit auction bid history (bid amounts are revealed in Dutch auction bid histories). Bidder identification and bid date and time are recorded in the bid history list. The sequence of the bid history list generally follows the date and time of each bid, with a few exceptions.

Bid Retraction

A reversal of a bid, usually a proxy bid that takes the highest bidder position (a bid that is outbid immediately on placement does not need to be retracted). A bid retraction is not condoned on the premise that the bidder should remain aware of the bid he is placing. More important, a bid retraction disturbs the competitive atmosphere of the auction by reducing or otherwise impacting the current price.

Bid Shielding

A situation where two bidders act in collusion. One bidder places a high proxy bid, usually early in the auction, with the objective of reducing competition in the auction, or at minimum, making it so that other bidders are very unlikely to outbid the high proxy bid. Then, the high proxy bid is retracted near the auction's close thereby reducing the auction's current price which in turn paves the way for the second bidder to place a winning bid. Bid shielding is a fraudulent manipulation of the auction and is therefore against the rules of conduct of online auction venues.

Bid Timing

The practice (and art) of placing bids in online auctions at such times that the bids obtain, improve or preserve the bidder's competitive position in the auction. The amount of a bid, as well as the time in the auction period when a bid is placed, depends on the strategy being used in the auction.

Bubble, Staying in the

Please see Staying in the Bubble. Also see Dutch Auction.

Closing Price

The price at an auction's close. Pertaining to single-unit auction's the closing price is the result of all previous bids (see *Current Price*) in consideration of any existing proxy bids when the auction closes. When a proxy bid exists that is higher than the second highest bid, the auction will be resolved at closing such that the auction closes at one minimum bid increment higher than the second highest bid, leaving the bidder with the highest bid (the proxy bud) the winner of the auction. If no proxy bid exists, the auction venue awards the auction to the bidder with the highest bid. Of course, the highest bid amount must exceed the seller's reserve if a reserve price exists. See Reserve Price.

Common Value

With respect to Internet auctions, the value of the item as it is generally thought to be, both in the auction environment and out. For instance, an auction item such as a numismatic coin might have a value established by an organization based on the current collector demand with that demand somewhat stable over time. An auction for such an item will tend to fetch a price consistent with the common value since the value is typically known by the interested persons. The retail price of new merchandise could be considered a common value, but usually only when the product has been consistently manufactured without substantial change. In that case, over time the market has generally become aware of the product and its typical pricing. It behooves sellers to understand the common value of their auction items and, of course, it behooves bidders to also know the common value to avoid over paying for the item.

Current Price

In single-unit eBay auctions, the price currently attributed to the auction based on previous bids. The current price increments according to specific rules of bidding. The current price is equal to the First Bid price if no bids have occurred in the auction. See Closing Price.

Disclosed Reserve Price

Where a seller who has placed a reserve on his auction states or otherwise reveals the reserve amount in the auction's listing body. When a seller's reserve price is known by the bidders, bidders have an understanding of what price the seller requires to sell the auction item and are more likely to bid up to that reserve if the reserve price is consistent with the bidder's valuation. As such, the current price in reserve auctions tend to reach the seller's reserve sooner, assuming that the reserve price is consistent with the valuation of the participating bidders.

Discovery Run

A sequence of small bids specifically intended to discover another bidder's proxy bid amount. See Proxy Discovery Run.

Discounted Target Price

A target price that has been reduced (discounted). Since the target price is based on recently closed auctions for the same of comparable auction article in the same auction venue, discounting proposes to lower the target price to account for the condition of the auction article, the seller's terms of sale and other factors that suggest that the auction article may have a lower value than recently closed auctions.

Double Proxy Bid

A bidding tactic where a two proxy bids are submitted close together in time. The objective of the second proxy bid is to increase the amount of a previously submitted proxy bid.

Dutch Auction

An auction format where a quantity of the same article is made available for bidding. Any single bidder may request (bid on) any quantity desired (at or under the quantity being auctioned). At the auction's close, all bidders win the quantity they requested at the lowest bid price *if* the total quantity requested by all bidders does not exceed the quantity being auctioned.

Dutch auctions do not utilized reserve pricing or proxy bidding.

Assume, for example that a Dutch auction has 100 items for sale. The opening price (or First Bid in the case of eBay) is $1.00 for each item. Assume that 25 bidders place bids, each requesting 1 item and each bidding $1.00. At this point, there are 25 items requested with a low bid of $1.00. If the auction were to close at this point, all bidders would win the quantity they requested (since there are enough to go around) and all bidders would win at the lowest bid price of $1.00.

However, the Dutch auction works a bit differently when the bidders request a quality, in total, that exceeds the auctioned quantity. In this case, earlier bidders would be awarded their requested quantity *if* later bidders do not bid a higher price than the earlier bidders. In the scenario, where the requested total exceeds the auctioned quantity and where all bid prices are the same, earlier bidders win their requested quantity and the later bidders do not – first come, first served.

But, the bidders who bid at a higher price position themselves in the Dutch auction so that, in the event the total requested items exceed the auctioned quantity, their bid price works to keeps them on the winners list. Bidders placing higher bids reverse the first come first served scenario – they buy their position on the winners list.

Assume that the same 25 bidders had each specified 4 items and each bid $1.00 as before. At this point, the auction quantity could satisfy all bidders if the auction were to close at this point (25 x 4 = 100). But, assume that 5 more bidders placed bids, each for 1 item, and further placed a $2.00 bid for each item. Now there is a specified total of 105 requested items which the auction cannot satisfy. In this situation, at least 1 of the earlier 25 bidders is going to get bumped to satisfy the bids for the 5 items requested over the auction's quantity. Earlier bidders with lower bids amount are pushed off the winners list to satisfy the bidders who bid at a higher price. By bidding a higher price, bidders are better positioned to not be pushed off the winners list should the total items exceed the quantity of the Dutch auction. However, since the lowest bid price was $1.00 all bidders, including those who bid $2.00, will win the auction at $1.00 for each item.

To recap; in a Dutch auction, all bidders win at the lowest bid price if the total requested items do not exceed the auctioned quantity. When the total requested quantity exceeds the auctioned quantity, earlier bidders are bumped by later bidders *who bid a higher price*. But, all winners win at the lowest bid price. The primary objective in Dutch auctions is to be positioned somewhere in the middle in terms of bid price to avoid being bumped if the total requested items exceeds the auctioned quantity. This is often referred to as "staying in the bubble" where the "bubble" is the winner's list. See Staying in the Bubble.

English-based Auction
Typically referred to as the single-unit auction. Among the many types of auction formats, the English-based auction mechanism starts with an opening price (see *First Bid*). The auction's current price increments according to specific rules as new bids are placed by participating bidders. When a single-unit auction is closes, the bidder with the highest bid (that matches or exceeds a reserve price if a reserve price has been set), wins the right to purchase the item. As such, the single-unit auction operates on the principle of price increase. eBay has modified the auction format from the purest English auction. One modification in particular is that bids in single-unit auctions are sealed (see *Bid History*) whereas in off-line auctions, the bid amount is typically known to the participating bidders.

Escrow
With respect to online auctions, a service offered by a third party that holds payment until the auction articles are delivered. The buyer (the winning bidder) forwards payment to the escrow service. The escrow service notifies the seller that payment is secured. The seller ships the item. The buyer then notifies that escrow service that the item has been received and is as represented by the seller. The escrow service forwards payment to the seller. There is often a fee for the escrow service which either the buyer or the seller pays, of the fee is shared between the buyer and the seller. Escrow services are one of several methods used to help protect the buyer, and the seller, from fraud or misrepresentation.

Failed Bid
A bid that is immediately outbid by another bidder's proxy bid.

Feedback
A method of self-policing an auction environment where bidders submit comments concerning the seller after a transaction is complete. Likewise, the seller submits

comments concerning the buyer (the winning bidder). The objective is to enable the parties involved in an auction transaction to publicly record comments about one another, from their respective vantage points, for the consideration of future participants with the seller or the buyer. Either party may submit a feedback statement with an associated negative, neutral or positive rating. Generally the online auction feedback system works, but is subject to misuse and abuse (see *Feedback Leveraging* as an example). In addition, should feedback be submitted prematurely, it cannot be withdrawn except under special circumstances. This requires that both parties use the feedback system responsibility.

Feedback Leveraging

This occurs when one party in an transaction waits for the other party to submit feedback first. By doing so, the second party has the benefit of knowing the first party's perspective in the auction transaction. If the feedback is negative, the second party can withhold a positive feedback statement, even if the first party deserves a positive feedback, or reciprocate with a corresponding negative comment. Sellers often leverage feedback by waiting for the buyer (the winning bidder) to submit feedback first. Typically, there are more performance demands on the seller at the time of the transaction, so the seller waits for the buyer to submit feedback thereby providing first indication of the buyers attitude concerning the transaction. It resolves to "You say nice things about me and I'll say nice things about you" – hence the feedback system becomes more of an exchange in the transaction, not an honest appraisal of performance. A more basic objective of feedback leveraging is that the seller can save the time and effort to submit feedback if the buyer does not himself submit feedback.

First Bid

eBay's term that indicates the amount required for the first bid in an auction. The First Bid amount is determined by the seller when the seller lists an item. The First Bid can be as little as .01 (one cent), per the seller's specification.

Floor Price

The minimum price the auction article can sell at. The Floor Price is set by the seller by the First Bid price (See *First Bid*) and by a reserve price if the seller places a reserve on the auction (see *Reserve Price*). The First Bid price sets an opening price and a reserve price establishes a minimum selling price. As such, the seller establishes a floor price, or the minimum the item will sell at.

Fraud

Any attempt to create an unfair or illegal advantage over another party. In Internet auctions, fraud is committed by intentionally omitting or misrepresenting information. Fraud is also committed by manipulating an auction or interfering with the fairness of the auction.

Gap Amount

The difference between the auction's current price and a bidder's personal maximum price. Essentially, it is the amount of money the bidder has remaining to continue to bid in the auction. For instance, if the auction's current price is $100.00 and the bidder's personal maximum price is $200.00, then there is a Gap Amount of $100.00. Therefore, in this example up to $100.00 remains that can be used for continued bidding during the remaining time of the auction. Note: There is a difference in purpose between a personal maximum price and the target price.

Highest Bidder

The person that currently has the highest bid in an auction. As it pertains to Internet auctions, the highest bidder may be in that position by having placed the First Bid, by having outbid another bidder or by having a proxy bid in place. See First Bid. Also, see Proxy Bid.

Highest Bidder's Seat

A term coined by the author to refer to the bidder who is the current highest bidder in an Internet auction. The current highest bidder is said to be in the highest bidder's seat.

HTML

Hypertext Markup Language. The term Hypertext is a metaphor for presenting information linked together to form a non-sequential web of associations. HTML therefore is a method of encoding textual information, graphics, sounds and data, possibly from various sources, to display in Internet browsers such that the user may link to other locations within the HTML page or on the web.

Immediate Market

The potential market that exists at the time the auction is running. The immediate market refers to the potential participants in the auction, not just the actual participants. For example, if a particular sporting article is not in demand at the time, the immediate market will be smaller than if the sporting article were in demand at the time. The extent of an immediate market can be estimated by reviewing recently closed auctions and observing the number or actual bidders and the closing prices of those auctions.

Indivisible Good

A tangible, manufactured item that is typically sold as a unit. The term Indivisible Good does not refer to a service being auctioned.

Inflection Point

As it pertains to online auctions, the point at which the required minimum bid increment increases. For instance, if the minimum bid is $1.00 at a certain current price range, when the current price raises to the next inflection point, the minimum bid increment rises to $2.50. See Minimum Bid Amount. Understanding inflection points facilitates strategic participation in an auction.

Internet Auction

A generic term that describes an auction that is hosted on an Internet web site. The Internet web site acting as an auction host receives, processes and manages bidding in the auction at that site. Interested persons preview auction listings via Internet software resources such as an Internet browser. Those who wish to bid in Internet auctions place their bids through the browser by completing and submitting forms. See Auction Venue.

Knockdown

Used in traditional (non-Internet) auctions to refer to the awarding of the auction item to the highest bidder when the auctioneers announces "Sold". See Highest Bidder's Seat.

Minimum Bid Increment

Except when bidding at the First Bid price, the smallest bid increment required above the current price of an auction. On eBay, the minimum bid requirement is

Current Price	Bid Increment
$.01 - .99	$.05
1.00 – 4.99	.25
5.00 – 24.99	.50
25.00 – 99.99	1.00
100.00 – 249.99	2.50
250.00 – 499.99	5.00
500.00 – 999.99	10.00
1000.00 – 2499.99	25.00 ·
2500.00 – 4999.99	50.00
5000.00 and up	100.00

The above information was accurate at the time this book was published. For the latest eBay bid increment information, please see the help pages at www.ebay.com.

GLOSSARY

determined by the current price (see table below as it pertains to eBay). Bids that do not meet the minimum bid increment are rejected.

Maximum Bidder

The Maximum Bidder simply places a bid at the maximum she is willing to pay for the item. Usually, the bidder knows the item's value to himself or has researched the auction item. Typically, a bid from a Maximum Bidder occurs once in an auction and that bid may be placed at any point. The Maximum Bidder is not interested in continuously checking the auction. He isn't concerned with placing multiple minimum bids, such as might the Minimum Bidder. He is not particularly interested in the activity of other participants in the auction. Maximum Bidders simply place a bid and, if they win, they will be notified when the auction closes.

Minimum Bidder

The Minimum Bidder's objective is to cause the smallest possible impact on the auction's current price. The Minimum Bidder operates from the stance that any bid they place in the auction will cost them more money should they win the auction. The logic is that if bids have the smallest possible impact on the auction's current price, then the auction will close at a lower price, at least in theory.

Maximum Price

The maximum price a bidder is willing to spend to win the auction.

Multiple-Item Auction

An auction where multiple units of the same auction article are offered in the auction. Please see *Dutch Auction*.

MSRP

Manufactures Suggested Retail Price. The price set by the manufacturer to provide a price guide for merchants and distributors. This price is also referred to a the "list price". In the United States and many other countries merchants and distributors may set any price they wish for most products. The MSRP is intended as a guide but is usually accepted as the upper price of a product where the manufacturer states an MSRP. Also see Street Price.

NIB

Usually refers to "New In Box"

Non-Paying-Bidder

A term used by eBay to describe a winning bidder who refuses to pay for an auction won by that bidder. See the eBay web site for additional information. *http:// pages.ebay.com/help/community/npb.html*

NR
Usually refers to "No Reserve"

Opening Price
Please see First Bid.

Opponent Bidder
Any other bidder who is active in the same Internet auction as yourself. For purposes of this book, all bidders in the same auction as yourself, including those bidders who have seemingly dropped out of the auction, are considered opponents since it is unknown the extent of their continued involvement in the auction.

Personal Maximum Price
Your personal maximum price is a contingency price and is used when an auction has exceeded the *target* price, but when you still desire to purchase the item. In effect, your personal *maximum* price is the most you are willing to pay for an item while the *target* price is what you base your strategic bidding efforts on. Your personal maximum price is determined by a number of considerations private to yourself including comparative price shopping, personal need and desire for the item, availability of funds, etc. Your personal maximum price is established to give you a predetermined spending limit for the auction.

A personal maximum price is higher than the target price. If you were to plan your strategic bidding efforts on your personal *maximum* price, you would be forced to justify a new and higher price should your bidding strategies not be effective in the auction. In addition, by thinking in terms of a target price, you tend to work to win the auction at less than you would be willing to pay at maximum. See Target Price.

Person-to-Person Auction
An auction environment where each seller (often an individual person) seeks to conduct a transaction with another individual person. The online auction venue serves as a venue to bring the seller and the buyer together. Typically, there are no middle persons in the transaction itself (but services are often provided to one or the other such as payment methods, escrow, etc.). Both the seller and the buyer take responsibility for the actual transaction. See Transaction.

Personal Valuation
The value that is assigned to the item by the prospective buyer (the bidder). A personal valuation is based on personal need, desire to own, personal assessment of worth, personal budget, etc. In other words, a personal value is subjective to the individual, although it may be based on external pricing factors such a published retail price, a price guide, etc. Compare with Target Price and Personal Maximum Price.

Price Point

The maximum price a bidder is willing to pay for an item – their personal valuation. Normally, you do not know the price point of your opponent bidders until the auction closes. In addition, your opponent bidders do not know your price point.

Private Auction

An auction in which only those specifically invited to participate may do so. Private auctions are not available to the public.

Profile

The score assigned to members of an online auction community based on feedback submissions and feedback ratings in past auction participation. Both seller and winning bidders have a profile in most online auction communities. The scoring system may vary slightly from one auction venue to another, but the objective is always to associate a numeric rating to a member to facilitate a quick assessment of past performance based on feedback.

Profile Points

The points assigned to a member of an online auction community. See Profile.

Proxy Bid

Where the auction venue places bids in an auction on your behalf until the proxy bid amount is exhausted or the auction closes. When you place a bid in an auction where the bid amount is higher than the minimum bid required, the bid amount in excess of the minimum required bid is then used by the auction venue as your proxy bid amount.

When an auction's current price has not yet met the seller's reserve price, should you place a bid that is equal to the seller's reserve price, the auction's current price is increased to match the seller's reserve and your bid is *not* considered a proxy bid. Should you place a bid that is greater than the seller's reserve price, the auction's current price is immediately increased to the seller's reserve price and the difference between the seller's reserve price and your bid is considered your proxy bid.

Proxy Discovery Run

A bidding tactic whereby you place a number of bids (which are typically at the minimum bid increment amount to avoid inadvertently submitting a proxy bid) for the specific purpose of determining the proxy bid amount of the current highest bidder in the auction. The proxy amount of another bidder is "discovered" when your nth bid exceeds the proxy bid amount of the other bidder.

Proxy Margin

The difference between the current price and the proxy bid amount, i.e., the bid amount that exceeds the current price. Until exhausted, the proxy margin amount is used by the auction venue to compete against other bidders on the proxy bidder's behalf, referred to an auto bidding. See Auto Bidding. When another bidder bids an amount over the proxy bid, auto-bidding is discontinued because the Proxy Margin is depleted.

Reactive Bidder

The Reactive Bidder certainly has a price preference, but is willing to re-think what she will pay for the item as the auction progresses. As the current price in an auction increases, the reactive bidder has a tendency to increase her personal valuation accordingly. Thus the Reactive Bidder tends to use the current price as her frame of reference, allowing the current price to determine (or at least influence) her personal valuation. The bid amounts of the Reactive Bidder are usually the minimum required. This is because the Reactive Bidder is not entirely sure of the items true value so doesn't want to place needlessly high bids. The price acceptance of the Reactive Bidder will continue until she can no longer justify any further price increase.

Reserve Auction

An auction where the seller has set a minimum acceptable price. Should the auction close without at least one bidder placing a bid at or over the seller's minimum acceptable price (the reserve price), the seller is not obligated to complete a transaction for that auction. See Reserve Price.

Reserve Price

The price below which a seller chooses to not complete an auction transaction. If no bids are received at or above the seller's reserve price, the seller is not obligated to sell the auction item. Sellers specify their reserve amount when listing with the auction venue. Sellers are not obligated to disclose their reserve price to bidders. An auction with a reserve price is called a Reserve Auction. An auction with no reserve price is called an Absolute Auction.

Retail Price

A predetermined price or price range that is usually associated with traditional (non online auction) commerce. A retail price is typically widely known or can be determined fairly easily. As such, the retail price is often used as a guide for the pricing of factory new merchandise being sold in online auctions. Often the price in the online auction is lower than the product's retail price, but this depends on demand within the auction market as well as the sales effort put forth to enhance the perceived value of interested persons. See Street Price.

GLOSSARY

Risk Averse

One who avoids risk. In Internet auctions, a risk averse bidder makes an effort to avoid overspending on the item. See Risk Neutral.

Risk Aversion

See Risk Averse.

Risk Neutral

One who does not consider an action to be risky. In Internet auctions, a risk neutral bidder places bid without the fear of risk, such as overpaying for an auction item. See Risk Averse.

Safe Bid

A bid placed in an amount that is unlikely to place the bidder in a position of being committed to purchasing the item for which the bid is placed. An example of a safe bid is a bid placed above the required minimum bid but below the seller's reserve price when the seller's reserve amount is known.

Seller

The person or organization which creates and posts Internet auction listings to offer a tangible good (or a service) in the auction venue.

Shill Bidder

With respect to online auctions, a shill bidder is a person who places bids in an auction with the intent of encouraging other bidders to place bids in the auction of a higher amount. This activity introduces competition to the auction with the objective of raising the auction's current price and ultimately the auctions closing price. Usually the shill bidder will simply stop bidding when the auction's current price has been raised sufficiently. On occasion a shill bidder will retract his or her bid which causes the current price to be adjusted down to the next highest bid amount. A shill bidder has no intention of winning the auction in which he or she places shill bids. A shill bidder usually works in collusion with the auction seller or could be the seller placing bids in his or her own auction using another registration identity. Auction mechanisms prevent a seller from bidding in her or her own auctions using the membership ID used to post the auction listing.

Single-Unit Auction

An auction listing that offers to sell a single unit of the item being auctioned. Compare with Dutch Auction.

Sliding Personal Price

A price point that increases in unison with the current price of an auction. Basically, a bidder continuously adjusts his price point as required by the auction's current price. By doing so, the bidder's willingness to pay an amount for the auction is directed by the competition in the auction which is the specific purpose of auctions. A better alternative is to have a target price that serves as an allocated budget for the auction. This allows more aggressive bidding free from the cycle of bid, no bid decisions. See Target Price.

Snipe Bid

As it applies to bidding in online auctions; a single bid placed within the final seconds of an auction. The term "snipe" means to strike quickly and without warning. A snipe bid is intended to give no other bidder the opportunity to respond or react with additional bids. To accomplish this, a snipe bid is placed within the final few seconds of the auction's close. By the time opponent bidders are notified of the snipe bid (or realize that another bid was placed), the auction has closed and no further bidding is allowed. Snipe bidding is generally thought to be unfair but the practice is quite common. In an effort to combat snipe bidding, some auction venue are programmed to automatically extend the auction if a bid is received with the final few minutes of the auction's closing time. eBay does not extend an auction in the event of a snipe bid.

Snipe Bidder

A bidder who places a bid very close in time to an auction's closing time. See Snipe Bid.

Sniper

The term "snipe" means to strike quickly, without warning. A sniper, in online auctions, is a bidder who places a bid very close in time to an auction's closing time. See Snipe Bid.

Stalker Bidder

The Stalker Bidder takes the lead of bidders who are known to have a knowledge of certain auction items. Most auction venues make it very easy to view all auctions that a particular bidder is currently bidding in or were recently won. This makes it possible for the Stalker Bidder to follow a particular bidder from one action to another. For determining value, all bidders have a certain level of trust in the bids of other bidders. The Stalker Bidder narrows his focus to one or a few bidders whom have demonstrated the ability to accurately access the market value of certain items.

Strategy

As it applies to bidding in Internet auctions; a plan of action intended to achieve an objective, in this case the objective is to win auctions at a closing price at or under the target price. A strategy consists of tactics which are techniques used to implement the bidding strategy. See Tactics.

Staying in the Bubble

Please review Dutch Auction first and then return here. In Dutch auctions, all bidders win their requested number of items if the total requested items can be satisfied by the quantity of items being auctioned. Should the total requested by all bidders exceed the quantity of items being auctioned, earlier bidders are dropped from the winner's list as long as new bidders bid a higher price. When the total requested items exceed the auctioned quantity, the bid price secures position in the auction.

For instance, if the total requested items by all bidders is 105 yet the Dutch auction quantity is 100, then those bidders who bid earlier in the auction are bumped from the bidders list as a result of new bidders placing a higher bid. The new bidders (who bid a higher price) essentially secure a position on the bidders list. Consider:

Scenario #1:

1. There are 100 items offered.

2. There are 100 bidders who have each requested 1 item and have bid $1.00 for each item.

3. A new bidder requests 1 item and places a bid for $2.00.

4. The new bidder bumps the first bidder in the auction off of the bidder's list because he placed a higher bid.

Scenario #2:

1. There are 100 items offered.

2. There are 5 bidders who have each requested 5 items and have bid $1.00 for each item (25 items).

3. There are 5 bidders who have each requested 10 items and have bid $2.00 for each item (50 items).

4. There are 5 bidders who have each requested 10 items and have bid $3.00 for each item (50 items).

5. There is now a total of 125 requested items, 25 over the 100 quantity being auctioned. To "stay in the bubble", you would need to bid higher than the 5 bidders who are scheduled to be bumped from the winner's list, who are the $1.00 bidders. Thus, to stay on the winner's list, your bid would need to be at least $2.00 (or higher). If this auction were to close at this point, the lowest bid would be $2.00.

Staying in the bubble simply means that you buy your way onto the bidders list when the total requested items exceeds of the quantity being auctioned. In that case, earlier bidders are bumped in favor of bidders who bid a higher price. As such, your objective is to bid higher than the bidders who will be bumped from the bidders list.

Street Price

Usually a lower price than MSRP (Manufacturers Suggested Retail Price) or the retail price, the street price is typically a competitive price offered by merchants and distributors. Street price is not normally attributed to the price set by private owners in pre-owned product situations. See Retail and MSRP.

Successful Auction

An auction that closes with a winning bidder. To win an online single-unit auction, the highest bidder must have placed a bid that 1) exceeds the First Bid price, 2) exceeds the bids of all other bidders, and 3) matches or exceeds the seller's reserve price, if the seller placed a reserve on the auction. In the event of a bid amount tie, where two or more bidders place the same bid amount, the auction venue will automatically determine the winner at the auction's close as being the bidder who placed the tie bid amount first.

Tactics

As it applies to bidding in Internet auctions; bidding methods or techniques utilized with the objective of positioning a bidder in the auction. Examples are proxy bidding, discovery runs, bidding of the dollar and adjustment bidding. Snipe bidding could be considered a tactic since it is normal bidding but which is timed to occur very close to an auction's close. See Strategy. Also, see Snipe Bid.

Target Price

A probable closing price of an item based upon recently closed auction of the same or comparable item and within the same auction venue. Alternatively, the typical selling price of the item being auction outside of the auction venue could be used.

The target price, being based on a realistic market price, is then used to establish a bidding budget with the objective of increasing your competitive strength. However, having a target price does not imply being willing to pay the full target price. Rather, provides a price guide for competitive purposes.

By having a target price for an auction, you are relieved of having to continuously justify the auction's current price as the purchase price. As the auction progresses, the escalating current price tends to cause bidders to increase their willingness to pay a progressively higher price.

GLOSSARY

In addition, since the target price is based on the closing prices of recently closed auctions, it helps you avoid relying upon another person's personal valuation, which cannot be know in single-unit eBay auctions.

Transaction

The completion of a sale resulting from winning an Internet auction. A typical transaction includes communications with the seller (typically via e-mail), making payment, escrow arrangements if escrow is utilized, arranging shipping, receiving the auction item, submitting feedback, etc.

Tripping the Reserve

As it pertains to single-unit auctions in which the seller has specified a reserve price, the bid that meets or exceeds that reserve price "trips" the reserve. On eBay, when a bid is submitted that meets or exceeds the seller's reserve price, the current price of the auction is immediately raised to the seller's reserve price and the bidder who placed that bid becomes committed to purchasing the item if she is not outbid before the auction closes. Since most sellers do not disclose their reserve amount in their auction listing, bidders are often caught by surprise when they trip the reserve. Savvy Bidders make an effort to not trip the seller's reserve price because auctions with the reserve not yet met tend to discourage serious bidding. This is because opponent bidders do not know what bid amount is required to exceed the seller's reserve. A tripped reserve provides a frame of reference for opponent bidders by which to better make a bidding decision. See Safe Bid. Also see Reserve Price, Disclosed Reserve Price and Undisclosed Reserve Price.

Undisclosed Reserve Price

Where a seller who has placed a reserve on his auction does not state or otherwise reveal the reserve amount in the auction's listing body. As such, bidders lack a frame of reference in terms of knowing what price the seller requires to sell the auction item. Lacking this frame of reference, bidders tend to either avoid the auction or place small bids in the auction. The current price in auctions with undisclosed reserve prices tend to climb slowly throughout the auction. In addition, during the early period of such auctions small bids are placed, usually from value Opportunists. Small, tentative bids imply lower perceived value which further discourages bidding. This is because bidders value the opinions of other bidders, those opinions expressed in the form of bids.

Valuation

The personal valuation given to a specific item. The valuation is determined by a number of considerations private to a bidder including comparative price shopping, personal need for the item, availability of funds, etc.

Value Opportunity

A perceived opportunity to purchase an item at well below its actual or market value. Bidders who make an effort to win auctions at below the item's actual or market value are referred to as "Value Opportunists", or more commonly "Bargain Hunters". Such bidders will place small bid amounts on items potentially having a much higher value and do so in the hopes that the auction will close at well below its actual value.

Winner's Curse

Simply stated, where a winning bidder realizes that he overpaid for the item. The Winner's Curse is a form of buyer's remorse, but has the additional attribute of the bidder having committed to an auction purchase at a higher than necessary closing price usually as a result of being caught up in the competitive situation of the auction.

Index

A

K

Knockdown. *See Glossary*

L

Laws of Strategic Bidding 120–245
Leverage Your Money 159
Luck, eliminating 144

M

market equilibrium 39
market's price level 39
Maximum Bid 36, 37
Maximum Bidder. *See Glossary*
Maximum Price 31, 36. *See also Glossary*
maximum price 36, 37
Maximum Price Objective 36–38
Maximum Target Price 44. *See also Target Price*
 determining 44–45
Minimum Bid 35, 36, 146
 avoid 199
 for stealth purposes 20
 to ferret out competition 157
Minimum Bid Increment 36, 79, 186. *See also Glossary*
 affected by cent value 210
 example of 79
Minimum Bidder. *See Glossary*
Minimum Bidding 20, 34, 82, 213, 216, 222
 increases bidding activity 82
 not normally competitive 83
 propensity for 79
 questionable competitive gain 83
 small bids increase competition 27
Most Comfortable Price Objective 35–36
MSRP 45. *See also Glossary*
Multiple-Item Auction. *See Glossary*
My eBay 195

INDEX

T

INDEX

Winning Is Easy

Bidder: You know, I'm really quite frustrated with those online auctions.

Friend: And why is that?

Bidder: Well, every time I place a bid in one of those auctions, it keeps telling me to place a higher bid.

Friend: I don't understand. You mean you are outbid so you have to bid again?

Bidder: No, no. As soon as I place a bid it comes back saying that I have to place another bid that is $1.00 higher.

Friend: Oh, that's just telling other bidders what's the lowest bid allowed at that time. It's called the minimum bid increment.

Bidder: Oh? No one told me that!

Friend: You mean you keep bidding the next bid increment?

Bidder: Yes! I wondered why I won all those auctions.

A Little Feedback Please

Bidder: I don't understand why eBay won't let bidders see the bid amounts in the bid history.

Friend: Oh, that's so you'll bid what you think the item is worth to you, not what someone else thinks it's worth.

Bidder: But, how can I know what the item is worth to me if I don't know what it's worth to others?

Don't Sweat the Small Bids

Bidder: I figured out the secret to winning on-line auctions at the lowest price.

Friend: Tell me more!

Bidder: Well, it's really very simple. Just bid the absolute minimum you have to. That way you don't cause the auction's current price to increase that much.

Friend: But, what if other bidders think the same way? Then they all bid small amounts too.

Bidder: That's the secret you see. It's easy to outbid their small bids.

Supply and Demand

Patient: Doctor, every on-line auction I see for Beanie Babies I have to bid in.

Doc: But you don't have to bid in those auctions.

Patient: Oh yes I do. If I don't, someone else will.

Doc: But, you don't *have* to buy every Beanie Baby up for auction.

Patient: Yes I do! You see Doc, there is such a limited supply that I have to buy as many as I can.

Doc: What makes you think there is a limited supply?

Patient: Well, the sellers must only have one each because that's all they ever auction off.

Ready to Bid to Win

Wife: You'd better bid in that auction before it closes.

Hubby: I'm ready. I just finished reading Bid to Win on eBay.

Printed in the United States
26134LVS00004B/93